Delhi

Delhi

ADVENTURES IN A MEGACITY

Sam Miller

St. Martin's Press   New York

Library of Congress Cataloging-in-Publication Data

Miller, Sam, 1962–
    Delhi : adventures in a megacity / Sam Miller. — 1st U.S. ed.
        p. cm.
    "First published in Great Britain by Jonathan Cape" —T.p.
verso.
    Includes index.
    ISBN 978-0-312-61237-5
    1. Delhi (India)—Description and travel. 2. Miller, Sam,
1962– —Travel—India—Delhi. 3. Delhi (India)—Social life and
customs. 4. City and town life—India—Delhi. I. Title.
    DS486.D3M54 2010
    954'.56—dc22

                                                    2010013043

    First published in Great Britain by Jonathan Cape,
        a division of The Random House Group Limited

        First U.S. Edition: July 2010

        10 9 8 7 6 5 4 3 2 1

To my parents, without whom I would be nothing;
and also to Homer, Prem Chand, Jane Jacobs,
Robert Darke, WG Sebald, the succulent one,
the ping pong prince, the plaster princess,
and anyone who has been happily lost in a city.

At night, I make plans for a city laid down
Like the hips of a girl on the spring covered ground.
Spirals and capitals like the twist of a script;
Streets named for heroes that could almost exist.

Josh Ritter
Thin Blue Flame
from the album *The Animal Years*; V2; 2006

Contents

Prologue   1

Chapter One: In which the Author is   15
dazzled by the Metro, finds a cure for haemorrhoids
and turns the tables on an unscrupulous shoeshine man

An Early Intermission   34

Chapter Two: In which the Author explores the mysteries   37
of the sodomitic gerund, monastic nudity and geocaching

A Second Intermission   58

Chapter Three: In which the Author is spat at, flirted   63
with and eventually beheaded

A Third Intermission   79

Chapter Four: In which the Author encounters a   83
digital Mahatma, unravels the mystery of Stella of
Mudge and engages in solvent abuse

A Fourth Intermission   102

Chapter Five: In which the Author discovers   107
a celluloid wardrobe, is described as a wanker and
meets some bestial shoe-cleaners

A Fifth Intermission   124

Chapter Six: In which the Author expectorates a carrot, meets an asthmatic goat and identifies a nappy thief   129

A Sixth Intermission   142

Chapter Seven: In which the Author rediscovers Tintin, prepares for the Olympics and locates the Hand of God   147

A Seventh Intermission   163

Chapter Eight: In which the Author is accused of queue-jumping, delivers a discourse on Mozart and considers the best way of disposing of a dead body   167

An Eighth Intermission   186

Chapter Nine: In which the Author visits Ludlow Castle, learns the meaning of choledocholithotomy and almost buys a packet of condoms   191

A Ninth Intermission   208

Chapter Ten: In which the Author tries to break into jail, falls into a manhole and encounters several tiny terrorists   211

A Tenth Intermission   226

Chapter Eleven: In which the Author is phlebotomized, meets a human yo-yo and avoids the cannibals of Noida   231

An Eleventh Intermission   246

Chapter Twelve: In which the Author climbs a   251
malodorous mountain, reflects on poverty and hope
and falls at the feet of King George V

A Twelfth Intermission   263

Chapter Thirteen: In which the Author is chased by   267
killer pigs, meets the 'Magnet Man' of West Delhi
and has a doleful wander through the Millennium City

Acknowledgements   283

Index   285

Copyright Acknowledgements   293

Prologue

DELHI WAS ONCE, several hundred years ago, the most populous city in the world. For better or worse, it may become so again. It is a city that has suffered many calamities, and has repeatedly risen from its own ruins. Delhi has been scoffed at, coveted, decimated, lionized, demolished and rebuilt. It is nearing its millennium—and all of its multiple avatars are visible through a thickening crust of modernity. It is the capital of a nation that is beginning to claim the twenty-first century as its own, whose struggle with poverty is incomplete, but whose aspirations for success seem unquenchable. Delhi is now a megalopolis, sprawling beyond its own borders, swallowing up villages and farmland, sucking in migrants, spewing out pollution. There are no natural limits to this rampant city, nothing to stop it growing except, perhaps, if it fails to live up to the new Indian dream. From all over India, they flock to Delhi. They want jobs and a brighter future for their children. Delhi, the once sleepy, boring, parochial capital, derided for decades by Bombayites and Calcuttans, has emerged from their shadows. It is becoming India's dreamtown—and its purgatory.

In 2004, Delhi's population passed fifteen million; more than twenty million if you include its suburbs. The following year, another, more significant, global landmark was passed. For the first time in history, the majority of human beings lived in towns or cities. The world had—by the narrowest of margins—become urban. And the great western cities of previous millennia, London, Paris, Rome and Athens, those archetypes of urban existence, are being dwarfed and prettified; and it is the new and ancient cities of Asia that are the pulsating giants of the twenty-first century. Delhi, the city of Sultanates and Mughals, of Djinns and Sufis, of poets and courtesans, is now also a city of cybercafés and shopping malls, of Metros and multiplexes. It is the past and it is the future. It is also my home.

Fragments of Delhi

As a child, I loved to be quizzed. I taught myself all the world's capital cities and performed a kind of circus act for my parent's friends. 'Albania? That's easy. Tirana, of course . . . Liechtenstein? Pea-sy . . . Vaduz.' And so on. One summer's afternoon with the tepid London sunlight on my arms and face, and suffused in the warming smell of jasmine from my parent's garden, an adult challenged me. It led to a brief but enduring moment of childhood shame. The grown-up asked me the name of the capital of India. I scoffed at such a simple question and said, quite correctly, 'New Delhi'. He replied, 'No, it's just Delhi.' I became confused. I declared, incorrectly this time, in an adamant manner, that Delhi and New Delhi were as different as York and New York. Another adult laughed out loud, and informed me that New Delhi was just a part of Delhi. I suddenly felt sick inside, eviscerated by failure. In my personal mythology, this was the beginning of a complicated relationship with Delhi.

I do have other early, minor, less palpable memories. I have tried and failed to reconstruct a half-remembered limerick involving Delhi and jelly and smelly[1] and I can vaguely recall a dark-haired woman mysteriously referring to diarrhoea as 'Delhi-belly'. It was clearly established for me as a city of abnormal bowel movements. My first visual encounter with Delhi was in cartoon form, thanks to a brief hectic stopover in the Indian capital by my childhood hero, Tintin, who was on his way to Tibet. Delhi re-emerges next for me, much later, in 1984 (by then I am a news-addict and would-be journalist), as the television backdrop for the assassination of Prime Minister Indira Gandhi by two of her Sikh bodyguards. I can recreate in my mind vivid indoor sequences of Sikhs in turbans of different colours; a red turban is unwound, followed by the cutting of long wiry hair with large tarnished tailors' scissors. 'Cut Sikhs' were less likely to be identified and murdered by mobs that targeted the Sikh community during the Delhi riots that followed the assassination

And then in 1987, I glimpsed my earliest sharp images of Delhi, in a video of the film *The Householder*—first of the Merchant-Ivory progeny—and the city began to gain some more solid qualities in my mind. The film is an unrushed, touching, comic portrayal of a newly wedded couple, in an arranged marriage, learning to compromise and giggle, before eventually falling in love.

Visually, the most memorable scene from *The Householder* was at

---

[1]The Brian Eno record, *Before and After Science* released in 1977, which I once owned, has the memorably meaningless lines:
'In New Delhi (smelly Delhi) and Hong Kong
They all know that it won't be long
I count my fingers (digit counter) as night falls
And draw bananas on the bathroom walls . . . '

Jantar Mantar, a group of huge open-air astronomical instruments that looks like a giant's playground. Prem, the hero (played by the pre-corpulent best-looking-actor-of-all-time, Shashi Kapoor) watched as his American friend, Ernest, jumped around among the shadows of the brick-built gnomons and equinoctial dials. It was one of the strangest urban sights I had ever encountered, and I pressed the pause and rewind buttons again and again. So, at the age of twenty-five, images of Delhi, my future home, had registered with me for the first time. In fact, those images were old ones; *The Householder* had been filmed in 1962, the year of my birth, closer to

© *Merchant-Ivory Productions*

British times than to the present. It was also in black and white, and it wasn't until I finally visited Delhi in 1989 that I saw the warm terracotta shades of the Jantar Mantar complex. Visiting Jantar Mantar, which turned out to be an early-eighteenth-century observatory in the middle of modern Delhi, was the highlight of that visit—indeed just about the only thing I remember liking about the city.

On that first visit, I had just come, bedazzled, from Calcutta, where I had traipsed the streets, paddling through late monsoon rains. I had also grown to love Bombay (almost as quickly as I had grown to love a Bombay woman) and had begun to contemplate the possibility of living there amidst the slums and penthouses, as close to the sea as possible. Both those cities, Delhi's Significant Others[2], seemed to have an energy and an identity which I did not sense in Delhi. Everyone in Delhi seemed irritable, they weren't (shame on them) so interested in me, and there was no clear centre, no heart to the city; I couldn't orientate myself in it. I even once, to my present-day shame, described it to a friend as 'loathsome'.

I later went on to live and work as a journalist in Delhi for two and a half years in the early 1990s. I would leave Delhi at every opportunity, and go back to my wife's home city of Bombay—or to anywhere in the subcontinent that wasn't Delhi. When asked, I would

[2]The official English-language names of Bombay and Calcutta changed to Mumbai and Kolkata in 1995 and 2001 respectively, though both are still widely referred to by their previous names. There have been suggestions that Delhi's name should be changed to Dilli, which is how Delhi is normally pronounced in Hindi.

describe Delhi as provincial and mean-spirited and *matlabi*—a word which here has the implication that people make friends only because of their ability to assist them in climbing a particular social or career ladder. Some of that was (and is) true, but it was also, as I now realize, a partial and incomplete account of a dizzyingly complex city undergoing rapid and unpredictable change.

Delhi's population has doubled[3] in the time I have known it. It has become, for better *and* for worse, a world city. It has everything that is old and everything that is modern. It still has its majestic, scattered ruins that, for me, equal those of Rome or Athens or Cairo. But it has largely lost the parochial quality I remember from the 1990s. Today, Delhi makes the city of my birth, London, feel quiet and peripheral. Delhi has a sense of continuous decay and regeneration that I have not met elsewhere. I find myself preaching to anyone who will listen that the world ignores Delhi's current experiments with modernity at its peril. Sometimes, because large cities are so large, and they can make us feel so small as individuals, we lose hope about changing anything. We forget that we human beings, have created these cities, these monsters; they are entirely our responsibility. And so in the end, my sermon continues, we will, collectively, get the cities we deserve. For that reason, we must come to believe that our great cities needn't be hell on earth, that they might even become better than purgatory. The world's urban pasts are brimming with failures—a world in which Delhi is an incubator for an uncertain urban future.

As for me personally, only now am I beginning to come to terms with that vacillating attraction and repulsion I feel for this monstrous, addictive city. Delhi has drawn me back repeatedly, a magnet and a temptation, and I tread its streets like a man possessed.

[3]According to the last census, the population of Delhi on 1 March 2001 was 13,782,976. Even at a conservative three per cent per annum growth rate, the population reached fifteen million by early 2004, and seventeen million by the middle of 2008. The UN Population Division has predicted a population of 20.9 million for Delhi by 2015. All these figures exclude huge contiguous urban areas (Gurgaon, Faridabad, Noida and Ghaziabad) in neighbouring states, whose total population is at least six million. In 1911, the year it became the capital of India, the population of Delhi was just 238,000. In the 1670s, during the reign of the Mughal Emperor Aurangzeb, Delhi was, according to the indomitable urban statistician, Tertius Chandler, the most populous city in the world with about 650,000 residents. A 2005 Google search for 'Delhi + population' produced Delhi, Louisiana with a population of 3,066.

On the importance of legs

Once upon a time cities were designed for the convenience of walkers, biped and quadruped. Legs, until relatively recently, were the main means of land transport. Longer distances could be achieved by water which tripled up as a means of sustenance and cleansing. But until the appearance of the train and the car, legs were hegemonic in cities. Even the bicycle is leg-dependent, a mere variation on a theme. These days, however, legs are things used only by fitness freaks, the eccentric and the poor as a means of substantive locomotion.

Now, this may be some lingering genetic memory of the days before the automobile, or just an unexpungeable idiosyncrasy—but I love to walk in cities. On arrival in a city, I need to walk. It's very much a physical thing; I feel that I have to do it; my instincts and my limbs command me to start walking. I will step out of my temporary residence as soon as I can after arrival and get my olfactory and visual bearings. I will work out the best way of navigating. If I have no map I will look around to see if is there a river, or a huge monument, or a distant hill, by which I can judge my position. I need to take in my immediate surroundings, so if I get lost (and I usually do) I can find my way back in the end. Then I start walking.

My earliest solo city walk was in Paris, where, as a teenager, I got stranded on the *périphérique*. Like most ring roads, and unlike most of Paris, the *périphérique* has few obvious charms. Because it is circular, however, there was no fear, if I kept going long enough, of getting lost. In fact, I grew to like something about the monotony of the *périphérique*; it provided me with a few lessons in architectural archaeology—and a sense of Paris as a living being, with the *périphérique* as its carotid artery. I would later walk happily through other more famous, more beautiful parts of Paris, along the river, or the long wide-open boulevards that were carved through the city by Napoleon III. But my early wanderings gave me the interest and confidence to walk off in the direction of some of the more ugly

tenement blocks, where impoverished migrants lived and argued and cooked and held parties; or to dying and rejuvenating industrial areas hidden from the average tourist.

The French have a word for someone who wanders aimlessly through cities, a *flaneur*. While the early English romantics devoted themselves to rural idylls, nineteenth-century French poets took a greater interest in urban life. Baudelaire, in his *Spleen de Paris*, wandered the streets of the city reflecting on poverty, madness, alcoholism, sexual depravity and, of course, love. His fellow poet, Gérard de Nerval[4], was a prince of *flaneurs*. He had a pet lobster that he took on walks through Paris on a pale blue ribbon; he preferred lobsters, he said, because they didn't bark and they knew the secrets of the deep. He later hanged himself with what he claimed was the Queen of Sheba's garter.

Not all *flaneurs* are eccentric—though it clearly helps. Non-*flaneurs* cannot understand why, if you can afford it, you should not travel by car, take a taxi, or ride the train; or perhaps even stay at home. I am not opposed to other forms of transport. But the arguments in favour of walking are impressive—though I have been accused of being, quite simply, ridiculous when discussing these issues with non-walkers. My first, most tendentious argument is that we are, after all, differentiated from other mammals by not having to crawl on all fours, so why not make use of that fact? Walking is also generally healthier unless, of course, you faint from heatstroke, or fall into a sewer; both quite possible in Delhi.

But there are larger, more important reasons for walking around cities. You will find out a lot more about a city by wandering through it than by visiting the homes of the well-off or by just exploring its

---

[4] Both Nerval and Baudelaire—less fashionable these days in the Anglophone world—were quoted by TS Eliot in *The Waste Land*, as were the Upanishads. These are last five lines of *The Waste Land*—the first of them is from Nerval's *El Desdichado*. The last two (in Sanskrit) are from the Upanishads.
Le Prince d'Aquitaine à la tour abolie
These fragments I have shored against my ruins
Why then Ile fit you. Hieronymo's mad againe.
Datta. Dayadhvam. Damyata.
Shantih Shantih Shantih
In *The Waste Land*, Eliot is greatly concerned with the fate of great cities and civilizations. London—which the poet traverses, like an all-knowing, god-like *flaneur*—is described as the 'Unreal City'.

ancient monuments. If you don't walk in Delhi, large parts of the city will be invisible to you. Its slums are mainly situated away from the main roads, hidden from the upmarket residential areas: so that most of the time the affluent are not embarrassed or troubled by the conditions in which the great majority of the population live. And Delhi has the great attraction, from a *flaneur*'s point of view, that, unlike so many western cities, so much of life is lived in the open. Flower sellers, chicken slaughterers, bangle vendors, children bathing, herds of cows, locksmiths, shoe repairers, mobile phone menders, sellers of computer peripherals, mendicants, tea drinkers, courting students, confectioners, quarrelling families and cricket players, all in one small stretch of an over-used city street.

However, Delhi is not an easy city to walk in. Its occasional and irregular pavements contain hidden hazards. It is unwise to wear open shoes, especially, as one Delhi *bourgeoise* pointed out to me, if you have just had a pedicure. In Paris, you pay to visit the famous underground city sewers; in Delhi they are open-air and free of charge. Walking in Delhi—especially if you're large and whitish, and clearly above the poverty line—can make you an object of disbelief and ridicule. In my earlier stay in Delhi, my attempts to walk were almost entirely in vain. Like a caged bear, I would pace up and down inside the compound housing the magnificent tomb of the Mughal Emperor Humayun——a peaceful place for a wander, but not for a proper city walk. There were a few crossing points on the major roads, but when I did try to cross I would be confronted with a wall of autorickshaws all hoping to receive my custom. They clearly resented the fact that by walking, I was losing them business. Whenever I asked anyone directions, in my newcomer's Hindi, I would be pointed not to the place I wanted to go but to the nearest taxi-stand. When I said 'No, I want to walk', most people would smirk, clearly believing I was challenging the order of nature and must be a little mad.

More than a decade later, it is possible to walk in Delhi. There are more underpasses. There are more foreigners living and working in the city, so I attract less attention. But the biggest revolution of all has been the *Eicher* map of the city—more than a hundred and ninety pages of maps in a book that I can carry easily. Now, for the first time, I can plan where to go, and I can begin to see how the little islands of affluent residential existence are connected.

And so it was that I began my first, tentative trek across Delhi, interrupted by laziness, the searing heat of summer and the monsoon rains. First, I walked from my temporary home in South Delhi to Kashmere Gate in the old city, in three separate tranches, carving an inelegant line from south-west to north-east across the city. At about that time, I came upon the works of the legendary London *flaneur* Iain Sinclair, who took a map of East London and drew a letter V on it. This became his route-map in his 1997 psycho-geographical travelogue *Lights Out For The Territory*—walking the streets marked by the lines of that letter. I remember deciding at the time that I was not quite as eccentric as *that*. Sinclair never even got round to explaining why he chose the letter V. But I then found myself continuing my Delhi perambulation by heading off on short strolls north and west in the winter months, before returning south to complete what turned out to be a nice little figure-of-eight through the Indian capital. I then began making plans for a more serious walk.

Heaven on earth

When I first lived in Delhi, in the 1990s, many residents behaved, like me, as if they were here on sufferance: just passing through, camping in Delhi for a few years, or a few decades. I returned to Delhi in 2003, as a second-time migrant, with children in tow, sent here by the BBC for six months—and with a definite plan to return to London. As the six months were extended to nine and twelve, this city seduced me, and we decided to stay. I became a warts-and-all devotee of Delhi. Apart from the tiny percentage of the population with roots in the old city, Delhi commands little loyalty from its citizens—particularly the newcomers. Some of its residents, of course, care intensely, even obsessively, about their building, their street, their neighbourhood. A few others care about Delhi's archaeological monuments, or its trees, or its disappearing wildlife—but the city as a whole still feels orphaned and unloved. This was not always the case.

There are few cities in the world which have seen their reputation and fortune fluctuate quite like Delhi's. According to the city's first great poet, Amir Khusro, Delhi was 'heaven on earth'. But within just two years of his death in 1325, Khusro's Delhi had been obliterated. The Sultan of Delhi, Muhammad Tughlaq, furious about a perceived insult by some of its residents, abandoned the city and destroyed it.

Half a million inhabitants were sent away to a new capital several hundred miles to the south[5]. They were then sent all the way back again two years later. Several centuries and several calamities later, in the 1670s, with the Mughal Empire at its apogee, Delhi

was briefly the most populous city in the world, and one of the richest. And Khusro's hyperbolic words about Delhi were proudly inscribed on the wall of the Emperor's audience chamber. But just sixty years later, with the Mughal Empire in decline, the Persian Emperor, Nadir Shah, plundered Delhi, killing as many as one hundred and twenty thousand people in a single night of bloodshed, and ran off with the Kohinoor diamond and the Peacock Throne. In the mid-nineteenth century, Delhi's last great poet, Mirza Ghalib, proclaimed that 'The world is the body, Delhi is its soul'. But in the wake of the Great Uprising or Mutiny of 1857, Ghalib witnessed his courtly Delhi fall apart, as the triumphant and vengeful British turned the streets of the old Mughal capital into a human slaughterhouse— and drove those who survived out of the city. The corpses lay so deep in Delhi's main thoroughfare that the horses of the victors had to tread on them.

After the Mutiny, Delhi became a poet-less, provincial backwater; a third-rank city that stagnated for a half-century while those other future megacities, Bombay and Calcutta, flourished as the economic and administrative centres of British India respectively. Bombay and Calcutta seemed modern, forward-looking. They had seaports, they were largely British-built, colonial creations. They had become great trading cities. Delhi—six hundred miles from the nearest port—was a fossil, an open-air museum of Indian history with no obvious future.

---

[5] Khusro, who spent most of his adult life in Sultanate Delhi, actually wrote, 'If there be heaven on earth—this is it, this is it, this is it', though there is some doubt over whether he was really the author of these words, and whether the original reference may have been to Kashmir, or even to India more generally. The Moroccan traveller Ibn Battuta, who became one of Muhammad Tughlaq's courtiers describes how only two people remained in Delhi: a cripple and a blind man. The Sultan ordered the cripple to be thrown out of the city from a giant catapult, while the blind man was to be dragged out of the city. According to Ibn Battuta, 'he fell to pieces on the road, and all of him that reached Daulatabad [the new capital] was his leg'.

And then in 1911, in an announcement that now seems whimsical, the visiting British King, George V, decreed that Delhi—or rather an unbuilt New Delhi, to be constructed alongside what was left of the city's previous incarnations—would replace Calcutta as the Indian capital. Delhi had been saved from obscurity, and turned into a building site. Large parts of parts of the city still feel like a building site, as successive waves of migrants—civil servants, building workers, Punjabis, north Indians and even a few foreigners—have encircled and swallowed the scattered remains of forgotten empires, and searched for new land on which to build their dreams.

In the popular imagination, Delhi is still unlike those other megacities, Bombay and Calcutta, whose unplanned vastness is the stuff of legend. Every year, books are published that challenge or reinforce the image of these younger cities as giant urban cesspits. Delhi is treated less seriously as a modern city, as if it were just some period-piece. Its contemporary reputation in India is as a place where people suffer lesser evils: power cuts and gastric flu, water shortages and road rage. It has become a cliché to describe Delhi as a collection of villages, as a home for corrupt or inept bureaucrats, or as the obsolete invention of long-dead town planners. Those who write about Delhi tend to evoke a sadness about a lost past, a dreamy admiration for old empires. They rarely deal with it as it is now— one of the largest and fastest growing cities in the world.

Of perfect numbers and Bernoulli spirals

Once upon a time, many moons ago, I was good at mathematics. Very good, my teachers said—but not much good at anything else (except capital cities). I learnt early on that I didn't want to be the kind of person who was good at maths, and eventually stopped studying it. In the society in which I grew up, in London in the 1970s, boys who were good at maths seemed to have lots of spots and no girlfriends. Their abilities were seen as impressive in some strange abstract way, but maths was boring—and mathematicians weren't really members of the species.

I still try to calm my occasional middle-of-the-night insomniac anxieties by blanking out my other thoughts and trying to find a formula that predicts the occurrence of prime numbers. Some people to whom I have told this look at me as if I am not of this world. Others dip their heads, and tell me about their secret night-lives, where they too play mathematical games in their heads, searching for the relationship between successive cubed numbers, or checking again that there really are only two perfect numbers under one hundred[6]. During my latest Delhi sojourn I developed a new middle-of-the-night game: the search for the perfect geometric method for exploring a city on foot.

I used Delhi—as wide as it is long, and vaguely circular—as my model. I was searching for a solution that was practical, mathematically sound, and aesthetically appealing. Circles, in the form of ring roads and *périphériques*, provide a simple, encompassing route around most cities. But, by their very nature, they leave out the heart, and are usually suffocatingly polluted. I considered other solutions: letters of the alphabet, as used by Iain Sinclair, a self-proclaimed proponent of 'ambulant signmaking'. The 'W' for instance, mapped on most cities, would give considerable variety. So does the 'S', in a rather more elegant way. But there was no logic to these solutions—and they left out too much. The figure-of-eight (geometrically-speaking, the lemniscate of Bernoulli) that I used for my preliminary wander through Delhi was also ultimately unsatisfactory, though very plausible. The holes in the two circles meant I had again left too much out; and it was too upright, leaving huge spaces to the left and right of the central junction of the '8'. There was an identical problem with the figure-of-eight's sleeping twin, the symbol for infinity (∞). I considered the Hindi ligature and mantra, Om, (ॐ), omnipresent in Delhi, which certainly seemed relevant but just a little aquarian, and discontinuous. One night, at three in the morning, I found the shape I wanted.

I had been staring at a book about Shahjahanabad—now known as Old Delhi—earlier that night, full of strange diagrams about how cities were formed. Muslim cities, I read, were formed in concentric circles. And there was a little drawing—six perfect earthly circles, orbiting around a central mosque. How could I visit each circle, and move between these circles? By spiralling. A closely packed spiral is, after all, hard to distinguish from a series of concentric circles.

[6] Six and twenty-eight are perfect numbers because they are equal to the sum of their factors. So 6 is divisible by 1,2 & 3, and 1+2+3 = 6. 28 is divisible by 14,7,4,2 and 1, which all add up to, yes, 28. It takes an extremely long period of insomnia to reach the next perfect number, 496.

Ask an adult to draw a spiral—and a good half of them will draw a wiggly line, a sine curve, or an approximation to a spiral staircase. Children know a true spiral, though some will draw it from the outside in. A spiral is special because it can be endless, but still under control. In fact, the spiral is not really a shape (though try telling that to a child), but just a curved line. My dictionary tells me that a spiral is a curve formed by a point which moves around a fixed centre and continually increases its distance from it. Suddenly I began to see spirals everywhere in Delhi, on mosquito coils, on Islamic tiles, in the design motif of the newish British Council building, in a range of tightly wound modern and ancient staircases, in apple peelings, on snail shells, in light filaments, on the staircase of a water tower, in emptying bath water, on the sandstone nautilus shells of Rajpath. In another sense, spirals are the stuff of life. The double helix of DNA is a doubled up 3-D spiral. And I discovered in the purple prose of Louise Bourgeois[7], one of the most inventive of

modern artists, an exaltation of the spiral as

. . . an attempt at controlling chaos. It has two directions. Where do you place yourself; at the periphery or the vortex? Beginning at the outside is fear of losing control . . . Beginning at the centre is affirmation, the move outward is a representation of giving, and giving up control; of trust, positive energy, of life itself.[8]

I had found both my device and my metaphor. A spiral through Delhi would give me a loose framework for my wanderings, always forcing me away gently from places I have already visited. Eventually, I would reach beyond the city. The tight spiral of the mosquito coil—green, silent, murderous, expectorating—became my first model. But it would take an eternity to reach beyond central Delhi because each

[7] Her 'Spiral Women' (2003) sculpture is a dark blue fabric body hanging from a meat hook. The top half of the body is a helix out of which emerge two naked legs.

[8] There is a curious Bourgeois-Delhi connection. Lawrence Rinder, a modern art curator, and author of *Louise Bourgeois; Drawings and Observations* (1996) has compiled a 322-line specimen of doggerel called 'Passages from India' which he posted with apologies on an Internet poetry site:

twist of the spiral is equidistant from the previous one. Then there was the nautilus, Bernoulli's *spira mirabilis*[9], the miraculous spiral the great mathematician asked to be carved on his gravestone in Basel, spinning larger and larger, but never losing control. I tried this on a large map of Delhi, inelegantly drawing a spiral that started in the centre of the city and curved off towards infinity into the countryside beyond the southern suburbs. It worked. There would have to be some deviations, I would not get permission to stroll across the runway at Delhi's international airport, and I was not going to swim the foul-smelling Yamuna river—but the basic pattern would take me to places I had never been. It would allow me to break with the normal arterial pattern of travel through this rapidly modernizing city; it would impose on me the experience of a cross-section of the outdoor life of this megalopolis. I now had a template for discovery, for chance meetings, for exploring this frightful, delightful city in flux. In the controlled randomness of a spiral embossed on the surface of Delhi, I hoped to make better sense to myself of a city I love and hate, all at once, in a way which, as I prepare to begin my walk, captivates and astonishes me.

We've assembled here in Delhi
Which is noisy and quite smelly
My throat is sore, my nose is runny
My stomach feels a little funny . . .
    It does get a bit better:
    Archaeologically speaking
Delhi's tough for those who're seeking
Simplicity in the march of ages
It's lacking in defined stages.

[9] The *spira mirabilis* of Jacob Bernoulli (1654–1705) is described geometrically by the equation $r = a \exp (8 \cot b)$ or pictorially by '◉'. In fact the stonemason carved a boringly uniform Archimedean spiral on his gravestone.

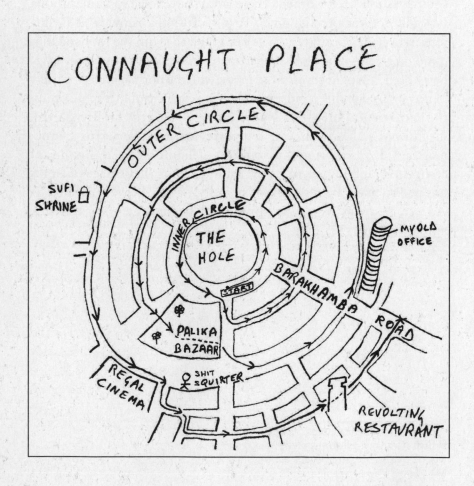

Chapter One: In which the Author is dazzled by the Metro, finds a cure for haemorrhoids and turns the tables on an unscrupulous shoeshine man

I WAS STANDING in a sleepy park in the centre of Delhi, struck dumb by what I could see beneath me. My face was pressed hard against the glass of a concealed skylight and I was gawping down into what seemed to be another universe. An enormous, pulsating cavern had been cut deep into the ancient rock and soil beneath Delhi's venerable Connaught Place, at the very centre spot of the Indian capital. Beams of dust-laden natural light illuminated the glistening steel and marble concourse below me. It was a hive of hyperactivity, milling with purposeful people—like the science fiction image of a subterranean city. This, then, is the dazzling new heart of Delhi.

Connaught Place, twentieth-century Delhi's commercial and geographical hub, has undergone irreversible change. It now houses a vast underground railway junction, the lynchpin of Delhi's new Metro system. The Metro is both a monument to modernity and a harbinger of change. India has ambitions of great power status, and its capital is now one of the most populous cities in the world. Once upon a time, the people of Delhi were accused of always living in the past, of romanticizing Delhi as a city of poets and courtesans; a city of empires—Mughal and British. Today, the emphasis is resolutely forward-looking. In this city of migrants, the congested, hypertensive older parts of Delhi are seen as squalid embarrassments or touristic culs-de-sac. And the new Metro, all steel, glass and concrete, is Delhi's latest offering to the gods of progress, to be placed alongside those other gifts for 'a modern future'—the convention centres, flyovers, multiplexes and shopping plazas. The Metro has become the icon of Delhi's uncertain future, carving its way above and beneath the city, overshadowing and undermining the forgotten and neglected mosques, temples, churches, forts and tombs of previous rulers.

From my secret window in the station's vaulted ceiling, high above the maze of footbridges and walkways, I stare, dazzled by this new world below. I track confident commuters as they weave their way, with some irritation, through gaggles of confused tourists. There's a miasma of electronic destination signs, and neon-lit bookshops and cafés. Police officers use hand-held metal detectors on impatient passengers. A young western woman with a backpack is struggling with the ticket-less token-operated entry gate; an elderly Sikh man shows her how to use it. There are wide staircases reaching down to the deepest level of the station, where the Metro's north-south artery runs—soon this line will go all the way to Gurgaon in Delhi's Deep South. The two visible platforms are broad and clean, and sleek trains slide elegantly into the station, briefly spitting out and sucking up passengers, before smashing their way through the darkness towards a distant suburb. A pigeon, stranded inside the station, flutters high above the concourse. It flies towards me, dashing itself against the glass of the skylight. It plummets towards the concourse, apparently unconscious and then pulls itself out of its fall, just inches from the ground—and flies drunkenly away.

The desperate pigeon has broken the hypnotic spell of the Metro. And I'm reminded of my purpose—that I should start my walk. As I peel myself away from the skylight, leaving a ghostly imprint of my face on the glass, there's a squirting sound behind me. A single jet of water lashes my back. Some fountains, behind which the skylight was concealed, are being turned on. I manoeuvre my way along a narrow parapet and stand, slightly damp, in the middle of Connaught Place. This is my starting point, the hub of my spiral.

The centre of Connaught Place is occupied by what looks, at first sight, like a fairly innocuous, well-kept municipal park. It has manicured lawns and pink footpaths, a few newly planted shrubs, a courting couple, five men playing cards, some faux-Edwardian street lamps, a small stone-built amphitheatre, and a series of ponds and unpredictable water fountains concealing the parapet that led to my skylight. But this sleepy park is, as I discovered when I peered into cavern below, not quite what it seems. It is, in fact, a landscaped lid covering a deep hole: an entirely artificial creation perched on the roof of the subterranean Metro station.

When I first lived in Delhi, in the 1990s, the centre of Connaught Place was a real park, the kind in which a dog can bury a bone, or where trees can grow roots. By my return to Delhi in 2003, it had become a huge construction site, with an enormous hole at its heart. I worked from an office which had a spectacular long-distance view over the hole, and would watch as construction workers eviscerated the old heart of Delhi. Most days at lunch time, I would stroll around the grey tinplate fencing that ringed the hole, painted with the circular red logo of the Delhi Metro. There were no gaps in the fences, and so the hole, and the shattered earth within, was invisible to most Connaught Place *flaneurs*. However, I am 6'1" and by balancing on a metal bollard I could peer over the fencing, through a tangle of steel, into the gloomy darkness that now forms the multi-level Connaught Place[1] Metro interchange—and try to assess how much progress had been made. Occasionally, as if by magic, the blue-white incandescent sparks of an arc-welder would briefly illuminate the bottom of the hole fifty metres below. And I would spot shadowy rebates in the levelled earth, convinced that they must be the Metro platforms of the future. And now, less than two years later, as I begin walking around the innermost circle of Connaught Place, the station is complete, and more unexpectedly, almost invisible: camouflaged from public view by the park I have just left.

Connaught Place has a very deliberate geometry. 'Stamped by foreign hands, concentric,' according to the Indian poet, Tabish Khair[2]. A near-spiral, Connaught Place, or 'CP'[3], consists of three

---

[1]Officially Rajiv Chowk Metro Station but always called Connaught Place (or 'CP') Station.

[2]Aarhus-based Khair's fourth volume of poetry, *Where Parallel Lines Meet* (Penguin 2000), is obsessed with geometry. It is divided into three sections: Squares and Circles, Straight Lines and Triangles, and Other Geometries. He shows no interest in spirals. Here is his description of pre-Metro Connaught Place—part of an eight-verse poem about Delhi.

Stamped by foreign hands, concentric
Runs its rush of cars and autos,
Breaking out now and then into a jangle
Of horns to break out of jungled metal
And pedestrians who dart like wet cats
From one end to another, linking shops,
Hotels and offices to the open
Park in the centre where the sky sits
Scattering peanut shells and playing cards
Or gossiping with sharp, straggly birds.

[3]The outer and inner circles are officially named Indira Chowk and Rajiv Chowk after two assassinated former prime ministers. Indira Gandhi was killed in Delhi by two of her Sikh bodyguards in 1984; her son and successor Rajiv Gandhi was killed in South India by a Tamil Tiger suicide bomber in 1991. CP was named after Prince Arthur, Duke of Connaught (1850–1942), Queen Victoria's seventh child, who was visiting Delhi as construction work on CP started.

circles, nestled neatly inside each other, spoked by seven radial roads. CP was completed in the 1930s, in the twilight of British rule. It was carefully inserted as the capital's new commercial centre into the forests and scrub that separated the newly built government buildings of New Delhi from the old Mughal city of Old Delhi. The inspiration for the double-storyed curving colonnades[4] of CP, the architectural historians tell us, was Bath's Royal Crescent and Circus, or even a decapitated, inside-out version of the Colosseum. CP still has a certain tarnished grandeur, a Palladian outpost suffering from modest urban blight. Hoardings and signboards have broken the careful lines and silhouettes of the colonnades, but the sense of circularity still exists, as anyone who has ever got lost in CP can tell you.

To my left is the circular park I have just fled, and to my right is a curving colonnade in white, two storeys high, emblazoned with the signboards of multi-national brands: Pizza Hut, Benetton, Reebok, TGI Fridays, Samsonite. It's still early—shops and offices are just opening. A guard sleeps on a chair inside a sports shop, the glass façade providing no shelter from intruding eyes. Above him is a sign with a picture of a cricketer and the words 'Proud to be Indian'. I take a picture, setting off my flash by mistake and waking him. He grants me an embarrassed smile, makes himself comfortable and goes back to sleep, hand on groin. Morning cricketers—affluent teenagers, boys and girls on school holidays, dressed in jeans and T-shirts, and speaking English—have taken over a parking lot; the boys titter as a girl in pink tries to bat. She is out first ball. A strutting youth with an incipient moustache and a sneer on his face then hits the ball down a Metro staircase. 'Six!' he proclaims, lifting his bat high in the air. A few seconds later, the ball returns on the same trajectory, courtesy of an unseen arm. There are more than ten such entrances to the Metro; like the station itself they are camouflaged: discrete half-hidden staircases cut into the pavement. But standing proud in the morning sun, glinting like a single silver tooth in an ancient jaw, against a backdrop of the peeling plasterwork of CP shops, is a

[4]The architect of Connaught Place was Robert Tor Russel (1888–1972), who as Chief Architect, Delhi was given some of the lesser buildings in New Delhi to design. They are all more neo-Classical, less influenced by traditional Indian architecture, and less monumental, than the more famous, earlier creations of Edwin Lutyens and Herbert Baker.

passenger lift for 'physically challenged' Metro customers. A striped grey squirrel shimmies up a nearby gulmohar tree, and runs down a drooping branch and drops onto the roof of the lift. A pariah kite hovers and swoops above, but does not find its prey.

Completing the first, innermost twist of my spiral, I veer outwards into the middle circle of CP, a service lane, a tangle of buildings and smells and autorickshaws. Steep stone stairs lead up to accountants' offices, tailors, employment bureaux and software developers. I hesitate, I can't visit them all. But one signboard intrigues me: 'Mail Massage services'. I go up. It's locked, and I peer through the glass door, discovering that the second word, not the first, was misspelled.

In the narrow service lane, there are reserved parking spaces, marked out in white paint, for the chairman and the managing director of DSIDC—which reveals itself, in a much smaller font to be the Delhi State Industrial Development Corporation. This public sector company has spread its wings in unlikely directions in recent years—and has divided its offices between two sideline businesses: a cybercafé and an alcohol shop, both managed by DSIDC. I choose the cybercafé—six small shabby-brown booths, all occupied, all quiet—just the energetic tapping of keys. The booths are far from private and all the computer screens are visible. Elsewhere in Delhi and in India, Internet cafés are places with curtains, or carefully constructed so as to allow privacy. One Indian journalist told me to go into any Indian cybercafé, and press the Back button, 'Always porn, hard-core stuff, or online dating.' But the DSIDC has a no-porn policy. A large notice above each computer: 'VIEWING OF OBSCENE SITES STRICTLY PROHIBITED'. I decide to wait for a machine to become free and pay for half-an-hour. I start pacing around, eyeing the users, all male Indians, and none of them looking at porn. One is writing up a CV, two others are e-mailing, one more is filling in a spreadsheet. This cybercafé is a place of work and aspiration, not pleasure. A man wearing a baby-pink tie and a maroon shirt stood up wearily and left. I plumped myself down. His seat was warm and the booth was ripe with aftershave. The Back button on his computer led me to a job recruitment site. After deleting Viagra-spam from my e-mail account, I still had seventeen minutes left. Looking around for inspiration, I punched in 'Connaught Place' and 'Internet'. The second search result, Trisoft.net caught my eye.

. . . Trisoft Systems and New Delhi Traders Association (NDTA) joining hands to host Asia's largest shopping complex, **Connaught Place** (CP), on the **Internet** . . . ."

www.trisoft.net/press/media/media1998.htm—18k—<u>Cached</u>—
<u>Similar pages</u>

Clicking through, I was able to enter the world of India's first Internet boom of the late 1990s. Hemant Sharma, a 'cyberbrat', according to one press cutting proudly displayed on the site, had left a good job at Microsoft to return to India and set up Trisoft. Among his projects was the creation on the Internet of a 'virtual Connaught Place'. Cpmall.com was launched in 1999, and meant shoppers around the world could 'visit' and purchase from 700 stores in CP without ever having to leave their homes or offices. But cpmall.com, when I searched for it on the Internet, no longer existed, and Trisoft's site had not been updated since 2002. Had it crashed along with hundreds of other early Indian dotcoms? I looked up Trisoft's contact details and e-mailed Hemant Sharma, at his ancient Hotmail address. The headquarters of Trisoft was listed as two blocks further along my spiral at E-30 Connaught Place. It was time to continue walking.

The sun was now high enough to shrink my shadow to an area no bigger than a laptop. I ploughed on in search of E-30. The wooden signboard listing the occupants of E block does not even include the number 30, let alone mention Trisoft. I drifted past a green-tiled open-air urinal, a chalk scribble showing it had last been cleaned four hours earlier. It was in use; two men, Little and Large, comically unaware of each other, but with perfectly synchronized arm movements, as they waggled their unseen penises dry.

I gave up on my search for Trisoft[5], and retreated to a more hospitable place. KI, the mother of a friend of mine, has lived in CP, in her current flat, for sixty-eight years. It was the first time I had seen English-style fireplaces and mantelpieces in a Delhi home. I was licked and nuzzled by KI's dogs, Inca and Khushi, as I devoured a Parsee[6]

[5]Hemant Sharma did eventually respond to my e-mail. Cpmall.com was still-born. Connaught Place traders were not willing to invest in the site, and too few customers were willing to buy over the Internet. It was a failed version of modernity. Trisoft, however, still exists, as a software development firm, and has moved to South Delhi.

[6]KI is one of Delhi's thousand-odd Parsees, followers of the Zoroastrian religion.

appetizer of *Papeta-par-eeda*—baked eggs and potatoes. She recalled moving into CP before it was complete, when jackals could be heard howling at night, and she said, grimly turning to her dogs, that the jackals would gobble up pets that weren't locked in. When I asked her about how CP had changed, she looked up to the heavens. She recalled the old bandstand in the central park, where a police band played every Saturday during World War Two. It was a beautiful park. 'The war years,' she began, with a nostalgic effusiveness that quickly dissipated into halting embarrassment, 'were lovely years'. Then came independence in 1947 and the partition of India. Most of the Muslims of Connaught Place, she told me, left for Pakistan. 'There was some looting', she said, 'but the army protected CP from the worst violence and there weren't killings like elsewhere.' She took me onto her balcony and pointed out a petrol pump. 'The Muslim owner asked my father for one thousand rupees for it, that's all. But he said "what would I do with a petrol pump?"'

KI helped out at a nearby hospital and looked after Hindu refugees from Pakistan, women who had been separated from their men-folk, and who'd been raped. 'We tried to get them back with their husbands, to reunite them. There was something that shocked me, though. Educated men would not take their wives back, if they had been raped; but poor men, illiterate men—they would. I couldn't understand that. Still can't.'

Over a rich mutton pulao, whose spices, cardamom and clove, were whirling their way out of the battered cooking pot and spinning around the room, KI continued, undeterred by my gluttony. 'Earlier, children could roam around CP freely, playing seven-tiles or rounders. Now there are so many call-girls; riff-raff, riff-raff.' Her voice trailed off. She fell silent, a trace of a tear in each eye. She sniffed, pulled her shoulders in, looked around and picked up where she had left off. Almost all the families she had known as a teenager had left; she herself had been offered a huge sum to move. But she would remain.

Although CP was designed as the new commercial hub for Delhi, it was always intended that families should live there too. The upstairs floors were built as homes, with large airy rooms, fireplaces and

---

Most of the world's one hundred thousand Parsees live in Mumbai. Rajiv Gandhi, after whom CP's metro station is officially named, had a Parsee father.

balconies. There were good schools nearby, and of course, the evanescent central park. There were few cars, and no high-rise buildings. CP had many of the elements of a model new development. However, Connaught Place was then on the edge of the city, which quickly encircled its circles, and grew and grew. Now Delhi stretches for many kilometres in every direction and CP shows all the symptoms of inner-city decay. In the evenings, it became the haven of the call-girl and the pimp. In the day-time, dazed backpackers still get harassed and cheated, and find the occasional bargain. A few older Delhi-ites still swear by the shops of CP, but most prefer to go elsewhere. Recently, the arrival of the Metro has encouraged brave talk about the rebirth of Connaught Place as the commercial heart of Delhi.

I stumbled back down KI's steep steps and out into the hazy punishing sun. I continued doggedly around the middle circle, the only one of the concentric triplets of CP whose geometry has been broken. In the space between two radial roads, is a lumpily landscaped mini-park, full of strange metallic and concrete protrusions, where lovers can rest and fondle, and where ear-cleaners linger with intent. Sirajuddin saw me coming. He dug a long, thin, pointed steel scraper into the ear of his smiling companion—and smiled up at me. '*Dekho*, look' (he provided his own translation). And then the scraper emerged from the ear with a piece of brown wax the size and shape of the body of a wasp. He offered to look into my orifices. He took out a tiny frayed notebook full of testimonials, '*Aap kahan se hain?* (where are you from?)'. During the 2003 Gulf War, I used to reply 'Finland' to this question—as a way of avoiding arguments—but now I had reverted to the truth. He flicked through his notebook and found an appropriate page. I began to read: 'Sirajuddin is a very persuasive man and is also a magician with ears. I could not believe the amount of crap that came out my ears. Rs 300 is very reasonable for this service. Mike. England 17/1/95.' Brandishing his scraper, he told me that his name was mentioned in the Lonely Planet guide to India, and that he had been cleaning ears for twenty-five years. He could see that I wasn't convinced. He flicked to the next page of his notebook. '23/5/95. After years of planning to get my ears syringed due to being almost deaf, I fell for having my ears done by Siraj. Well worth it. Rs 600 and a whole lot more hearing. Go for it, its safe and relaxing. Julia, Charge Nurse,

London'. I, a regular cotton-bud man, decided not to go for it. I had already steeled myself to the idea that I might have to walk through a sewer if necessary as part of my perambulation, but I would not, on any account, have a pointed metal object stuck deep into my ear. Instead, I disappeared into an opening in the ground, and tripped my way down a spiral staircase.

The carbuncular protrusions in the park that I'd just descended from are actually air-vents, waste-pipes and sky-lights serving the labyrinthine, sleazy, electronic, underground world of Palika Bazaar. This is Connaught Place's alter ego, its sunless and shrunken doppelgänger, built like CP in circles. Palika Bazaar is, in the modern vernacular, a grey market, with dodgy goods galore. Neon-lit stalls, set into this concrete underworld, sell fake perfumes, Minnie Mouse wall-hangings, *101 Dalmatians* T-shirts, plastic jewellery, hair-tongs from China bearing the label 'Intellectual Ionic Hair Permer', bust-developing cream, pirated DVDs of new Hollywood films, Indian and European porn movies on VCD, mobile phones without guarantees at 60 percent of list price, and, as I discovered precisely 57 minutes later, a watch battery that didn't work for more than an hour.

I wandered into a shop called Astro-Scan, which promised computer horoscopes within five minutes. I handed over Rs 125, and the date, time and place of my birth. A young woman dressed in a crimson *salwar kameez*, entered the details into her late 1990s PC, using special *pandit-ji*[7] software. In three minutes, twenty seconds, I had received eight closely typed pages of horoscope. I learned that I am a) 'jolly natured', b) proficient at mathematics c) a 'glib talker', d) like to spread religion through music e) have drooping shoulders f) like cardamom, g) am attracted to the opposite sex, h) have a skin disease i) am good at interior decoration and j) have a 'unique and weird nature'. 6½ out of 10, I thought. Not bad. As I left, thanking the crimson lady, she eyed me—and said with a malevolent smirk 'you will have many girlfriends'. Exit 4 from Palika Bazaar led me up and out into the blinding sunlight of the outer circle of CP. It was too hot—and I hailed an

---

[7]*Pandit* can mean a learned man, a Hindu priest (many of whom are also astrologers), and it's widely used as a synonym for Brahmin. It is also the source of the English word 'pundit'. *Ji* is an honorific, similar to Mr, but used as a suffix.

autorickshaw to take me home to the quiet, tree-lined, cattle-filled streets of South Delhi.

I resumed walking from Exit 4 three days later, heading past Statesman House, a fourteen-storey circular office building, whose malnourished Palladian columns pay minor homage to CP's colonnades on the other side of the road. It has a curious seventeen-storey companion on the next corner, Gopal Das Bhavan, its cross-section like a pinched ellipse, and closely modelled on a tall stack of dirty dinner plates. This was my place of work, on the thirteenth floor, for thirteen months. It had a good long-distance view of the Metro and the great hole of Connaught Place. Gopal Das Bhavan entered the national consciousness for a brief period in 1997 as the backdrop for a legendary act of incompetence and brutality by the Delhi police. A team of undercover officers pumped 31 bullets into a car, occupied by suspected criminals, waiting at the traffic lights outside Gopal Das Bhavan. According to one witness, 'they opened the doors and dragged the bodies out. They were kicking the bodies to make sure they were dead.' The police then realized they'd got it wrong. It wasn't bearded Mohammed Yaseen, dangerous kidnapper, in his cobalt blue Maruti Esteem, but bearded businessman Jagjit Singh, in a different cobalt blue Maruti Esteem. Jagjit Singh, and the car owner, Pradeep Goyal, were dead. The prime minister ordered an inquiry, some police officers were reshuffled, others were charged with murder[8].

Beyond Gopal Das, I pass the fire station, then a whimsical police notice-board—'with you, for you—always . . . Delhi police'—and a fruit stall with four varieties of mango. The buildings get smaller: lamination shops, rubber stamp shops, take-away restaurants with kerosene stoves on the pavement, railway property fenced off by red-brick boundary walls, perfect as a urinal—and in constant use. Amidst the pissers, a disconsolate cobbler is seated beneath this sign in English, 'Urinating prohibited. Defaulters will be prosecuted.'

A little further on, a narrow, partly covered passage leads to an unexpected open space, home to one of Delhi's youngest Sufi shrines,

[8]On 11 June 2004 the real Mohammed Yaseen was shot dead in an encounter with the police in South Delhi. In October, 2007, ten policemen were convicted of murder for the killings of Jagjit Singh and Pradeep Goyal—and sentenced to life imprisonment.

predating CP by just thirty years. Inside a blue-washed sideroom sat Maulana Mohammed Omar Faridi Salimi Fakhri Chishti, President of the Sufi Council of India, mobile phone and business cards at his side. He signalled that I should sit on the floor close to him. Opposite the Maulana were two women, a mother and daughter, to each of whom he dispensed a little packet containing a grey powder, and a piece of paper on which he wrote some Arabic words in brown ink. I asked the women if the paper was a prescription for medicine. They looked at each other coyly. The

daughter eventually responded, in an upper-class Indian-English accent: 'Yes, in a way . . . but much better than that.' She wouldn't tell me more. They got up to leave, nodding gratefully. The Maulana turned to me and began his explanation, with the two women just within earshot. 'You see, the mother . . . well, she has very bad piles.' He pointed helpfully at his own bottom. 'And, the daughter . . . she just can't get pregnant, however much she tries.' The two women seemed to speed up their departure from the room, as the Maulana continued. 'The powder is a herbal medicine, made from the bark and leaves of a tree over there,' he continued, pointing to the shrine compound. The piece of paper had words and verses from the Quran, he explained, and each word had a numerological significance. The paper must be kept close to the body. He then went into a long digression on Islamic numerology, and the numerical value of each Arabic letter, and ended by providing me with a mathematical formula for converting the Muslim calendar into the Christian calendar[9]. I asked him about the success rate of his fertility treatment. 'Ninety-five per cent' he replied

[9]Multiply the Muslim year by 32, divide the result by 33 and add 622. The result will be the date according to the Christian calendar.

immediately, without batting an eyelid. 'And piles?' I persisted. He looked at me suspiciously, as if I was mocking him, and said nothing. He lapsed into meditation, and I gathered my belongings, ready to leave, feeling that I had caused offence. He looked up at me again, and gave me a hard, wary stare. There was something he wanted to say. 'Let me tell you, I have almost 400 patients a week, almost all of them are Hindu—not Muslim. Do you understand? Those ladies, the ones who were just here—they are Hindus; the one with piles, she had been coming to me for thirty years.' I felt like saying it was about time she tried another doctor, but I bit my tongue, recognizing that he was making an important point about Hindu–Muslim relations in CP, and indeed in Delhi generally. He presented me with two boxes of joss-sticks, and a business card complete with e-mail address—and one of his numerology students accompanied me out into CP.

I was coming towards the end of the Connaught Place twist of the spiral. I hurried past Hotel Alka ('the best alternative to luxury'); and more municipal corporation signboards, 'Say No To Plastic Bags'; and a large cartoon of a man spitting, a gob of saliva suspended in mid-air, with a big red cross, like the Swiss flag, drawn over his face. The next block is dominated by one building: the Regal, one of Delhi's oldest cinemas, built at the same time as the rest of CP. It was briefly famous around the world. In 1998, a group of self-proclaimed defenders of Hinduism ransacked the Regal for showing an Indian film in which two Hindu women, sisters-in-law, fall in love. A few weeks later, a counter-demonstration outside the cinema saw the slogan: 'We are Indians, Lesbianism is our heritage' deployed for the first time on the streets of Delhi.

In pre-independence days, one acquaintance told me, there were daily matinee shows at the Regal—for the British women, 'all good family films'. These days, mornings are for masturbators. Outside the cinema was a poster for *Love Affairs* showing a near-naked, western woman arching her back, her breasts lightly sprinkled with silver glitter. 'Randy, Raunchy & Hot For You', 10.30 a.m. show only. I looked around nervously for anyone who might know me, ready with my explanation that I was working on a story. My ticket cost Rs 40. Inside, already showing, was a very bad print of a German film, with English subtitles. It was a comedy of sorts. The main character was wearing dark glasses and carried a white stick. He was pretending to be blind, going up to unknown women in the street, touching their faces with his fingertips, as they smiled kindly and slightly nervously. He then lowered his hands and—to the audible delight of my fellow cinema-goers, all of them men—fondled his victims' breasts. There was no nudity, a fair amount of groping and a lot of rustling in the back rows of the stalls. I left early—emerging into the mid-day sun, as the queue built up for the main Hindi feature film. I walked past another of my circle of circle restaurants: DV8 (say it out loud)—proclaiming itself to be 'away from the ordinary'.

Nearby stands one of the unheralded glories of modern

Indian architecture, the Indian Life building. It is a majestic triumph of asymmetry, like a huge goalmouth viewed from the right-hand side of the penalty area, with a steel pergola as its roof netting. There are four separate upright structures, with huge gaps between them—connected only by the pergola. A central column, plain and solid and white, flanked by two vast wings whose scale and floor space are modestly underplayed by great darkened reflective sheets of glass. These mirrors give space and grandeur to the rest of CP, and create a legion of virtual trees. On each side, there is red-tiled masonry, a Mughal colour, and far to the right, toward DV8, a red column, knife-edged, cutting through the Delhi haze. The building is, in the best possible sense, a waste of space. Unlike so many of Delhi's modern buildings, there is no attempt to squeeze in as much floor area as possible. It is low density. The building has space to breathe and so does Connaught Place[10].

[10]The Indian Life, or Jeevan Bharati, building was designed for the Life Insurance Corporation of India, by one of the country's most celebrated architects,

Outside on the pavement amid the trees, I feel less comfortable. For this marks the site of my moment of greatest shame in Delhi. Here I once rubbed faecal matter from my right shoe onto the torn jeans of a poor man. Let me explain. Three times I have been caught by the phantom shit-squirter. On the first occasion, I was approached by a shoeshine man. He pointed at my right shoe, on which sat a perfectly formed slug of mud. 'Shit,' the man said, offering to clean my shoes for me. I pulled off my shoe and ascertained rapidly that his surmise was correct: I had a strange worm of shit on my shoe. I wiped it off with a leaf. It happened again, a month later, as I emerged from the same underpass. I realized this time that here was some scam, a way of encouraging tight-fisted, dirty-shoed foreigners to exchange some money for a good polish. I shouted at the shoeshine man, there was a minor scene—and eventually I sloped off, shit still on shoe. Then the third time, I decided I would try to take a photograph of the person who put the shit on my shoe in the first place. But I was daydreaming as I wandered through the underpass—and was squirted again. The same shoeshine man appeared, clearly not recognizing me. I was both furious and embarrassed to have been caught again, especially since I was attempting to catch the scamsters out. To the consternation of passers-by, who hissed at me but did not intervene, I grabbed the man by one shoulder and cleaned my shoes on his less than spotless trousers[11].

Delhi's highest restaurant is just a market-trader's scream away from the Indian Life building. Getting there, however, proved complicated. I headed twenty metres south down Parliament Street and plunged left into a busy, unnamed street market. Many of the traders seemed to be looking, with some concern, in my direction. I

Charles Correa. It was never finished. An elevated pedestrian walkway was intended to be built through the central gateway of the building.

[11]An Internet search for 'Connaught + shit' produced eleven separate accounts of finding an unexplained turd on one's shoes while wandering in Connaught Place. The more genteel 'Connaught + dung' and 'Connaught + muck' got three and two entries respectively. Nondot.org even has some pictures. The scam goes back at least twenty-five years. One tourist who paid to have her shoe cleaned, then discovered that the stitches binding the upper to the sole had been mysteriously cut. An American, who describes with some pride how he pushed and swore at the shoeshine man, concludes: 'All in all, I feel pretty enlightened that I didn't make him lick it off.' For me, I have come round to thinking of it as a minor peril of whiteness, but am still determined to catch the shit-squirter in action and on camera.

gently lifted my hat as if to indicate that I intended them no harm. They began furiously packing up their goods, mainly clothes, gathering them together in huge sheets of jute. I looked behind me, and realized that I was not their object of concern. There was an open mustard-coloured truck now blocking the route by which I had entered. Six men, the leader wearing a pink-and-white bandana,[12] got down from the truck, and started pushing their way into the market. They deliberately overturned a ramshackle table covered with shiny plastic belts. A woman began to howl and wail in an unexpectedly assertive and aggressive manner. Suddenly, the bandana man spotted me, and looked a little sheepish. I didn't say a word, although I did reach for my camera. 'Illegal, all illegal,' he told me in English. Another man, a trader, whispered 'NDMC' to me; he spoke these letters as if the New Delhi Municipal Council[13] was the KGB. The bandana man asked to see one other trader's market permit, and then he and his gang sloped off.

I sat down on a low wall next to a man who was picking his nose vigorously. Between excavations, he told me that the market inspectors normally just demand money—or confiscate goods. My presence had stopped them. I looked away and up, and saw a huge building looming above me. I identified it as the southern face of the Indian Life building. It was no longer a curtain of mirrors but a wall of red, punctuated with deep-set sun-excluding windows. It seemed to be an entirely new creation, appropriate for the side of a building that faced and endured the punishing pre-monsoon sun. As I reflected on this work of architectural brilliance, a large, desperate woman interposed herself in my line of vision and tried to sell me three pairs

[12]From the Hindi *bandhna*, to tie. The reference to tying, however, is to the tie-dyed cloth (*bandhni*), rather than the manner in which a bandana is affixed to the head.

[13]The New Delhi Municipal Council is the governing body for large parts of the centre of the city. New Delhi is still widely known as Lutyens' Delhi, after the architect most strongly connected with its construction. The status of Delhi and its various administrations is more than confusing. Most of the rest of the city comes under the Municipal Corporation of Delhi or MCD. Delhi is officially called the National Capital Territory—which means its status in terms of self-government is somewhere between a state and the centrally governed union territories. Like a state it has a chief minister and an elected assembly, but it does not have full executive power in a number of key areas, such as the control of the police force or urban development. Then there is what is known as the National Capital Region, a virtual entity used largely by planners which includes urbanized parts of neighbouring states.

of different-coloured luminous socks for Rs 100, or, for Rs 50, a toddler's 'Buffy the Vampire Slayer' T-shirt. I hurried off, brushing through the middle of a group of lawyers, in black and white, and with tie-less buttoned-up wing collars, emerging from a back stairway that led to the National Consumer Disputes Redressal Commission.

I had spotted my next place of succour, Antriksh Bhavan, sticking up from behind a decaying jawful of fang-like unplanned high-rise office buildings, an orthodontist's nightmare. There were still two broad New Delhi radials to be crossed, originally named after a royal wife (Queensway) and a viceroy (Curzon Road). They'd been Indianized since independence into the populist Janpath (People's Way) and a tribute to the long-suffering wife of the father of the nation (Kasturba Gandhi Marg). Both are now sluggish, congested tourist traps lined with trinket shops and airline offices. I pass a flower shop called 'The Green Revolution.' 'We bring nature closer to you in this concrete jungle.' A young cyclist in a green apron, and, from my vantage point, no other visible clothing, emerged from a side lane with a bunch of red carnations, wobbling as he steered one-handed through the oncoming traffic.

Antriksh Bhavan (or Cosmos Building) is a tall concrete cuboid with lots of smaller space-age protrusions. Stuck on its roof is a close approximation to a lunar landing module. It's unmissable—Delhi's first revolving restaurant. I should have guessed what was to

come from a signboard at ground-floor level. A freelance restaurant critic had, with a magic marker, crossed out the second 'v' of revolving and replaced it with a 't'. I approached the lift. Just ahead of me was a man with a long, rounded black beard who entered the lift. He pressed an unseen button—and to my surprise another set of doors opened, through which the bearded man immediately exited. The lift not only served as a means of going up and down but also as a corridor through the middle of Antriksh Bhavan.

Now, I was a first-time visitor to revolving restaurants. I had always supposed that the whole restaurant would—well—revolve. Not this one. Only the floor moved, with a disconcerting jerk. Five millimetres forward, two millimetres back, I estimated. *Derh*[14] *ganta*—one and a half hours—I was told, for a full circle. The walls, the windows stayed where they were; the tables, the chairs and I were, in fits and starts, on the move. The carpets were not quite wall-to-wall—and close to my feet was a small gap through which I could have squeezed my multi-paged cardboard menu, and allowed it to parascend on to the fortified precincts of the neighbouring American Center. The well-thumbed menu had several innovative features: there were, for example, samples from past meals on many of the pages (and on the napkins), and the text—in English—had clearly been translated by a computer loaded with early 1990s software.

I had sat myself down at a window, with a quite spectacular view over Connaught Place, and its clearly delineated concentric circles. Only from this height does the design of CP really impress or make sense; or does it feel like the heart of a megacity. Perhaps CP's architect only intended his creation to be fully understood—in those pre-skyscraper days—by the gods and by aviators. From above, the rest of Delhi does appear to radiate out, miraculously, from CP. To the north: railway stations and Old Delhi, the Red Fort and the minarets of the Jama Masjid. To the east: silvery slug-trails of water marking the Yamuna river, once Delhi's *raison d'être*, now little more than a sewer; and beyond that the huge settlements of east Delhi. To the west, the modest hills of the Ridge—still green and barely visited—which, not long ago, with the Yamuna, provided Delhi with its natural borders. Now the city stretches for miles beyond the Ridge. And although it was a clear day, I could not see the borders of this city of *derh crore*, fifteen million people. To the south—where I hoped to

---

[14]Hindi and its related north Indian languages are unusual in having a separate word for one-and-a-half, *derh*. So 150 becomes *derh sau*, or one-and-a-half hundred. I have been unable to find any other language group which does it. There are also separate words for one-and-a-quarter (*sava*), two-and-a-half (*dhai*), one hundred thousand (*lakh*) and ten million (*crore*). The last two words are widely used in Indian English.

make out the distant skyscrapers of Gurgaon, Delhi's most modern incarnation, I could not see more than thirty metres. My view was blocked by a thirteenth-storey junkyard, a repository for broken chairs and ancient typewriters—the top floor of the offices of the *Hindustan Times* newspaper.

As I prepared to order, I could hear an Italian couple arguing with a waiter about their food, which had not reached, they seemed to be saying, the basic level one would expect of a restaurant. Fussy tourists, I thought to myself—gazing around, noticing that there were no Indian diners—usually a sign that the food is less than satisfactory. I ordered simply: chicken kebabs and *naan* bread. Both were inedible, the former leaked visceral fluids, had more gristle than meat and looked as if it had been carved from a living chicken a few minutes earlier. The *naan* would probably have been rather nice on the previous day. I had been brought up not to complain in restaurants, and decided to move on to the next course. Fresh fruit salad, I thought, was a safe choice. Two minutes later, an elegant, cracked cocktail glass arrived containing what was clearly tinned fruit. I did complain. The waiter hurried off and brought back the manager, who turned out to be the same bearded man I had briefly encountered in the lift-cum-corridor. He was carrying a tin. He pointed politely to the writing on it. 'Fresh fruit salad', I read. I was lost for words. There was no look of victory in his eyes—and I was very hungry. I downed the tinned fresh fruit salad as the kindly manager looked on.

Delhi has more cars than Bombay, Madras and Calcutta combined. That's partly because it has bigger, more open roads; but also because it had an appalling urban transport system. The Metro is supposed to change all that. But for now the construction work had made things worse. The land around Antriksh Bhavan had been turned into an office-workers' car park. The cars were parked five rows deep; often so close that one could not walk between them. Handbrakes are left off, and car-park attendants rolled the cars back and forth, undoing and reorganizing their vehicular logjam, guessing which car they will have to move next. Viewed from above, it becomes a complex mathematical puzzle. How many other cars need to move to get that Skoda from the back row out of the car park? A shirtless boy, thirteen perhaps, had had enough of trying to find a pedestrian route through the car park, and was stepping from car bonnet to car roof and making fine progress. The attendants started shouting at him. In vain, of course: to catch him, they, too, would have had to walk on the cars. As I struggled to find my galumphing way through the tangle of cars, I envied the nerve and nimbleness of that boy.

Eventually I cleared the car park, and reached Barakhamba Road, eastward-leading, the last of the CP radials. Barakhamba Road is central Delhi's only true street of skyscrapers. Thirty years ago, there were only British-built bungalows[15] on this part of Barakhamba Road. Now there is just three-quarters of a bungalow left. The old house at 20, Barakhamba Road[16] has had one side of it torn away by bulldozers. The rest still stands as a vacant ruin, dwarfed by its neighbours, a decaying reminder of Delhi's recent past, gradually returning to dust.

[15]Bungalows in Delhi are lived in by politicians and the super-rich. 'Bungalow' comes from a Hindi word, meaning 'a house in the Bengali style', and traditionally describes a single-storey free-standing house surrounded by a verandah—also a Hindi-origin word. Both words entered English during the nineteenth century. The word 'bungalow' today has very different connotations in India and in the UK. According the Encyclopaedia Britannica (2004) 'In Great Britain the name has become a derisive one because of the spread of poorly built bungalow-type houses'. Some Delhi bungalows have two storeys.

[16]The house has an interesting history. In the 1950s this bungalow became a crucible for the revival of political Hinduism in Delhi. The assassination of Gandhi by a Hindu fanatic in 1948 had resulted in the banning of the RSS, the umbrella organization for an eclectic range of Hindu cultural, political and religious groups. The Hindu right appeared to be in decline, tainted by allegations of complicity. Hans Raj Gupta, an RSS official and an iron magnate whose family had made their money from renting out sugar-cane crushing machines, was the owner of 20, Barakhamba Road. He was a key figure in its revival and eventually became Mayor of Delhi in the late 1960s. The partial destruction of his former residence was, according to a watchman, the outcome of a property dispute between his sons.

An Early Intermission

I AM STRUGGLING, disconsolate. I have been out on the streets of Delhi at dawn to escape the May heat. It has reached 45°C; that's 130°F in the language of my childhood. The sun parboils my brains, desiccates my skin. The undersides of my feet, cracked and crispy, have become a red cherry *mille-feuille*. But there is worse. I am suffering self-doubt, barely known to me. I find it hard to admit to myself what I am doing. I am stealing time to wander around Delhi in a spiral. There is no slower way to explore a city, no other route through a city that is as purgatorial. It is as if moving continents has left me a little unbalanced. Understandably, I command no sympathy from others.

And I *have* become a little obsessed with spirals. Yesterday I met a charming young undertaker, who was holding forth on the problems  of refrigeration in the Delhi heat, when I spotted, on his van, his ersatz hearse, a spiral. Or a near-spiral: it was helical, a snake wrapped round a staff. He explained to me that it was the international ambulance symbol[1]. The red cross, he told me, had been reclaimed by the Red Cross. We got so caught up discussing the politics of symbols, that he forgot to show me his morgue and I forgot to ask him why a hearse was carrying an ambulance symbol in the first place.

I also realized that I had embarked on a spiral that is anti-clockwise, without consciously deciding to do so. This has troubled

---

[1]The snake and staff are the symbol of the son of Apollo, Asclepius, who, according to Greek mythology, possessed the art of healing—hardly, it would seem, appropriate for a hearse. From about 300 BC the cult of Asclepius became popular. His followers set up healing temples, called *asclepieion*, where non-poisonous snakes were left to crawl on the floor in dormitories where the sick and injured slept. According to legend, Asclepius was killed by his grandfather, Zeus, for raising the dead—so perhaps it is after all an imaginative symbol for an undertaker's vehicle.

me unnecessarily, I think. But I have, in autistic mode, been working it over in my mind. I have a bad right knee, an uncured veteran of six surgical interventions.[2] It is fine for walking, but I dare not twist it, lest the thigh bone should become visibly and painfully detached from the kneecap. I naturally rest greater confidence on my left leg, and lean in on it—and therefore tend to veer slightly leftwards unless corrected. This delivers a natural anti-clockwise tendency to my movements. My brother once had an Eastern European car which had what he described as a leftwards 'wag' to its steering, which needed constant vigilance and clockwise adjustment. I seem to have my own leftwards wag. The only time this matters is when I meet an insurmountable obstacle to continuing my Bernoulli spiral. Then, I have decided that I must veer to the right, not the left, and ensure I never touch the trail of the previous whorl-twist.

I will go on, through this heat and through this self-doubt, and probably take some pride in deceiving people about my ambulatory activities. And I find unexpected solace and inspiration from the world of spirals, and occasionally from the poems of the dead. I found these lines, of a recently deceased poet, that I have learnt and repeated back to myself.

At worst, one is in motion; and at best,
Reaching no absolute, in which to rest,
One is always nearer by not keeping still.[3]

These words seemed to defend my madness and perversity, and encourage me to continue. They might even be construed as a description of a spiral walk.

---

[2]A reconstruction of my anterior cruciate ligament, an Ellison repair to my lateral collateral ligament, a medial meniscectomy and three arthroscopies.
[3]From *On the Move* by Thom Gunn (1929–2004).

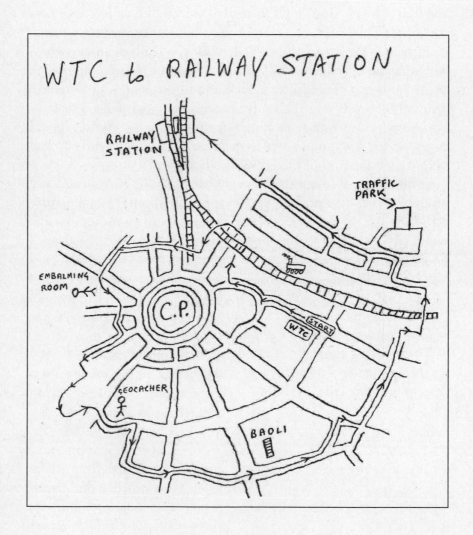

WTC to RAILWAY STATION

RAILWAY STATION

TRAFFIC PARK

EMBALMING ROOM

C.P.

START
WTC

GEOCACHER

BAOLI

Chapter Two: In which the Author explores the mysteries of the sodomitic gerund, monastic nudity and geocaching

BARAKHAMBA ROAD IS the last of the Connaught Place radials. Beyond it, as I continued on my anti-clockwise mission, the symmetry was broken. Suddenly the ripples and spokes of CP are no longer the dominant force shaping the heart of Delhi. Instead, a railway line, linking north and south Delhi, had imposed its rectilinear will on its vehicular neighbours. The streets are suddenly straight, and right angles proliferate. Once upon a time, I worked in an office building here, with a totally inappropriate name: the World Trade Centre; it bears no relation, in size or design, to its deceased New York namesake. Cowering in the shadow of the giant Intercontinental Hotel is instead an unremarkable five-storey building, smelling of Dettol. It contains foreign currency dealers, travel agents, and, exasperatingly, photocopy shops whose owners are too mean to change the ink in their machines until the copy is indistinguishable from a blank sheet of paper. I occupied an office previously inhabited by the Everlasting Media Company, which had by then disappeared without a trace; nearby was the Heartthrob Marketing Agency whose name touched me beyond reason, but which always seemed bereft of custom.

From the World Trade Centre, I was forced by the line of the railway tracks back towards Connaught Place. I reached Campa Cola House, once the headquarters of a major competitor to Pepsi and Coke, now derelict. Coke had been forced to leave India in the pre-globalization, socialist 1970s. India, its rulers argued, was on a path to self-sufficiency and had absolutely no need for foreign fizzy drinks. Coke was replaced by Campa Cola and later was joined in the buzzing fizzy drinks market by every tourist's favourite Indian spelling, the legendary 'Thums Up'. In the early 1990s, with economic liberalization in India, Pepsi and Coke were allowed to enter and, in doing battle with each other, destroyed or bought up the local competition. Their marketing and distribution budgets were gargantuan, and I (a cola-agnostic) am assured they even tasted a little better. In 2000, Salman Rushdie, returning to India after more than twelve years in seclusion, remembered Campa Cola as 'a disgusting local imitation' and exulted in the triumph of Coke. By then Campa Cola House had closed, and become victim to the kind of interminable multi-party property dispute that affects so many Indian businesses.

Today, there is no water and no electricity in the four-storey building but dozens of employees still come to work each day. They sit in the few ground-floor rooms that they have managed to keep open, playing cards and smoking cigarettes. Swaraj Walia, a 'purchasing executive', told me that he and his companions are engaged in a court case against their former employers, and are demanding several years of back pay. For legal reasons, too complex for me to understand, they dare not miss a day's 'work' and so each morning they gather outside Campa Cola House. Swaraj Walia took me inside, despite the protestations of a security guard. Each floor was a wreck, with five years of dust, overturned filing cabinets, ancient advertising billboards. 'Taste It For The Fun Of It'; 'The Great Indian Taste—Campa'. All advertisements proudly declared that Campa contained no fruit juice or pulp. Outside, above the main entrance, the huge Campa logo, as long as a man and as tall as a table, with the red cursive calligraphy copied originally from Cola-Cola, was on its last legs. The large capital 'C' had fallen, leaving a ghostly grey trace on the wall behind, so too had the 'p'; the other three letters were still visible, but the 'm' had slipped and was pointing downwards, only

the two 'a's held fast. Campa Cola is all but dead; it is on sale outside Campa Cola House (rather tasty, I thought, less fizzy and with a bouquet of lemon tea), but barely available in the rest of the country. Anti-globalization activists campaign[1] against Pepsi and Coke, accusing them of hydropiracy (better known as water-stealing) and of poisoning the masses with toxic chemicals. Some call nostalgically for

[1] At the World Social Forum in Bombay in 2004, there was a big campaign and rally against Coke and Pepsi. Among the slogans were 'Not Coke but Coconut' and the delightful Hinglish ditty, 'Killer Cola, Toxic Cola; Clean Up Your Act, Public *Ne Bola*' (the public says).

the return of Campa Cola. In the battle for control of the Indian soft drinks market, the West has won. In other areas, generating even larger revenues, such as computer services, India has a much stronger position.

From the roof of Campa Cola House I had finally seen the railway lines which had exerted such influence on the layout of the neighbouring streets. I was a little perturbed that I could see no way through for myself without turning back into CP. Back on ground level, I began ferreting away down various back alleys, all on railway property, and eventually found myself inside a large building. I asked a young man where I was. '*Ardiyesso*' came the reply. *Ardiyesso*, I repeated back, none the wiser. It was a new Hindi word for me, and I got out my little black vocabulary book. The young man looked at me as if I was an idiot and took me to a signboard where I read 'R.D.S.O. S&T (Insp) Cell'. Ah, I said, what does RDSO stand for? He didn't know[2]. As I left the RDSO building, whose many rooms appeared to be serving as some kind of hostel, I found myself entering another world, a railway colony, a vast empire of real estate and acronyms under the ultimate control of the Indian railway ministry. After all, Indian Railways does employ more than one million people. In the area north of CP, the railway empire spreads out in all directions, and includes a hospital, a sports stadium, a railway officers club and a computer training centre; the empire has its own language, in which frog gaps, swing noses and python rakes are part of everyday speech and where a job on the railways has always been a job for life.

However, I had not yet seen a train. I walked under a rail bridge and then up some steps that seemed to lead in the direction of the railway tracks. Ahead of me were two men each carrying the bottom half of what had once been a plastic bottle of mineral water. I followed them, clumsily swaying as I edged along a thick black metal pipe that broke through the wall guarding the tracks. From the pipe they climbed up onto the wall, and then jumped down—carefully resting their makeshift water-carriers so as not to spill their contents. I followed them over. They went to the left and found a nice open

[2]Later I punched RDSO + India + railways into Google and discovered rdso.gov.in, the website for the Research, Design and Standards Organisation of the Indian Railways. It has a cute homepage, with a small train that runs along the bottom, breaks down every 30 seconds, even stops at a red signal, and restarts at a green one. S&T (Insp), is Signals and Telecommunication (Inspection).

space where they would be in full view of any passing trains. One of them untied the ribbon that held up his loose, off-white cotton pyjama trousers, crouched and began to shit. The other one got ready to follow suit. Their little jugs of water, their *lotas*, were for cleaning themselves afterwards—paper is rarely used in India, and is seen as just a bit insanitary. I looked away, towards the right, and started walking alongside the tracks; stopping, watching nervously as several crowded express trains sped past. I crossed the tracks eventually, following three young boys, who clearly knew where they were going, and showed me how they listened to the sound of the tracks to know if a train was coming and it was unsafe to cross. I then tailed them into a gap between two huge engineering sheds.

Thanking them, I crossed on my own to a siding and, beyond it, a ghostly platform. There were no signboards or porters or railway officials or hawkers or train schedules or passengers—it was if I'd been magically transported to the Delhi equivalent of JK Rowling's platform $9^3/_4$. There were clothes lines strung out between the windows of a single train carriage and the struts and pillars of the platform. Sarong-sized chequered sheets, pink starched saris, and assorted Victorian-style underwear hung from the lines. This carriage was

clearly not going anywhere in a hurry. I ducked and began to brush my way through the sea of cotton—and was met by three more waves of clothing. I looked on my right into the cabins. In the first, two old women were trying to brush each other's hair at the same time and laughing lightly at the tangles they were creating; when they caught my eye their laughter became hysterical. In the second, *bidi*-smoking men were playing cards, each concentrating so fiercely on the game that I, for once, went unnoticed. In the third, two men were asleep on bunks, with huge contented smiles on their faces, as a woman swept the floor, collecting the debris of a meal onto a broken piece of pink plastic and throwing it out onto the tracks. Then a small chain of men began to emerge from the door at the end of the carriage.

I spoke to them in Hindi, asking what they were doing there; they turned to each other in a huddle, there were a few nods and shakes, and a few exchanges in what sounded like a South Indian language. Then the huddle broke up and a bare-chested spokesman burst forth. 'I am SR Krishnamurthy of Ramalingam stationery stores in Bangalore.' He told me that he and 59 companions, thirty couples all over the age of 50, had rented a railway carriage, a 'bogey' in Indian English, and were travelling extremely slowly around the country, on a 'sight-seeing cum pilgrimage' tour. They had been to the temples of Tirupati and Puri and had just come from Hardwar. Next was Agra—Indian railways would hitch their bogey to the scheduled train and off they'd go. They were on day 23 out of 37, and they all slept throughout on the train. They were spending two days in Delhi, a chance to stock up on basic provisions in Connaught Place and wash their clothes. But, SR Krishnamurthy told me, Delhi didn't interest them—it was too hot and the people were very rude. They were happy on the special platform at New Delhi railway station. They could wash their clothes and make *dosas* and everybody left them alone. 'Except you,' he said, without a note of embarrassment. 'And them', he added pointing at another bogey at the special platform, 'the railway accountants'.

Sure enough, twenty metres up the platform was another carriage—full of railway accounts assistants from all over India. Every three months, they told me, they meet for three days in a different part of the country to reconcile their quarterly accounts. They stay on a train, saving their accommodation allowances. Their self-appointed spokesman, TVSR Murthy, was a man of carefully ordered thoughts,

41

each of which he counted with his fingers. He told me they all liked these meetings 'because, point number 1, we get away from our wives; point number 2, we get to see new bits of India; point number 3, we are all good friends by now; point number 4, we make a profit on each trip.' He was about to move on to his thumb and point number 5, when I entered the train. Inside, the cabins, unlike those of the pilgrims, were a mess; half-eaten food, empty bottles of Indian whisky, a partly melted plastic cup piled high with cigarettes and *bidi* stubs. This was their last day, and they all looked a little haggard. Mr Murthy clearly saw nothing to apologize for. Next time he said, putting on an excessively morose look, 'we're in my home town, Bhubaneswar, so I will have to stay at my residence.' 'When do you go back to Bhubaneswar?' I asked. 'Buggering-off time is twenty-three hundred hours', he said, in what I later learnt was the best Indian railway demotic, using the sodomitic gerund as if it were a polite and precise legal word for an impending departure.

Much of the land occupied by the railways is surprisingly quiet and green. There are very few footpath businessmen here. I am still within the acoustic footprint of CP; but there is little more than a low buzz punctuated by honks; quiet enough, though, to hear the stridulating of invisible insects, and the sound of my own phlegm working its way up into my throat, a protest at the despoiling of my lungs by the heavy, pollutant-laden inner-city air. I pass the

headquarters of the monthly '*Railway Worker*' magazine, the Karnail Singh Stadium, home of the Railways cricket team. Without incident, I slip out of the railway empire into a hospital colony. It's too hot and I'm too tired to explore any more. I promise myself I'll visit a hospital later on in my spiral. But I do note down the names of the buildings I pass. First, a nurses' hostel, a dispensary, then a busy leprosy clinic, and lastly a slightly less busy embalming room, and back out into the midday madness of Delhi roads. An autorickshaw careers towards me aggressively and I climb in and head home.

I resume the following morning. A brief storm has brought pre-monsoon rains and the temperature has dropped. The reek of rotting vegetation has replaced the stench of eye-watering diesel fumes, as central Delhi's dominant aroma. I find a temple, belonging to the Digamber sect of the Jain religion. Inside, a student lawyer, Vikas Jain, introduces himself. He tells me that Jainism is much tougher than Buddhism, to which it's often compared. All strict Jains are not only vegetarian, but they also eat no potatoes or onions and will not eat after sunset. All water must be filtered to ensure that small creatures are not imbibed. Similarly, some Jains wear facemasks to ensure that they cannot swallow a fly or, more commonly in Delhi, a mosquito. Digamber literally means sky-clad, and the most holy Jains of the Digamber sect wear no clothes at all; they just carry a little flywhisk to ensure they do not tread on any animals. Vikas points high up on the wall to a row of photographs of Jain *sadhus* or holy men. All of them are naked, with an array of shrivelled penises that testify to their ability to withstand the temptations of this world; a few however had hidden their genitals from the camera lens with a carefully positioned knee. 'What about women *sadhus*?' I ask, casually. 'Because of menstruation they must wear clothes,' he tells me firmly. 'They cannot go bleeding all over the place.' There are a few moments of silence. I wander over to some white, delicately carved statues of cross-legged naked men. Vikas follows me. Jainism is not, he informs me, a religion, but a principle. We have no god, no prophets. The statues are of the twenty-four teachers of Jainism, of whom the greatest and most recent was a former prince called Mahavir[3], a contemporary of Buddha and Confucius, who defrocked himself at the age of thirty and proceeded not to speak for 12 years. There are today about 100,000 Jains in

---

[3] Mahavir is portrayed as a gold-cloaked septuagenarian by fellow iconoclast Gore Vidal in his 1980 novel *Creation*. In *Creation*, Vidal, who doesn't have much else in common with Mahavir, tells the life story of Cyrus Spitama, the fictional grandson of Zarathustra, who wanders around the world meeting lots of famous people who were Mahavir's contemporaries: Darius and Xerxes, Buddha, Confucius, Lao Tse, Jeremiah, Pericles and Herodotus.

Delhi: 'none of them are poor,' Vikas told me proudly. I recounted the legend that no Jain has ever had a criminal record. Vikas shook his head, 'That may have been true once; but then there was the Big Bull.' This was the nickname of the stockbroker, Harshad Mehta, who became the envied hero of India's great stock market boom of the 1990s (he owned 32 cars) and then became the jailbird villain of its greatest financial scandal (his cars were auctioned off). Unlike Mahavir, he was rather keen on tailored suits.

I have a sentimental attachment to Jantar Mantar[4], my first image of Delhi, revealed to me in *The Householder*. It makes me chuckle, deep in my throat, every time I pass it by on Parliament Street. I adore it because it seems so eccentric, so unexpected, and so ludicrously post-modern in the middle of commercial Delhi. At first glance, from the road, Jantar Mantar is a small park, with a scattering of huge pinkish abstract sculptures which people can climb all over. It fact, it is one of several open-air observatories built by the Maharaja of Jaipur in the early eighteenth century. Each of the six 'sculptures' is actually a scientific instrument—for measuring azimuths, declinations, meridians and zeniths. The tallest of the buildings is simply an unadorned staircase leading to nowhere—portrayed by Thomas and William Daniell in their two 1808 aquatints as if it were a stairway to heaven. The Daniell's aquatints are the earliest representation I

have been able to find of Jantar Mantar. Artists, architects, photographers and filmmakers have been inspired by the complex ever since. The Japanese-American artistic polymath, Isamu Noguchi, created his '*Slide Mantra*' (which is both a children's slide and a sculpture, and sits in a Sapporo park) as a tribute to the strangest of the Jantar Mantar instruments, the Misra Yantra. This curvaceous construction resembles a stylized

[4] Pronounced Junter-Munter, to rhyme with hunter. Jantar Mantar, is thought to derive from the Sanskrit words for instrument and calculation respectively. It is now used as the Hindi equivalent of Abracadabra.

upside-down heart, though one male travel-guide writer, with an unschooled sense of female anatomy, compared it to a yoni or vulva. It has two sets of walls, or *labia*, I suppose, and a staircase that runs up through its middle (a zip, perhaps?). The Misra Yantra was converted into a logo for the 1982 Asian Games in Delhi, and has since been borrowed for publicity purposes by the PR company 'Jantar Mantar Communications' of Toronto. Now Professor Barry Perlus, of Cornell University, and webmaster of jantarmantar.org, has undertaken 'a multimedia project . . . which will use 'interactive panoramic "VR" photographs, time-lapse sequences, and 3D models, as well as articles, drawings, and historic texts', to explore the Jantar Mantar site in Delhi, and its cousin in the city of Jaipur.

On a recent visit to Jantar Mantar, I came across a tourist who seemed to have lost something inside the baby-Colosseum-like Ram Yantra. He was on his hands and knees in the dust, moving between the starburst slices of masonry that emanate from its central column.

'Hello,' I said, in my special kind voice for unfortunate tourists. 'Have you lost something?'

'Nope. I'm looking for a cache.'

'What's a cache?'

'Hidden treasure. Geocaching. Look it up on the Net.'

I did. Geocaching is relatively new to India. It bills itself as one of the fastest-growing leisure activities in the world. It's a kind of global treasure hunt, based around the Internet and a small electronic device (a GPS) that tells you where you are. Someone puts some worthless objects inside a small plastic container and hides it somewhere (there are caches in almost every country in the world). Clues and map co-ordinates are entered into geocaching.com and geocachers have to find it. My unfriendly dust-grubbing tourist was chasing a cache that been hidden in the Jantar Mantar complex. I later discovered he'd not looked carefully enough at the instructions. The cache hidden at N 28° 35.033 E 077° 10.870 (the coordinates of the Jantar Mantar) was a virtual one[5]. Which

---

[5]According to the rules of geocaching, virtual caches should only be used occasionally. 'Although many locations are interesting, a virtual cache should be out of the ordinary enough to warrant logging a visit.' Five geocachers have visited Jantar Mantar, including Honupohaku (from Hawaii) who wrote 'Yippee! This is my first international cache. And man is this place cool; the ultimate in art, science and functionality.'

is to say that it did not exist. Apparently, in India, city caches rarely survive the day—acquisitive locals take them away, or they get eaten by goats.

I spiralled east from Jantar Mantar in a brief early-morning respite from the monsoon rains. I stepped over a sodden sleeper, comatose on a traffic island. For a moment, I wanted to wake him and ask him his story; but thought better of it. I dipped down a side lane past the unimposing 'Kook-a-doodle-do' restaurant, specialist purveyors of chicken *biryani*, and soon found myself at the back door of the Imperial Hotel, my first place of residence and nourishment in Delhi. Unlike almost everything else obviously connected with the British Empire, the name has remained the same. By the 1920s, New Delhi needed a new hotel. The Imperial, with its largely Art Deco design, was inaugurated in 1933, and played a major role as a place of rest and comfort for some of those involved in the independence struggle. By the 1960s it had become legendary for its ballroom and for its lobster thermidor—more than six hundred miles from the nearest lobster pot. It had fallen on hard times by the late 1980s, and when I first stayed there it was more famous for food poisoning and its large open-to-the-public collection of that distant cousin of the lobster, the Delhi cockroach[6]. On that first visit, I complained to the management—and was sent a wiry old man, who took off his sandals at the threshold, leaving one of them at the door. He skipped across my cavernous bedroom and with the other sandal he crushed at least a dozen bathroom cockroaches, scooping his dead victims up with the edge of his sandal and dropping them into a small plastic bucket. He left with a smile and Rs 20. The crime scene remained; each murder marked by a small stain of cockroach juice and the occasional russet limb.

On my last stay at the Imperial, the cockroaches had gone. The Imperial has had a makeover, and is doted upon by many regular visitors to Delhi, particularly the British. It somehow represents the India of the Western imagination, a land of maharajas and high tea. Unlike the other luxury hotels of the city, it is unashamedly backward-looking, and, well, imperial. There's a new bar, Daniells, named after

[6] The cockroach and the lobster are both members of the phylum *arthropoda*; a biologist points out to me that humans and rats have an even closer evolutionary relationship.

the artists who painted Jantar Mantar, and Daniells' prints can be found in almost every recess. The staff are dressed in imperial costumes of startling complexity and tidiness, and they have been taught to perform their duties with such overbearing obsequiousness that they almost appear rude. The Imperial is for me the last gasp of the Empire, a pastiche of the past, bottled and conserved for future generations.

Either side of Janpath are the Eastern and Western Courts—designed as Neo-classical palaces of justice but now serving as guest houses for MPs. Then I entered 'P&T' land. Like the railways, the Posts and Telegraphs department has its own colony in the heart of Delhi. Schoolchildren dressed in the all-white uniform of the P&T School leap about me, demanding to be photographed. I give in and scurry off to a little-known place I have visited once before. Hidden away behind the construction site which was, until recently, occupied by the Maltese High Commission (what did they do all day at the Maltese High Commission?[7]) is Agarsen's Baoli, central Delhi's oldest building. Six thousand years old, and built by the uncle of the Hindu god, Lord Krishna, according to its watchman. A mere seven hundred years old, according to historians. Agarsen was probably a thirteenth century chieftain and a *baoli* is a rectangular step-well. Through a padlocked gate opened by a taciturn, *bidi*-smoking watchman, I climbed up onto a large plinth from where one hundred stone steps lead down to the bottom of the well.

Although this is only my second visit, it is a view I have seen many times before, thanks to a Delhi photographer called Raghu Rai, with a Cartier-Bresson-like instinct for the decisive moment. In a photograph taken in 1976, a young boy is caught at the moment of launching himself from a wall into the waters of the *baoli*, a dive of at least twelve feet. Above loom some of the newly constructed high-rises of Tolstoy Marg and Barakhamba Road, but beneath is the ancient step-well. I ask the watchman if he has seen the photograph, and he

[7] An Internet search for India + Malta brings up lots of links for Malta India, 'a very nutritious non-alcholic drink from Puerto Rico.' $5.95 for eight small bottles. Buried among these links, is an Indian ministry of external affairs fact-sheet about Malta, which tells its readers that there are six Indian restaurants in Malta, and that the Indian mission there closed in 2002. Malta (see next footnote) has 19 Seventh-Day Adventists.

© *Raghu Rai*

stuns me by saying that he, Bagh Singh, grizzled and grey-haired, was that diving boy. He sends a young girl off to get a copy of the picture he has cut from a magazine and gets me to photograph him holding it. In the thirty years in which Bagh Singh has aged so rapidly, the water level at Agarsen's Baoli has fallen by twenty feet. A shortage of water is one of the biggest problems facing Delhi today.

As I left, the air became very still, and the skies darkened. I turned into Hailey Road. A few drops of rain began to fall, not the pale, gentle raindrops of a London shower, but rotund, green-tinted, heavy ones that augur the full onslaught of a monsoon downpour. I ran along the broken pavement, searching for shelter, knowing that in a few moments the full monsoon storm would break. I caught my right foot on a small piece of metal that protruded from the pavement. My knee twisted and gave way. I tumbled to the ground. My knee had partially dislocated. My lower leg was pointing in the wrong direction. Now I have dealt with this kind of situation before, but never in such weather. It was as if buckets of water were being poured over me. I grabbed my lower leg tightly, pinioning it by pressing my thumbs into the shinbone and levered my tibia back into its normal position. I got up slowly, feeling the synovial juices within my knee begin to spread, swelling up and cushioning the damaged joint. I could limp on to a small tea-shop, a *dhaba*, with an awning of blue plastic sheeting and no customers. Not a single part of my body was dry. The rain had turned into a frosted glass waterfall, so dense that I could not see beyond the modest river that had once been Hailey Road. I asked for some tea, and declared uncontroversially, in the English fashion but the local vernacular, '*Bohut baarish hai*', there's a lot of rain. I was immediately contradicted and reminded that this had been a very late monsoon, and the tubewells were still empty. My interlocutor described how drought was turning his village in nearby Rajasthan into desert; as he spoke, rainwater was pouring in through gaps in the awning. I looked around for better shelter and saw a modern brick building. Through the rain, I could make out the words: Northern Indian Union of Seventh-Day Adventists.

I entered, limping, bedraggled, muddy-trousered and sodden. I was desperate to be wrung dry and air-conditioned, but I would have to make do with Jesus Christ. Garish paintings of a very Caucasian Jesus, in sallow yellows and beige, leapt off the wall. There was no receptionist—I followed the sign to the 'Auditorium', a large room, enough for two hundred people. Ahead on a dais, peering over a lectern were a young couple, Filipinos I guessed, with huge toothy smiles and demoralizing good humour. They were singing 'Come let us reason, that is what God said.' I was given a wave of encouragement and my lips began to move silently. There were now three people in the audience. A very short African man, gazing heavenwards, mouth firmly closed; a forty-something winsome south Indian woman in a green sari, swinging in her pew and, myself, one decidedly worse-for-wear succour-seeking agnostic standing in a pool of rainwater. When the singing stopped, the pretty Filipina at the dais asked me my name. 'Sam' I said, sotto voce, as quickly as I could, as if I could somehow make my name even shorter. 'Again,' the Filipina said, 'Say it out loud. Sing your name to me.' 'Oh my God,' I said to myself. I felt an inner implosion, as if my soul was being crushed. At that point, there came, like a gift from God, a modern miracle. My mobile phone rang—and I had an excuse to exit.

The caller was a journalist asking me to write a review of some short stories by Khushwant Singh, son of the builder of Connaught Place, whose writings display an obsession with the size of women's breasts. I asked my caller (actually, my saviour) why she always got me to review books about breasts and penises. As I spoke, I took a step backwards and trod on the feet of the winsome woman in the green sari—who, unknown to me, had snuck out of the auditorium and was listening to every sinful word of my telephone conversation. She shrieked and so did I. I dropped my phone and Winsome picked it up, switched it to mute (it took me several minutes to work out how to do that, I thought), took me by the hand and led me, still dripping, back into the auditorium. She beckoned for me to sit and whispered, 'Martin, my nephew, will give his first sermon now.' A Brylcreemed teenager with a kipper tie had appeared from nowhere and was proudly standing at the dais. He thanked his 'auntie' for showing him the way of the Lord and proceeded to deliver a sermon on, of all subjects, the pitcher plant, renowned among 1970s London schoolboys for trapping and digesting insects. More than intrigued, I remained, rapt. Martin began reading out what seemed to be a college essay about the taxonomy of carnivorous plants. But he gradually revealed a side to the pitcher plant that had never occurred to me. Rather than being just a more than normally active member of the plant family, it should be seen as the devourer of innocently inquisitive but godless insects. Like Satan, it is a source of temptation; something all of us, insects and humans, would do well to avoid. We all clapped, Martin smiled broadly and nobody asked me to sing my name out loud. I hadn't been converted, but, carrying a large number of proselytizing leaflets[8], I did promise to return.

I wobbled outside, the sun now shining, but large parts of the street still under water; empty crisp packets and other urban detritus were river borne and floating off in the direction of the not-so-modern Modern School[9]. I followed the crisp packets past the school entrance, its buildings invisible from the main road—and, as the crisp packets disappeared into an open sewer, I headed for Bengali Market, where I knew I could get tea and Delhi's most visually impressive range of sweet snacks in air-conditioned comfort.

To continue the spiral I needed to tiptoe across the railway line again, and on the other side I found myself in a showcase of disastrous urban planning. Here the land between New and Old Delhi has been handed over to a collection of NGOs, state government ministers, institutes and hospitals. And ripping through the heart of it is Deen Dayal Upadhyay Marg, a long straight road, adored by speeding trucks, and named after a politician who fell out of a train in mysterious circumstances. For pedestrian visitors to the Gandhi Peace Foundation it is almost compulsory to be involved in a traffic accident. I suppose I was lucky that I was only lightly grazed on my left hip by an almost stationary cycle rickshaw. It took my mind off the swelling knee on the other side of my lower body. I headed down a side street, under

[8] According to their statistics-obsessed website, Adventist.org, the Seventh-Day Adventists number more than 800,000 in India, 690 of whom are in Delhi. The world assets of the Adventists are more than $13 billion. The SDAs were originally known as Millerites, after a non-relation of mine who predicted that the world would come to an end on 22 October 1844. They were wrong and the period that followed that non-event became known to Millerites as the Great Disappointment. Undaunted, they regrouped as the Seventh-Day Adventists—still predicting the imminent end of the world—and distinguished themselves from other Christian sects by declaring Saturday, not Sunday, to be the Sabbath.
[9] Gandhi was not entirely happy with the name. He visited the school in 1924, four years after it opened, and six years before it moved to its current location. 'I have only one fear. If in the flush of the modern, the ancient is lost it would greatly harm the young girls and boys.'

a painted sheet strung across the road with the words 'International symposium of electronics in cancer surgery' and reached Bal Bhawan, Jawaharlal Nehru's pride and joy.

India's first Prime Minister is always said to have been particularly keen on children, as if this were a wholly unexpected and abnormal aspect to his character—akin to Ayatollah Khomeini's little-known love for deep sea diving or the veil of secrecy that surrounds Bill Gates' collection of nineteenth-century false limbs. Bal Bhawan was built on the site of Delhi's old jail in the 1950s. It is encompassed by a mini-railway, within which various other child-friendly mini-things co-exist. The mini-zoo has some plump, tasty-looking, well-groomed full-sized white rabbits. The mini-technology park has seen better days: a square wood-framed white-flecked steel mesh, which had clearly been used recently for sieving cement, is described as a solar energy panel; rust has overtaken most of the rest of the exhibits. The museum was closed, except for the poorly lit caverns of its Sun Gallery. Inside was a word-heavy, exhibit-light exhibition, a black and white photograph of the Newgrange Spirals[10] holding my attention. A cohort of blue-shirted six-year-olds was being frogmarched past. No time to look or read—their teachers had to get them through all the exhibits by closing time.

At the back of Bal Bhawan is what is known in India as a traffic park, set as far away from any traffic as is possible in central Delhi. The park consists of a patch of land, four metres by six, with Lilliputian road junctions, a small mesh of mini-roads and blanket-sized carpets of grass with six inches of pile swaying gently in the wind. Sprouting out of the grass on each junction is a half-sized set of traffic lights. It was intended that children would visit the park in order to learn how not to get run over. But it is now five o'clock on a Thursday afternoon and I am the first visitor of the day, the second of the week (the first, according to the visitors' book, was a dentist from Geneva). The traffic park supervisor, Sub-Inspector

---

[10] Rock-cut spirals in county Meath in Ireland. More than five thousand years old, they are the earliest spirals I've been able to find and one of the most impressive examples of Neolithic art. According to the Bal Bhawan museum, the Newgrange Spirals represent the rebirth of the sun at the winter solstice.

Satpal Singh, is the loneliest policeman in Delhi. He begs me to come inside a small concrete building and watch his video. There, amidst levitating dust and patched-up electronic equipment, I sat down and watched a public information film showing a young woman and a child weeping dramatically at a graveside. This fades, in that ghostly manner which indicates a flashback, into  images of a brash young man drinking alcohol straight from a bottle with the gusto of the most swashbuckling of amateur actors. Then he is driving his car, erratically swerving back and forth across an implausibly empty Delhi road in the pattern of a sine wave. The film then cuts back to the graveyard scene. And finally—in bold—across the screen the words: 'Your car may run on alcohol, you can't.' It took me a moment to work that one out. There aren't many cars in Delhi, or anywhere else, that run on alcohol—but I suppose I was visiting a technology park. I watched six more information films—showing a wide range of genres of overacting, all resulting in the tragic death of one or both parents. I told Satpal Singh I wouldn't want my children to see these videos. 'These are old ones,' he told me, 'I have apprised my seniors that I want some new videos, with real accidents and real blood. They are not granting me funds for shooting.'

Kabari Bazaar is both a rubbish tip and a home to more than one thousand people. It is a small slum by Delhi standards, hidden away behind Bal Bhawan and not far from New Delhi railway station. Kabari Bazaar literally means Rubbish Market, and here and there are neat piles of old battered car doors, arranged by size; large stacks of wood off-cuts, empty Campa Cola crates; piles of crushed plastic mineral water bottles; huge ostrich nests of multi-coloured shredded waste paper; open drains clogged with an efflorescent oil-tinged sludge; and, up above, a web of electricity and telephone wires, slightly lower to the ground than the top of my head, bringing light, information and the danger of electrocution to inhabitants of the slum. Small barefoot children run around, and scoot away when they see me; one tiny girl in a red dress bursting into tears of terror at the sight of this green-hatted monster, limping about, taking photographs, trying to find a friendly face.

The residents of Kabari Bazaar are a suspicious lot, who did not take easily to my questions about their lives and their homes. But I had time to kill and a knee to rest. Gradually, a few—all of them men—began to talk. And I began to understand their suspiciousness. They were grimly aware of the implications of living in what is known as an unauthorized settlement. They had no title to the land on which they lived, and on which they had constructed their makeshift shacks. One day, the authorities will send in the bulldozers, and then their homes and possessions will be rolled and crushed into the dust. In these ramshackle huts, they run their businesses, shelter from the monsoon rains, make love and raise their families. The land they occupy was once a Muslim graveyard. Most of the residents are Muslims too, some of them refugees from an infamous

slum clearance from the nearby
Turkmen Gate area in the mid-
1970s, others more recent
migrants from the countryside—
exchanging rural destitution for
urban poverty. They are full of
aspirations for their children,
but grim in their knowledge that
no one really wants to give them
a chance. One man proudly
showed me his son's school
textbook, full of English words
which no one there could read

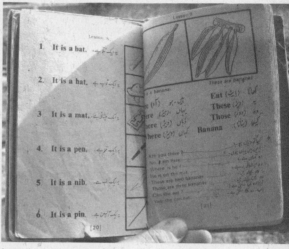

but me. They encourage me, laughing, to read Lesson 8 out loud. 'It
is a bat. It is a hat. It is a mat. It is a pen. It is a nib. It is a pin.' (Lesson
9 of this ancient textbook introduces the letter 'o'). I looked up and
around at the group, suddenly silent, and sad-eyed. Surely, I wanted
to tell this wary group of determinedly hopeful slum-dwellers, this
was not the best way of learning English. But I couldn't. I was caught,
dumbstruck again, in that ugly vacuum between hilarity and despair.
It was as if, for the briefest of moments, I had a sense of what their
lives were like and would be. And I saw less hope than they did.

New Delhi railway station was built in the 1950s, at a time when
internal air travel was very rare, and trains were for all. It remains
hugely congested, a place where different worlds coalesce, and where
notice-boards abound. First-time escalator-users get special help in
Hindi and English: 'While climbing escalators put right leg on moving
stairs and hold handrail (black belt) and put another leg immediately
on moving stairs. While climbing down put right leg on comb plate
and leave the handrail and put another leg on comb plate.'
Unfortunately, this escalator was not moving—and judging by the
number of fag-ends and beribboned *bidi* stumps on the comb plate,
it had been inactive for some time. I leant against a nearby wall,
trying to be inconspicuous (successfully for once, because of the
abundance of so many varieties of foreign tourists). Dazzled by the
activity of this city in miniature, I began writing down everything I
saw. Bare light-bulbs of low wattage. A human of indeterminate
gender, covered in sackcloth, asleep on the tiled floor. A pigeon with

55

its head inside a crisp packet. A railway official strutting past, stiff with self-importance. Bedraggled children, squatting in a nook, sniffing something, perhaps glue, and playing cards. A European tourist openly smoking dope, fiddling with and twisting his dreadlocks. *Paan*-spattered marble, stained crimson. Emaciated, scarlet-shirted porters—still known as coolies—joshing each other. Two pleased-with-themselves policemen escorting a baby-faced captive in handcuffs. An anxious British man (for a moment I thought it was me), following a coolie, and in turn followed by a chain of three children clinging to each others' hands as if their lives depended on it. 'Da-ad, wait,' I heard the rearguard cry. A grand Indian family, with servants, led by a woman barking orders in execrable Hindi— and parting the human waves as miraculously as Moses.

And a large notice headlined in blood red:

Attention of Foreign Tourists:

Beware of touts. Do not listen to those who attempt to tell you the ticket office for **international** tourists is closed. Please proceed to the **international** tourist bureau on the first floor at New Delhi railway station building and ignore those who attempt to lead you to a booking office elsewhere.

I was, at this point, grabbed at the elbow by a man who had appeared out of nowhere. I immediately presumed this was the tout of whom I should beware. 'I am not a tout. I am a helper,' he pointed out, helpfully. 'Come with me to the international tourist bureau.' He pointed to an alternative, functioning escalator—up which I ascended, alone, tout-less. I entered a chilled room, rank with the smell of unwashed human flesh. Inside were at least thirty assorted foreigners, not a smile among them: shattered by days of continuous travel, unconfirmed bookings, and failed attempts to find the right queue. Up above, huge posters exalted 'the Romance of Travel'. Underneath, a sign saying 'reservation forms', and in place of any forms there was a large, thick book garrotted to the wall with two loops of industrial-strength wire. The title, *When There Is No Doctor—A Health Guide*, caught my eye. It was an alphabetical compendium of all the maladies that might befall an unlucky tourist: anal fissures, bewitchment, cholera, dengue fever, elephantiasis, food poisoning, genital warts, hookworm, insomnia, jock itch, kidney stones, leprosy, meningitis, nausea, obstructed gut, piles, questions to ask a sick person, rickets, scrofula, testicular swelling, unconsciousness, vomiting, xerophthalmia, and yeast infection. They had clearly given up on Z, a distinct failure of the imagination. The entry dealing with jock itch had been particularly well-thumbed. I suddenly felt it was time to leave, and reflect elsewhere on the pleasures of travelling in India.

A Second Intermission

THE RICH AND powerful of Delhi used to flee to the mountains for the summer. With a troupe of servants, they would ensconce themselves in the Himalayas, as Delhi's British and Mughal rulers had done before them[1]. There, they would laze around, go boating and take long afternoon strolls. Today, many of them travel the world. Every spring, the Delhi newspapers carry front-page advertisements for 'Europe in seven days', with superimposed cartoon images of the Eiffel Tower, the Leaning Tower of Pisa and Big Ben, with an improbably exhaustive itinerary and a promise of 'Pure Veg' Indian meals at all hotels.

I too fled for Europe this summer, extracting my overcooked children from the Delhi heat, and found myself in several of the effete cities of the old world. London, where I have lived most of my life, appeared to have shrunk and become cute. Parts of it are being turned into an urban toyland, a post-modern parody of itself. My first evening was spent at a party in an old water-pumping station in North London. Its reservoir had been turned into a moderately majestic yachting marina, its old pump house had become a indoor climbing centre, speckled with fluorescent plastic footholds, and the main building had been turned into a party venue, with discreetly positioned lilac lighting to show off the intestines of this relic of the industrial age. A waitress, carefully disguised as a guest, walked up to me carrying a plate of immaculately presented sweet chilli seafood salad, with an enormous tentacle of octopus balanced on top. I reached out and stuffed the tentacle into my mouth. 'That's the decoration, sir,' she said. The tip of the tentacle was still visible when I reopened my mouth to say sorry. To my embarrassment, I found myself adding, by way of explanation, 'I've just come from India.' I felt a sudden longing to return to Delhi, as if I was a self-consciously gauche migrant who had just arrived in the West.

---

[1] The Mughals would head for Kashmir, where they built the formal gardens of Srinagar. The British built hill stations such as Simla, which became India's summer capital and is today the capital of the Indian state of Himachal Pradesh.

I went in search of places that are as unlike Delhi as possible. Brussels and Geneva, *soi-disant* international cities, felt like over-nourished hamlets, though Brussels did have one of the world's best collections of underpasses and pastry shops. And in Geneva early one morning, prevented from spiralling by the waters of Lake Leman, I accidentally wandered out of the city and walked into France. Heading in the opposite direction, was a multiracial *peloton* of power-dressed cyclists of both sexes: suit and ties, or jackets with impressively padded shoulders, presumably heading for the United Nations. Towards the back of the *peloton* there was a single tandem, with a besuited rear rider, typing one-handed on the keyboard of his personal organizer and talking over his hands-free mobile. I felt like an extra in an environmentally-aware, science fiction B-movie of the 1970s.

I also climbed several minor Swiss mountains. One day, I struggled through a blizzard, dressed in fluorescent green and blue Gore-Tex, and came upon a small, perfectly formed steel-and-glass hut way above the snowline. Inside, I found a surly Swiss waiter and, to my astonishment, two disconsolate, frozen Indian families pretending to ignore each other[2]. They had each, I discovered, been delivered to this remotest of places by a cog-railway from the town of Zermatt; each family was a willing participant and then a victim of different 'Europe in seven days' programmes. The smaller family group, more accustomed to travelling, I felt, was made up of a husband, wife and a wild plump son who was responsible for the waiter's surliness. They were all dressed in jeans, and T-shirts (the son's intimated a recent visit to Disneyland). The other, larger family—five of them—were nervously well-behaved. The grandmother was wearing three cardigans over her sari and was shaking with cold. They were talking in a mixture of Punjabi and English and had come from Delhi; they couldn't wait to get home from their Grand Tour.

[2] Two hundred thousand Indian tourists went to Switzerland in 2003—the numbers continue to rise. Many recent Bollywood films have had scenes shot in Switzerland, partly because the insurgency in Kashmir has deprived filmmakers of India's best known snow-capped backdrop. This has been a major reason for the recent dramatic increase in the number of Indian tourists visiting Switzerland. All the Indians I met complained how cold and expensive it was.

I returned to a late but hyperactive monsoon, which had turned the roads into rivers, gardens into jungles, dust into mud. And we moved from the rancid plushness of one of the smartest colonies in South Delhi to a flat that had known many tenants, and which abuts the crumbling walls of Siri Fort, built seven hundred years ago to enclose the second of Delhi's seven cities[3]. Here, I decide, I can make my home. I try to organize a regular supply of water and electricity, as well as a broadband wireless Internet service. All is possible, though it's an unseen neighbour who unknowingly supplies me with a wireless connection. I can read, thanks to the time difference, the British papers online while my London relatives are still asleep; my inbox receives regular vowel-deficient missives by e-mail and Messenger from my pre-teen North London nieces. Photos from anywhere can reach me within minutes of being taken. I've even found myself staring at webcam pictures of London's traffic hotspots in order to check on the weather. Homesickness is easier to conquer these days. I am a beneficiary of this shrunken world.

I gaze from the windows of my new home at the ancient walls of Siri, realizing that our remoteness from the past cannot so easily be shrunk. Siri was built by the Khilji dynasty in 1303 and so named, according to Delhi legend, because hundreds of heads (*sir* in Hindustani) of defeated Mongol invaders were interred in the city walls[4]. These crumbling ruins today serve, in decreasing order of importance, as a pissoir, a source of free building material, a children's hiding place, an ersatz hillock for local goats, a minor city landmark and, last of all, one of the most romantic evocations of Delhi's

[3] Most guidebooks refer to the seven cities of Delhi—the first (Lalkot/Qila Rai Pithora), the second (Siri), the third Tughlaqabad, and the fourth (Jahanpanah) are all in the southern part of the modern city. Delhi's centre of gravity moved northwards and the fifth (Ferozebad or Feroze Shah Kotla), the sixth (Dinpanah) and the seventh (Shahjahanabad, or what it now known as Old Delhi) are grouped along the Yamuna river. Others have made the case for many more avatars of Delhi. The traditional seven cities ignore evidence of settlement prior to the eleventh century AD, as well as the twentieth-century British-built city of New Delhi, and the Indian capital's post-independence incarnations.

[4] Descendants of those Mongol invaders, who had converted to Islam and were known as Mughals, re-invaded Delhi two centuries later, and established an occasionally interrupted hegemony in Delhi that lasted officially until the 1857 Uprising.

extraordinary history. I have come to love these ruins, and show them off proudly to visitors.

My fellow Delhiwallahs do not seem terribly interested in their city's past. Most of them have never heard of the Khiljis, and only know about Siri Fort because it has given its name to a large auditorium. This city lives for the present and the future—and has little time for nostalgia. It is a city of migrants and the growing city-pride of its inhabitants relate to its aspirations, not its history. India's most venerable newspaper, the *Times of India*, has become the latest proponent of Delhi's global ambition with a marketing campaign whose tagline proudly proclaims, 'Delhi—from Walled City to World City'.

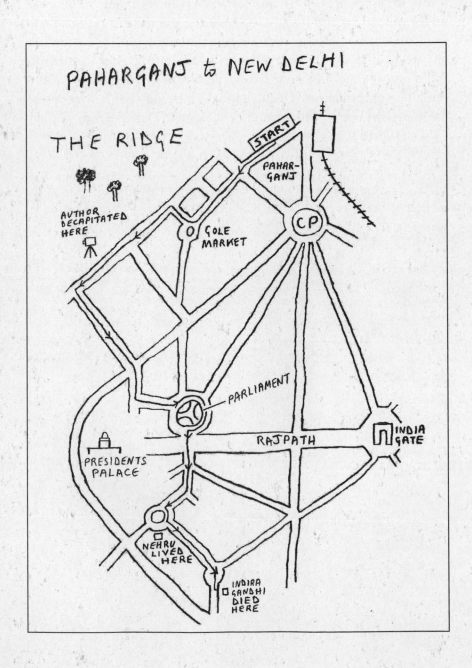

Chapter Three: In which the Author is spat at, flirted with and eventually beheaded

I AM SITTING in the Everest Café in the backstreets of Paharganj and I feel uncomfortable, torn. I have entered backpacker-land and I wonder whether this is a world to which I belong. I live in India and I am married to an Indian; I speak, like many Indian migrants to this city, a corrupted version of Hindi—and yet I always stick out, as a white man. Now I have entered a room, a small café, in which I am for once not an object of curiosity, not under scrutiny. And yet I feel a wave of nausea coming over me. It is as if 'No Indians Allowed' were written on the wall. It is as if I have left Delhi through a mysterious portal marked Everest Café and entered a purgatory for western travellers, full of un-Indian comforts and terrible tortures. On sale are cappuccinos, cheese cake, muesli, porridge, cornflakes, avocados, mosquito sprays, diarrhoea pills and toilet rolls. Foreigners, I was once told by a mystified Indian hotel manager, use up three times as many toilet rolls as Indians—'Are their motions very different?' he enquired.[1] I look around, unnoticed. A silent couple (German-speakers, I deduce from the unopened novels in front of them) are both staring into space, one up, one down. The woman, whiter-than-white, and almost as broad as she is tall, has a red smear in her hair parting, and is wearing a maroon bridal sari. The man, wan-faced and wraith-like, is wearing a T-shirt whose legend I read with a series of sideways glances, and scribble down surreptitiously in my notebook

OM
No hashish
No boat
No change
No rickshaw
No problem

---

[1] An Internet search for Paharganj + diarrhoea will explain all. I'm afraid it gets even more revolting if you enter Paharganj + vomit.

On the table, between their books is a half-used toilet roll. The woman gets up, the *pallu* of the sari falls off her shoulder and she wraps it round her waist. She picks up the roll, gives a look of unparalleled grief to her companion, and heads towards the bathroom. An Israeli woman looks up briefly from her Hebrew guidebook, and bellows incomprehensibly at the waiter. This is the first human sound I have heard since entering the café. The waiter comes over. The Israeli stands up, a good five inches taller than the waiter. Her turquoise T-shirt clings to her, and across her chest are the outlines of two hands, as if her breasts are being grabbed from behind. Up above, her face bears a scowl of quite formidable proportions, a surreal contrast to the message of her T-shirt. She jabs at the menu with her index finger. 'Salat Israeli. Look . . . [jab, jab, jab] Get it.' The waiter scuttles away. (I look at the menu; and there it is, to my surprise: Israeli salad[2].) He returns with a few chopped vegetables on a plate. She picks up a long sliver of raw carrot, and dangles it like a pendulum, and then lays it down as if it were a dead goldfish, carefully placing it so it bisects her triangular paper napkin. 'No carrot,' she barks, pronouncing the final syllable as if it were a description of the quality of the food. The waiter brings the plate back without any carrots, and she doggedly eats her medley of vegetables (I can see cucumbers, tomatoes and coriander) with a look of unforgiving disgust on her face.

As she was finishing, I decide I would be failing as an intrepid explorer if I didn't try to interview her. I nervously went up and asked if I could talk to her about Delhi. 'No English,' she said decisively, but in such a way that I was left pondering whether she was rejecting me on ethnic grounds, or because she could not speak my language. She stared hard at me, as if to assess whether I was an enemy, and then said, with a dismissive sweep of her arm. 'Delhi . . . Khhugh [the sound of phlegm being expectorated] . . . Shit.' And then she

---

[2] According to the website jewz.com an Israeli salad is simply a mixture of cucumbers and tomatoes cut up very small. However, israelioliveoil.com adds green peppers, parsley and, unsurprisingly, olive oil. The most exotic Israeli salad I have been able to uncover is at prostatepointer.org, quoting a recipe from the San Diego Prostate Cancer Support group, which includes onions and as optionals, feta cheese and olives. Most Israeli salad recipes bear an extraordinary similarity to what is also known as Arabic salad.

rounded her lips and made as if to spit so realistically, and with such an impressive sound effect, that a glob of saliva actually flew out of her mouth and landed on my cheek. She was as surprised as me. She grabbed her napkin, sending her rejected sliver of carrot skywards, and tried to dab my cheek at the same time as my finger touched the errant glob. Somehow, our fingers and the napkin became intertwined, and then, for what seemed like half an eternity, but actually cannot have lasted more than two seconds, we both gently stroked my cheek. 'Pardon, pardon,' she said. I laughed out loud, and sat down. 'It's OK, it's OK.' And then somewhere from the recesses of my brain came the words 'mazel tov[3]'. She began to cry. I realized that the Hebrew phrase that had come out of my mouth, meaning congratulations or good luck, was totally meaningless in the context of the two of us trying to remove saliva from my cheek, but it had turned her from a screaming monster into a weeping wreck. And she had an arm round my shoulders, and was trying to tell me something in Hebrew. 'No Hebrew,' I said. I realized that our language gap meant that I would never learn why she hated Delhi so much, and, extricating myself, got up to pay for a croissant, which I had asked for and no longer had the stomach to eat. As I left, I noticed that the rotund German had returned, her sari now in use as a shawl and a comfort blanket. She looked more disconsolate than ever.

Outside, disoriented, I asked a man loitering next to a garish hotel how to get back to the main Paharganj Bazaar. Instead I was offered hashish, then cocaine, and when I turned these down, sex of an unspecified variety. This is not Delhi at its best, I thought, as I fled Paharganj, and yet it is the Delhi so many new foreign visitors first encounter, and yet again it is a part of this city that few of my Indian friends are aware of. I eventually found refuge in a Christian cemetery

---

[3] I knew this phrase from the 1971 film version of the schmaltzy musical *Fiddler on the Roof*, which I saw as a special treat on my tenth birthday. There are two delightfully obscure Delhi connections—Vernon Dobcheff, who played a Russian official in *Fiddler on the Roof*, later played the viceroy, Lord Willingdon, in the 1998 movie about the founder of Pakistan, *Jinnah*. (The long semi-circular road, a kilometre away from Paharganj, that marks the boundary of the Presidential palace is still known as Willingdon Crescent although it was recently renamed Mother Teresa Marg.) And *Fiddler on the Roof*'s make-up artist, Wally Schneiderman, also worked on the 1963 movie '*Nine Hours to Rama*' about the assassination of Mahatma Gandhi in the heart of New Delhi in 1948.

I had visited months before, when I had traipsed from grave to grave, absorbing the normality of early death, and wondering less metaphysically why quite so many Indian Christians had the surname Massey. Was there some Englishman of that name, who could have spread his seed so widely? And this time it came to me, a sudden bolt of understanding: Massey is an anglicization of Massih, which is the Hindi (and Urdu and Arabic) word for Christian, and has the same root as the word Messiah. Re-energized by my etymological discovery, I set off again, crossing another CP radial, Panchkuian Road, passing under the huge concrete stanchions that support the railway track of Line 3 of the Delhi Metro. Determined to put Paharganj as far behind me as possible, I marched on past a single-storey office building: the firmly closed North End Complex, home to the National League of Pen-Friends and the All-India Sports Council of the Deaf; and then down towards the officially circular, but actually octagonal, Gole[4] Market, and the headquarters of the Communist Party of India (Marxist) with its proud hammer and sickle, the home of the kingmakers of modern Indian politics[5].

I then veered off right, concerned that my spiral had become too constricted (I was still less than two kilometres from the heart of Connaught Place and that at this rate I might forever keep getting marginally further from CP but would never reach outer Delhi. And so I arrived at Mandir Marg, or Temple Street, with at least eleven places of worship and five schools, constructed parallel to the thorn-and-rock scrubland of the Ridge, which until the middle of the last century formed the western boundary of urban Delhi. The Ridge itself is more than 500 million years old, part of the Aravalli range, which is reverentially described by school textbook writers as the oldest mountain range in India, as if this were some kind of consolation for being not very big. The Himalayas are mere

[4] *Gole* means circle.
[5] The Communist Party of India was formed in 1925, and split in the 1960s into pro-Russian and pro-Chinese factions. The latter formed the largest faction, the Communist Party of India (Marxist) which has been elected to power in three Indian states, and was the third largest national party in the 2004 elections. The Congress-Party-led ruling coalition was only able to form a government because of CPI(M) support. Both of India's main communist parties have performed dismally in Delhi city elections. No communist has been elected to the Delhi assembly since 1972.

babies, at less than 100 million years old[6]. There appeared to be no easy way to approach the Ridge from Mandir Marg. So I entered the compound of the Harcourt Butler[7] Boys Secondary School, which seemed deserted. A small boy came up to me, and asked me what I was doing there. I said

he looked a little young to be at secondary school. His father, he said, was the watchman, but was having a sleep, and had asked him to make sure there were no intruders. He told me that the school was closed for a public holiday, *choti Diwali,* the day before Diwali. I told him I only wanted to look around, and, with a small theatrical bow, he allowed me in. Above each classroom door was written a deeply disagreeable English saying, designed, it seems, to inculcate fear into the students. Many were on the theme of mortality. Class 7 had the simple 'Do not forget death', and next door was 'Death keeps no calendar', and after that 'Everything is under the sway of death and decay'. I could barely believe this was not a joke. Then came others that were only slightly less fatalistic or bleak: 'Misfortunes never come alone', 'Hunger is the best sauce', 'All relations are chains of bondage', 'Enjoyments are our fatal diseases' and 'Desires are a tantalising mirage.' Out at the back of the school was a playground, backing on to the Ridge, with teenagers playing volleyball, all students from Harcourt Butler. I

---

[6] The Ridge is the northern tip of the mainly quartzite Aravalli range, which runs for 650 kilometres southwards into Rajasthan. The Himalayas were created when India (an island which had broken off from a supercontinent known as Gondwana) crunched its way into the larger Eurasian continent, buckling the land and throwing up the largest mountain in the world. The summit of Mount Everest was a seabed at the time of the formation of the Ridge. Everest continues to grow by a few millimetres each year, while the Ridge is getting progressively flatter and less ridge-like because of quarrying and encroachment.

[7] Harcourt Butler was a British Lothario-cum-civil servant who, among other things, opposed the transfer of the capital of British India from Calcutta to Delhi in 1911.

asked them about the slogans above the classroom doors—but it was clear that most of them thought it a strange kind of question and were untraumatized by their pessimistic view of life. I climbed, unskilfully, up on the Ridge, alone among the rocks except for a family of black pigs, and gazed over central Delhi's skyline—picking out Gopal Das Bhavan and the India Life building to the east and, to the south, the puce, circumcised dome of Rashtrapati Bhavan, the Presidential palace, New Delhi's flagship building, and a key landmark for the next twist of my spiral.

First I had to return to the main road, where I was set upon by several postcard- and trinket-sellers outside Delhi's main tourist-route temple, the Birla Mandir. I had shown what I thought was a casual interest in a wafer-thin pamphlet about the temple, but was quoted a bizarrely absurd price and decided, to the dismay of the vendors, that I didn't want the book, or anything else, after all. They weren't going to give up, though, and I was only able to escape by entering a gate at the side of the temple—where a severe watchman turned away my pursuers. I discovered that behind the Birla Mandir is a park, with an impressive collection of large multi-coloured concrete animals. The creators of Indian parks are keen on these animals, whose underbellies provide useful shade and cover in the hot and rainy seasons. This one, however, was special. Several of the animals are conjoined mysteriously beneath a man-made hillock, and there is a warren of man-size, earth-clad tunnels that can be entered through bestial orifices. I was able to enter, unbent, through the mouth of a dragon, brushing past a pair of real-life amorously entwined humans, and to exit, still standing, from between the rear legs of a lion. And just beyond the lion's backside I encountered Raman photo stall.

Raman had strung up a maroon bed-sheet from a tree as a photographic backdrop. Two children were seated on a bench in front of the sheet, and a man, presumably Raman, had buried his head under a black cloth, using a box camera of a kind that became antique early in the twentieth century. Throwing off his shroud, Raman emerged, beaming, and invited me to look at examples of his photos pinned on a display board. He turned out to be a devotee of the little-practised art of black-and-white photomontage, in an unusual way that was appropriate to his location, behind the Birla

Mandir. Raman offered his customers a choice of which Hindu god they could be photographed with. I selected the most violent and bizarre photo, in which I would prove my devotion to the goddess Durga by decapitating myself and offering Durga my head as a gift. Raman took a photograph of me holding out my hands, cut out my body and then my head with a pair of nail scissors. He then glued my body next to a pre-printed image of Durga riding a tiger, positioned my head precariously on my hands, and re-photographed the photograph. The final result was dramatic, if not particularly convincing. And there was something about my decapitation that delighted my children when I showed them the photograph later in the day.

Raman, a cheery man addicted to tales of woe, was a refugee from Lahore in Pakistan. He was born just before independence in 1947, when millions of Hindus and Sikhs crossed to India—as millions of Muslims headed in the opposite direction. His father and grandfather were photographers before him in Lahore, a sister-city to Delhi with a similarly strong Punjabi and Mughal heritage. Raman's son was now in the same business, though he used a digital camera and worked down the road at the Presidential palace. Raman was proud of his son, but even more proud of his grandfather, who had set up the stall behind Birla Mandir, with some help from his contacts in the controversial Hindu cultural organization, the RSS[8]. There were

[8] The Rashtriya Swayamsevak Sangh was formed in September 1925 as an organization for Hindu activists in the widest sense of the word. They can be seen, dressed in khaki shorts doing physical exercises in many Indian parks. However, it is the political activities of the RSS which have received more attention over the decades. The organization was accused of involvement in the assassination of Mahatma Gandhi—and many politicians from the Hindu nationalist party, the BJP, are also members of the RSS.

four photo stalls in the Birla Mandir Gardens in the 1950s— and they used to move around every year so that each would have a turn at the plum location. Now there were only two stall-owners left—and though they'd once been close friends they no longer acknowledged each other's existence. Raman said his former friend had refused to move from the best spot, there had been a fight, and they'd both ended up at the police station six hundred metres further up Mandir Marg. So now Raman's stall was permanently near the lion's backside, and business was bad. Even worse, he found it hard to find silver bromide paper for his ancient camera. Delhi had gone digital, and even the slightly more modern 35mm photography stalls were suffering. I left clutching my sacrificial photographs, three copies expertly coiled so they could dry without sticking. Raman followed me for a little, checking, I think, that I wasn't paying a visit to the other photography stall.

I marched to the end of Mandir Marg, passing the Swati Working Girls Hostel (not—I checked with the watchman—a euphemism) and then took an enforced left turn, reaching a junction where I

was faced with a choice. On the right: Willingdon Crescent, both a genuine arc of a circle, and central Delhi's greenest road, sandwiched between the Ridge and the vast, overgrown compound at the back of Rashtrapati Bhavan. On the left, Imperial Delhi: the palace itself and new city built by and for the British—and a few carefully chosen Indians. To take Willingdon Crescent would mean encounters with monkeys and peacocks and fresh air; it would also shorten my spiral, broadening the gap between each twist and quickly allowing me to escape the gravitation pull of central Delhi. To turn left would mean confronting the most tangible legacy of a group of imperialists who bore the same nationality as me (but with whom I feel little in common). I chose the psychologically more daunting course and headed for Imperial Delhi.

The heart of British New Delhi has three huge rectilinear government edifices, and, to one side, a whimsical, circular afterthought. Those three main buildings are built on a vast plinth created by simply slicing off the top of what was once Raisina Hill, as if it were a hard-boiled egg. At the back, the British built the Viceregal palace, with the interior of a huge English country mansion, designed to remind 'the natives' just who was boss. On either side came North and South Block: two symmetrical red hulks of buildings in a hybrid Mughal-European style which sweep down the hill and dominate the great open area below, and which were designed as a place of work for the all-powerful Indian Civil Service. Then, rather late in the day for New Delhi's architects, it was felt necessary to grant Indians an increased amount of self-government. And so came the afterthought, a Parliament House with three semi-circles and a little circle inside a big circle, as if drawn with a schoolchild's compass, and placed insecurely on the northern side at the bottom of Raisina Hill. The whole forms a dramatic and unforgettable mess, and its architects knew as much.

The most striking feature of all is the amount of empty space on the plain below Raisina Hill. A huge broad avenue sweeps up from the east. It is as if a runway had been laid in central Delhi, so wide and flat and deserted that it is a daunting place for a solitary walker. Once a year, on Republic Day, India's home-made missiles, liveried soldiers and un-Scottish bagpipers are paraded along what the British called the King's Way, officially to celebrate the day when they rid themselves of the British King. In reality it has become a display of India's military might, what one polyglot diplomat called 'a willy-waving display of *machismo* aimed at its *frère-ennemi*'—a reference to Pakistan. At the western end are the great looming ministerial buildings of North and South Block, and barely visible, as if shamed

71

by the power of the bureaucracy, is the Presidential palace, set far too far back to provide the sense of 'awe and majesty' that the British had intended. Edwin Lutyens, the chief architect, had wanted the palace to sit alone on top of the hill—but he had been persuaded to allow the secretariats to share that position. Lutyens then placed a 145-foot column in front of the palace, further obscuring the view, and constructed a dome that is uncomfortable with its own proportions, as if it desires to be a tower when it grows up. But most embarrassing of all, the slope of the avenue up Raisina Hill is a little too steep, so that, at the moment of its intended triumph and majesty, the palace suddenly disappears almost entirely from view. Lutyens and his colleague Herbert Baker argued so bitterly over the gradient of the slope of Raisina Hill that they did not speak for six years. The former French Prime Minister, Georges Clemenceau, visiting India in the 1920s, uttered his famous *bon mot* about the great buildings of Imperial Delhi: they will, he said, make magnificent ruins.

The British never really got to enjoy New Delhi. The new city took twenty years to build, and less than seventeen years after it was inaugurated, the British had left, tails between their legs, to return only as tourists, journalists and spouses. The Viceregal palace was not, as Mahatma Gandhi would recommend, turned into

a hospital; the huge family quarters of what became Rashtrapati Bhavan (the Presidential palace) was occupied until recently by a bachelor nuclear scientist. The bureaucrats of North and South Block still reign supreme on Raisina Hill— a tribute to the continuing power of the Indian civil service. But they are barely visible. The minor potentates, file-shuffling princelings of the

Licence Raj[9], enter from below through side doors; the big shots, the VIPs and (to use the Delhi demotic) the VVIPs, arrive in white air-conditioned Ambassador cars. There is something eerie, inhuman, about the whole area. Authoritarian, like Nuremberg, declaimed one writer about Delhi. I find its silent emptiness even more striking. Here is a huge, landscaped, open public space in the centre of one of the biggest cities in the world, and it is desolate. No one is here, except for me. It as if Clemenceau's prediction had come true and I was visiting a ghost city.

Originally, all central government ministries were to be housed in North and South Block, but they became far too bloated. And so began the construction of many a ministerial *bhavan*, some of them of quite breathtaking ugliness. My favourite eyesore of them all, astonishing for its total lack of grace or aesthetic sense, is the bleak, scab-encrusted, moulting, death-grey eight-storey cattle shed called Sena Bhavan, or Army House, which loomed over me as I headed south from South Block, towards the heart of the land of the bungalows, known officially as the Lutyens Bungalow Zone or LBZ.

LBZ is home to judges, generals, diplomats (ambassadorial rank only), occasional wealthy members of the public and, of course, politicians. The first task of any new minister is to move into a large single-storey 1930s building surrounded by well-tended lawns, contained within a forbidding red-brick boundary wall, and generally guarded by stir-crazy constables of the Delhi police force. There are many hundreds of these bungalows. I tried to take a photograph of a corner bungalow, in huge grounds at 1 Kamraj Lane, home to the Minister of State for Human Resource Development, Mohammed Ali Ashraf Fatmi, but was ordered away by a pistol-toting man in a denim suit who was wearing sunglasses in midwinter. Next, I chanced

[9] Licence Raj was a shorthand term invented to describe the complex regime of government licences and regulations, overseen by the civil service in post-independence India. The term was popularized by the south Indian politician, Chakravarti Rajagopalachari, or Rajaji, who saw the Licence Raj as a cause of corruption and slow economic growth. As Governor-General of India (1948–50) Rajaji was the first Indian occupant of Rashtrapati Bhavan. In 1950, the post of Governor-General was abolished, and India became a Republic, with a President as Head of State.

upon the home of Surgeon Vice-Admiral VK Singh, AVSM, VSM, DGMS (Navy), more than five hundred miles away from the nearest ship. Then, the unguarded bungalow of a dapper ex-foreign minister, and the extremely well-guarded home of a Delhi MP who became briefly known as the tsunami minister, and who already—like many bungalow occupants—has a perfectly adequate home in Delhi.

It is this Delhi of bungalows that seems to glow with authoritarianism, for it is here that many of the most powerful people in the country live, a large number of them cut off from the rest of India. These bungalows are allotted under a Byzantine procedure which seems to cause far more rancour among politicians than the ideological differences that ostensibly separate them. The LBZ today is one of most tangible vestiges of a dying British Empire in India, a place which was deliberately designed to exclude the ruled. The trappings of those last days of authoritarian rule have survived in a VVIP culture which is deeply divisive. And the LBZ is the epicentre of that culture, where democratically elected politicians can retreat into their rent-free or low-rent compounds, where they can intrigue to get an even better bungalow, where they can escape from their constituents, where they can avoid being reminded of the lives of the poor (from amongst whom many of them have risen). It encourages the powerful to believe themselves omnipotent, as if they were gods or belonged to a different species from their fellow Indians. And maybe some of them do. After all, no other democracy has produced three generations of prime ministers from the same family.

Jawaharlal Nehru ruled India for sixteen years from Teen Murti House, intended as a home for the British Commander-in-Chief, with the second best private gardens in Delhi, and a direct view of the Viceregal palace. Today, it is a ghostly cavernous museum. There were two other visitors when I turned up. We three politely nodded as our paths crossed. A silent young man, bored, trying to pass some time. An older woman, perhaps sixty, in a green sari, repeating to herself, 'Marvellous, marvellous', as she examined a slightly moth-eaten black gown and mortar-board worn by Nehru when presented with an honorary degree at Columbia University by 'President' Eisenhower[10] in 1949.

[10] In 1949, Eisenhower was president of Columbia University. He only became President of the United States of America in 1953.

She wanted to talk. The young man had failed to respond to her opening gambit, and a little later she sidled up to me. 'I could spend the whole day here. Nehru was the greatest Indian, much greater than his witch of a daughter, and now people have just forgotten him,' she said, gesticulating in the direction of an empty room. 'Look at this . . . ' and she dragged me over to a photograph of Nehru, 'Isn't he handsome? I just worship him. Sometime I even dream about him . . .' And she stopped speaking and giggled shyly and became embarrassed, as if her dream had become a little too vivid and personal. We moved together through the galleries, scrutinizing laminated wall-mounted copies of old newspapers, describing the long haul of the freedom movement and Nehru's increasingly important role. There were dozens of faded reproductions of old photographs, more of his daughter Indira (her distinctive nose identifying her at any age) than of his wife Kamala, who died thirteen years before he became India's first Prime Minister. The lady in the sari continued to follow me, silently but sometimes pointing to pictures of Nehru that she clearly found particularly attractive. As I prepared to leave, she giggled again, holding my hand tight, and spoke again with the intensity of someone who has had an unexpected amatory experience. 'That was lovely. Thank you so much.'

Indira Gandhi lived and died a short stroll away at 1 Safdarjung Road. The house, an immaculate whitewashed bungalow set in well-tended gardens, has become a kind of temple, with long queues outside and hushed crowds within. There the pilgrims from all over India file through a series of rooms, gazing respectfully at possessions: her travel Scrabble set, her unfinished knitting, her binoculars for bird-watching, as if they were minor relics of a saint. The major relic is further on: the rust-coloured sari she was wearing when she was killed near the front gate of this house by two Sikh bodyguards in 1984. Next to the sari are her multi-coloured shoulder-bag and a pair of simple black sandals with half-inch heels. The sari has been pressed and loosely folded, but not cleaned. There are blood stains and several bullet holes. Beant Singh and Satwant Singh[11] shot her

---

[11] Beant Singh was shot dead shortly after the assassination. Satwant Singh was hanged in 1989 in Delhi's Tihar jail. Many Sikhs objected to Mrs Gandhi's decision to send the army into the Golden Temple in Amritsar to capture or kill

at least thirty times. The crowds are thickest here. An old Sikh man in a ragged tweed jacket puts his cupped right hand to his head and then opens it like a flower in the direction of the sari, as if to ask, 'How could they?' A family of south Indians jostles him out of the way, but he is lost in his thoughts, too preoccupied to care. He wanders on in a daze into a room of strange, unusable objects from around the world: a crystal pineapple from Jamaica, the key to the city of Bogota, a red lacquer plate bearing the avuncular, long-bearded likeness of Ho Chi Minh, and nearby, a signed photograph, 'To my dear Niece Indira Nehru. Loving Greetings! 7.2.58. Uncle Hochiminh.'

There are also hundreds of photographs, marking every stage of her roller-coaster life. Some of them are remarkably dull, as she meets a huge number of po-faced suited male leaders (and Margaret Thatcher) from around the world. But there are others that are quite extraordinary. In 1924, she is a shy six-year-old in a white dress sitting on the bed of an emaciated old man with a huge grin on his face, who is grasping her arm as if his life depended on it. The old man—in fact only fifty-five at the time, but midway through a fast that had made him even skinnier that usual—was Mahatma Gandhi. Both would

become by far the most influential Indian political leaders of their day, and both would die violent deaths in the heart of Delhi. Seventeen years later, Indira is alone with that other Gandhi in her life, her Parsee fiancé Feroze (they married the following year), in London during the Blitz. He took a series of touching photographs of her—a skeletal recently released patient at a

Sikh militants. According to the Indian government, 2,733 Sikhs were killed in Delhi in the riots that followed her assassination. The website carnage84.com puts the figure at 4,000.

Swiss tuberculosis clinic—skipping and pouting and posing and flirting unselfconsciously on a London roof top. Then as her marriage falls apart, Feroze disappears from the photographs—and Indira becomes her father's full-time companion and de facto First Lady of India. In 1966, two years after her father's death she becomes Prime Minister, and displays the full range of human emotion to the lens of her camera. We see her distraught, angry, teasing, victorious, giggling and nervous. But for me there is one image that is missing. It is of Indira the autocrat, the

world's most powerful woman, ruling over a coterie of spineless men, captured mischievously by Raghu Rai, (who photographed the diver of Agarsen's Baoli) in a famous photograph, tellingly absent at the Indira Gandhi memorial.

Her son, Rajiv, had been an airline pilot and a very good amateur photographer before he succeeded her as Prime Minister, and was the kind of person about whom, unlike his mother, one might use the word 'nice'. He, too, was killed, as he was about to make a political comeback, and much less is left to see of the clothes he wore on his final day. On the campaign trail in southern India,

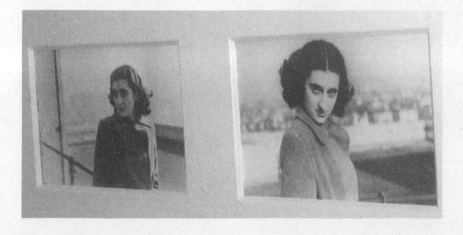

he was, quite literally, blown to pieces[12], as were his trousers. In an ante-room at the back of the Indira Gandhi memorial museum, the fragments of his pyjama-style trousers that were recovered from the bomb site have been fixed to a cloth, and reassembled as if it were an inherited jigsaw of which half the pieces are lost. The grisly ensemble has been hung like a translucent curtain, his red-and-white Italian-made high-ankled Lotto basketball shoes carefully placed below, as if ready to be worn by his ghost.

[12] Rajiv's assassin, Dhanu, was a member of a Sri Lankan rebel group, the Tamil Tigers. She and at least fifteen other people died in the explosion. The Tamil Tigers had objected to the presence of the Indian army in northern Sri Lanka, ostensibly as a peace-keeping force, when Rajiv Gandhi was Prime Minister in the late 1980s.

A Third Intermission

V.S. NAIPAUL made his first trip to India in the year of my birth, 1962. He was appalled. 'For the first time in my life I was one of the crowd.' In Trinidad, in the UK, in Egypt he had stood out as an Indian; he was, in one of his favourite words, 'distinctive'. In Bombay, he rails, 'I entered a shop or a restaurant and awaited a special quality of response. And there was nothing. It was like being denied part of my reality. Again and again I was caught. I was faceless[1].' This is a perfect description of the exact reverse of my situation, and I think I now begin to understand why Naipaul minded so much.

Life in Delhi has brought me a new kind of freedom. I am no longer one of the crowd. I no longer feel the need to conform, or to measure myself against London contemporaries. Here it is taken for granted that I am different, eccentric. I stick out wherever I go. As a *firang*[2], I have discovered a multiple role: I am a source of amusement for small children who follow me around the streets of Delhi as if I were the Pied Piper (unless they are very young, in which case they burst into tears). I am a source of additional revenue for rupee-pinching shop-keepers who take great pleasure in being excessively polite and extracting a small tithe in return (I am now reconciled to paying a premium of at least ten per cent for being strange and foreign). I am a source of income and consternation for wide-eyed household workers who discuss my unusual foreign ways with next-door's servants (I sometimes make my own tea. I also prefer not to turn the packing of my suitcase into a group activity).

My size, my colour, my gait, my accent, my demeanour, my body language, my facial expressions mark me out as a foreigner. And I always will be a foreigner, however long I live here. The more Indian I wish to become, the more eccentric I appear. Because, unlike most foreigners here, I speak and read some Hindi, I appear even more

---

[1] Naipaul then buys himself a pair of dark glasses in order to make himself more distinctive.

[2] *Firang* or *Firangi*, slightly disparaging words for white foreigners, originally refer to the Franks, from whom the French derive their name. It probably came via the Arabic *ifranji* which was used to describe Frankish Crusaders and then became a word that was applied to all Europeans.

unusual. My Hindi teacher has taught me some literary words such as *girja*[3] *ghar* for church, or *chhayankan* for photo. These words coming out of my mouth can reduce an Indian adult to a giggling wreck. *Chaarch* and *poto* are the preferred everyday words, an Indianized English which I often find myself, out of some pointless vestigial pedantry, too embarrassed to use. Sometimes there is no alternative.

I have tried hard to say 'toast' in a way that most Indians will understand. My strike rate is not disastrous—I will be understood about sixty per cent of the time—and yet it has become enough of a problem for me to forego, when feeling unadventurous, what my stomach desires and order some other food. There is no Hindi word for toast—leavened bread having been introduced by Europeans. And so the English word makes do, in most Indian languages, with a variety of pronunciations, each slightly different to 'toast', as I, a long-vowelled, diphthonged Londoner, might normally say it. Often when I have tried and failed to order toast, my wife has stepped in, and with gleeful gusto, repeated the word in a way that is identical, to my uncultured ears, with the word as I had uttered it, but which also magically results in the arrival of several slices of lightly toasted bread. There are two kinds of problems I face here: one is the

expectation that I, being foreign, will not be understood, and that my wife, an Indian, will be understood. But this is only part of the story. I have realized how important it is not to say 'toast' with an English accent. In Hindi, there are four different 't' sounds[4]; so there are sixteen possible combinations for the opening

---

[3] *Girja* actually comes from the Portuguese *Igreja* which (like the French *église*) comes from the Greek *ekklesia*.

[4] The four Hindi Ts are: the retroflex unaspirated plosive ट, the retroflex aspirated plosive ठ, the dental unaspirated plosive त, and the dental aspirated plosive थ. The most common English pronunciation of the letter 'T', the alveolar unaspirated plosive, is not used in Hindi. All plosives are single, non-continuous sounds (you cannot 'hold' the letter 't' as you can the letter 's'). For dental consonants, the tip of the tongue is placed against the teeth. For retroflex consonants, the tongue is rolled back against the roof of the mouth. For alveolar consonants the tongue touches the alveolum or ridge above the upper teeth. Aspirated sounds are more breathy.

and closing consonants of the word in question. But hardest of all is the vowel sound, shorter and rounder than the English 'oa', in a language that is short on diphthongs. My latest middle-of-the-night insomniac game is to try out as many different Indian-language variations of the pronunciation of toast as I can formulate. It helps me practise my four Hindi 't's, but I have quite gone off toast.

The worst response to the negative aspects of being a foreigner is to become angry. I have learnt instead to take pleasure at others finding me amusing or incompetent; and there are rewards. If I am lost, a crowd will gather to help me. If I enter a forbidden building, I only get a mild reprimand—as if I, a foreigner, would not know better. I am often dragged (only a little unwillingly) to the front of a queue when buying a ticket. I am, for better or worse, distinctive.

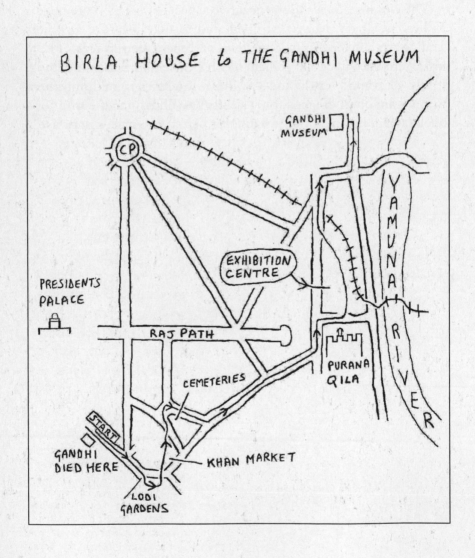

BIRLA HOUSE to THE GANDHI MUSEUM

CP

GANDHI MUSEUM

PRESIDENT'S PALACE

EXHIBITION CENTRE

RAJ PATH

YAMUNA RIVER

CEMETERIES

PURANA QILA

START

GANDHI DIED HERE

KHAN MARKET

LODI GARDENS

Chapter Four: In which the Author encounters a digital Mahatma, unravels the mystery of Stella of Mudge and engages in solvent abuse

THIRTIETH JANUARY STREET is a ten-minute walk from Indira Gandhi's place of death. It contains two Delhi landmarks, one of them the place of death of an even more illustrious Gandhi. On the northern side, set back from the far-from-busy tree-lined road, is the neo-classical National Defence College[1], its martial purpose underlined by three menacing howitzers stationed outside its gates. I lean against one of these small cannons, painted green and khaki as if ready for battle, looking around to ensure that I am not observed. Bending down with my neck twisted to one side, I peer up along the howitzer barrel as if I were taking aim, and try to visualize the parabolic path that would be traced by a shell launched from its muzzle[2] . It would, I adjudge, score a direct hit on the second, more famous landmark, on the other side of the road. I've been spotted, not by an officious guard, but by a relaxed two-star General, stroking and pulling at his moustache, ensconced in the rear seat of his black Ambassador with its two golden stars affixed to the number plate. He looks at me and gives me a nervous quizzical wave. I smile back as if we were old friends, and point across the road to make it clear that I'm actually going to the building opposite. I step across the road to Birla House,

[1] The National Defence College building has had several avatars. It was built in the 1930s as a home for a horse-loving Indian Muslim princeling (who would eventually opt to live in Pakistan); then it was rented out as an army hostel during World War Two, before becoming the British High Commission at the time of Indian independence. The former colonial power eventually moved out in the late 1950s into its current 33-acre estate in the diplomatic enclave, and the National Defence College, a training school for senior officers, moved in.

[2] A Howitzer is a large mounted gun, which fires shells, and has a shorter barrel than a cannon. The word comes from the Czech word *haufnice*, meaning catapult. The words pistol, dollar and robot also come from Czech. I have since discovered that the range of the howitzer is more than 15 kilometers, so unless fired at a very low angle, a shell would travel well over Birla House, reaching beyond Delhi airport.

which had been reduced, in my hyperactive imagination, from a mansion to a pile of howitzered rubble.

Birla House, once the Delhi home of the same businessman who financed the Birla Mandir, was the place where the world's most influential cheek-turning peacenik since Jesus was murdered. I have long admired Mahatma Gandhi, but not only for the usual reasons. He was a great walker; indeed one of the hardiest, most determined walkers of all time. Walking was both exercise[3] and political protest. He walked as a child, instead of playing cricket, which he disliked. In London, as a student lawyer he would walk eight to ten miles each day, and was convinced that it kept him healthy despite the privations of a vegetarian diet in a carnivorous country; in Bombay as a young barrister he would walk one and a half hours each day. In Paris, as an Eiffel-Tower-hating tourist, visiting the Great Exhibition of 1890, he walked almost everywhere. On the salt march of 1930, he walked more than two hundred and forty miles as an act of political and economic protest against British rule; and he died walking at the age of seventy-eight, supported by his two great-nieces, Abha and Manu, whom he referred to as his 'walking-sticks'. His last steps from his bedroom in Birla House through the garden are immortalized in stone. One hundred and eighty two foot-shaped concrete lozenges, each one inch thick, have been cemented into the pathway, as if his feet had been divine and had left terracotta weals upon the paving stones. Impiously, I stepped upon the lozenges, one by one, counting them, tracing the final seconds of his life. He was walking to his place of evening prayer and discussion, where large crowds would gather each day, when he was shot dead by a pistol-packing Indian journalist, Nathuram Godse, who believed that Gandhi had been too nice to Pakistan in the aftermath of partition.

[3] In his remarkable 1942 pamphlet *Key to Health*, Gandhi declares that 'a brisk walk in the open is the best form of exercise. During the walk the mouth should be closed and breathing should be done through the nose.' The nose, he points out, is an air filter that requires daily cleaning and suggests this alternative to the widespread subcontinental and British practice of public nose-picking. 'Draw clean water up through one nostril, the other remaining closed, and expel it through the other by opening it and closing the former.' I have failed, and once almost drowned, in my attempts to master this procedure.

And so Birla House has become another museum for another Indian hero. Like the prime ministerial memorials to Jawaharlal, Indira and Rajiv, it is full of photographs. Unlike theirs, however, there is almost nothing else; for Gandhi was a man of practically no possessions. Everything he owned is in one very empty room. Mounted on the wall are a small sickle, a pumice stone, a knife, a fork, a spoon, his trademark pebble glasses and glasses case, a walking-stick, and the pocket watch that fell to the ground as he was shot, and stopped, dead, at seventeen minutes past five. In the same room are his bed, writing table and spinning wheel. Here, on 13 January 1948 he had begun his final fast, his infallible means of getting his way. Delhi was being torn apart by Hindu-Muslim rioting—as large numbers of Hindu refugees arrived from Pakistan, and beleaguered Delhi Muslims fled their homes. 'Gay Delhi,' he declared, 'looked a city of the dead.' Five days of fasting brought an end to the violence— and Gandhi was able to resume his normal frugal diet of fruit, vegetables and a drink made of ginger, lemon, aloe juice and strained buttermilk. Twelve days later he was dead, a victim of the Hindu chauvinism and insecurity that still haunts India .

Less than twenty metres from Gandhi's room is a shop selling a wide range of overpriced cotton clothing, and some non-perishable foodstuffs and bottled lotions. The commercialization is modest. There is apple jam and mango pickle, as well as 'Eco-Friendly Honey of Wild Bees' from Sewagram, the commune in central India where Gandhi lived (and consumed honey[4]) for many years. However I can't quite believe Gandhi ever used Brahmi Ayurvedic Shampoo[5] —

[4] In *Key to Health* (1942) he recommends hot water, honey and lemon as a 'healthy nourishing drink, which can well substitute for tea or coffee.' He was also a proponent of the 'scientific collection' of honey in a way that did not kill any bees.

[5] The English word 'shampoo' comes from the Hindi verb *champna*, to press, as in a massage. Charles Dickens in *Dombey & Son*, uses the word in its original sense to describe Miss Pankey 'a little blue-eyed morsel of a child, who was shampoo'd every morning, and seemed in danger of being rubbed away, altogether.'

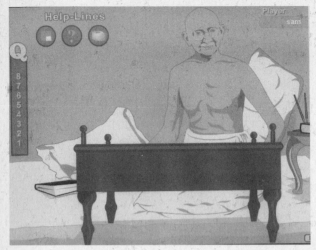

'to make the hair long, lustrous and disease free.' If he did, it was disastrously ineffective. But the Gandhi shop in Birla House comes nowhere close to matching the goodies and 'edutainment' available on the Internet. Mahatma.org has T-shirts in beige or red carrying Gandhi's signature in eleven different Indian languages, for US $15; or more inappropriately, for only US $12, a mouse-pad from the American pro-gun website libertyoutlet.com, with the words 'Mohandas Gandhi—Famous Gun Nut[6]'. But best and worst of all is an interactive quiz, at gandhiserve.org. It's an Internet version of *Who Wants to be a Millionaire*, presented by a cyber-Gandhi sitting next to a spinning-wheel. His square-jawed digital mouth opens and closes and we hear a disjointed American accent say '*Namaste*. Hello. I am Mahatma Gandhi. Let's play a game.' For each question there are four possible answers; and once you've decided, the robot-Gandhi mutters inanities like 'Let's lock it and see,' and 'Let's check it out.' All the questions are about Gandhi, and they're very difficult. It took me many attempts before I was allowed to print an e-certificate proclaiming that I had successfully passed the Mahatma Gandhi quiz designed by ZMQ[7] Software Systems, Delhi.

Today in Delhi there are more than twenty-five streets, localities and institutions named after Gandhi. He has the indignity of having one of the city's longest, most congested and most cursed roads,

[6] Libertyoutlet.com justify their use of Gandhi by quoting him as saying, 'Among the many misdeeds of the British rule in India, history will look upon the act of depriving a whole nation of arms, as the blackest.'

[7] ZMQ are based in the Pitampura area of north-west Delhi, where they specialize in what they call 'edutainment'. Their on-line games include Happy Meal in which players have to catch a McDonalds burger, a soft drink and a gift by moving their mouse around the screen. The object of the game is to get the highest McScore possible. ZMQ are also responsible for Coca-Cola Checkers, an Internet game played with Coca-Cola bottletops. Gandhi would not have approved.

MG Marg[8] , named after him. Gandhi himself does not seem to have liked the city much, but then he wasn't keen on cities in general. He first visited Delhi, at the age of forty-five, four years after it had been made the capital of British India. He had to make regular trips there, for political reasons, but always seemed in a hurry to get the first train out. Modern Delhi seems to reciprocate that feeling. Gandhi is admired in name only; Gandhian has almost become a term of derision, a description given to people who are seen as impractical and backward-looking dreamers. But the monuments and tributes abound. Less than six hundred metres from Birla House, at the entrance to the Lodi Gardens, I encounter a large, unappealing, water-stained block of beige stone erected (or just dumped there) for Gandhi's birth centenary in 1969. Carved on one face are three monkeys[9] in bas-relief, and Sanskrit words from ancient Hindu scripture chiselled into another, overwritten with graffiti. 'Mohit', we learn, 'loves Jyoti'.

The Lodi Gardens were briefly the Lady Willingdon Park, after the viceregal wife who had the area landscaped around some impressively intact tombs and mosques from pre-Mughal Delhi. It is now home to some of Delhi best-kept lawns and flowerbeds, as well as a suitably diminutive compound containing the National Bonsai Park. It is a place where diplomats, politicians and senior civil servants network and exercise (I saw two elderly men performing what used to be known as physical jerks, their faces contorted in agony) and where courting couples are to be found gymnastically entwined in the shrubbery. There's a jogging path, intended not only for humans. A noticeboard requests, 'Dog lovers: Lead your pets preferably on jogging track'. And then, below, an afterthought perhaps: 'Kindly ensure droppings are removed from track.' I moved stealthily along the track, encountering no faecal matter, and doubled back towards Khan Market, where exotic European foodstuffs like a packet of bacon or a punnet of raspberries can be purchased for significantly more than the daily wage of a labourer.

[8] MG Marg is better known as the Inner Ring Road. Ho Chi Minh, Gamal Abdul Nasser and Olaf Palme are among those who have the honour of having parts of the Outer Ring Road named after them.
[9] Gandhi was very fond of the Japanese legend of the three monkeys who could see no evil, hear no evil, and speak no evil. He kept a statuette of the 'no evil' monkeys by his bedside, as a symbol of peace.

Khan Market, quite justifiably, has a reputation as Delhi's most up-market market. Yet everything is on a small scale, with lots of little shops grouped together in a U-shape. It is far from stuffy, and provides a distinct break from the empty anodyne quality of bungalow land. Suddenly there are lots of purposeful and purposeless people milling around, creating loosely interconnected networks of activity. In this respect, it is like the rest of India and quite unlike Lutyens' Delhi. Khan Market is an idlers' dream: two delicatessens, three camera shops, four bookshops, five cafés, toy shops, magazine stalls, juice sellers, boutiques, a temple, even an animal dietician ('Royal Canin— nutritional programme for dogs and cats'. The shop even has its own vision statement: 'Knowledge of the pet. Commitment to the owner. Respect for both.'). And Khan Market's hinterland spreads to its north and east, with busy roads, a mosque, a hotel, a street of restaurants, a taxi stand—before succumbing once again to the funereal atmosphere of bungalow land. Even the cemeteries here have more life—and there is a triad of them, adjoining each other; one each for Christians, Jews and Parsees. In the Christian cemetery, full of visitors, gravediggers, coffin-makers, masons, overseers and gardeners I chance upon the strangest of headstones. It says simply

A gardener tells me she was a foreign princess, but knows no more than that[10] . I peer over a wall into the much smaller Jewish cemetery.

[10] An Internet search for Stella + Mudge helped solve this mystery. She was, it turns out, the second wife of the eighth Maharaja of Kapurthala. Stella Mudge was the stage name of Alice Villiers, a Kent-born cabaret dancer, the daughter of a wire-walker-cum-publican, who married the Maharaja of Kapurthala in London in 1937.

A young man beckons me to climb over, and getting a toe-hold on a broken slab of marble I am able to stand on the wall. I'm so seized by what I see that I wobble and almost fall off. Amid a tennis-court sized cemetery, with headstones inscribed in Hebrew and English, many bearing a Star of David, I see a small hut, with two swastikas daubed in red paint on the wall. No attempt has been made to remove them, and they have clearly been there some time. And then it dawns on me. I realize this was not the result of act of anti-Semitic vandalism, of neo-Nazi racism. It must be the only Jewish cemetery in the world where the presence of a swastika would not be considered an act of desecration; where this ancient Hindu symbol is interpreted as sign of good luck rather than a symbol of genocide[11]. The two swastikas are in fact part of a small Hindu shrine attached to a hut at the back of the cemetery. I climb off the wall on to a marble bench inscribed 'in memory of our dear father, Menacheim Daniel Moses 1908– 1964'. The young man who had encouraged me to take the shortcut introduced himself as Anand, explaining to me that the hut with the swastikas is his home, where he lives with his parents and grandparents. His grandfather is the cemetery caretaker. I asked him if anyone had objected to the swastikas.

'No, why should they? It is a sign of good luck.'

'But in Europe it the symbol of the Nazis, of Hitler, who killed many Jews.'

'No, you are wrong. It is a Hindu sign. It has nothing to do with Jews.'

'And what about the families, have they said anything?' I ask pointing at the gravestones, with their inscriptions in English and Hebrew.

'Not many left,' he responds almost resentfully.

I ring several times at the doorbell of the synagogue, and a man wearing striped nightclothes eventually emerges, rubbing his eyes. I check my watch—it's 10.30 a.m. 'Sorry, it's a holiday for

[11] The Sanskrit word 'swastika' for both the anti-clockwise symbol 卐 or the clockwise symbol 卍, (occasionally also referred to as a sauvastika) first appears in the Hindu epics the Ramayana and the Mahabharata and means well-being, or good fortune. It only took on negative connotations after the rise to power of Adolf Hitler. Previously it had been used as the symbol of the Finnish air force, a Chinese sign for vegetarian food, as the repeating pattern for the floor mosaic of Amiens cathedral, and even as a decoration in medieval synagogues.

me today, I was sleeping in,' he tells me in English. Introducing himself as Ezekiel Malekar, honorary secretary of the synagogue, he takes me into the synagogue, pointing at the pile of skullcaps for me to choose from.

'Are you Jewish?'

'Not really[12]. Are there many Jews in Delhi?'

'There are only about ten Jewish families now, but there never were very many,' he told me, 'it's not like Bombay and Cochin where there are some very old Jewish communities. They probably go back thousands of years, but so many Bombay and Cochin Jews have gone to Israel. In Delhi, there are actually more Jews these days, because of all the embassies. There are about one hundred Jewish diplomats, not just Israeli, and some of them come here on the big Jewish holidays, at Passover, Yom Kippur.'

Above the trees of the streets leading eastwards, I could now make out the elegant cupolas perched on the towering stone walls of my

next destination, Purana Qila, or the Old Fort—yet another place of famous death. Of all Delhi's surviving forts (and there are at least ten[13] of them) the Purana Qila most resembles the crenellated, impregnable fortresses of my childhood imagination, like something out of *The Lord of the Rings*, casting great looming shadows over the land beneath. A moth-eaten modernity has brought some

---

[12] One of my grandparents, my maternal grandmother, was Jewish. By the matrilineal laws of Orthodox Judaism, I am Jewish; though my children—whose mother is a Zoroastrian—are not. Parsee Zoroastrianism is patrilineal. So my children are also not recognized by Orthodox Indian Zoroastrians as members of their mother's religious group.

[13] Oldest first: Lalkot; Qila Rai Pithora; Siri Fort; Tughlaqabad; Adilabad; Jahanpanah; Feroze Shah Kotla; Old Fort; Salimgarh; Red Fort. The first six are all in South Delhi, largely overgrown and ignored by the local population. For the poor they often serve as latrines and dumps. The Old Fort, Purana Qila, is actually the third youngest of the forts.

changes. The moat has been turned into a murky boating lake, the path next to the moat is a fitness trail, with rusted chin-up bars and vandalized exercise beams, and the grasslands to the south are now a worse-for-wear  zoo, where the keepers will poke a stick at the still-as-death cobras to prove to onlookers they are not stuffed. In the car park, a stall sold Pepsi and Coke, crisps and English-language educational cassettes. An English language maths revision tape was playing, and a bright-voiced woman was jauntily reciting the rarely practised seventeen times table. 'Join me, children. Sing along and say after me. 'Six seventeens are one hundred and two; seven seventeens are one hundred and nineteen . . .' I bought a cassette, for Rs 50, and marched up to the western gate of the Purana Qila, faltering as I tried to recite in silence, yet with my lips gently moving, the eighteen times table with as little hesitation as Ritu Sharma (MA, B.Ed), the narrator of my latest invaluable purchase. I looked up, as if for divine help, and was struck by another presumably Judaic mystery: two Stars of David[14] have been inlaid into the face of the stonework of this Muslim fort. I carried on inside the Old Fort, a huge open grassy space, the size of twenty football fields.

The Purana Qila has had many names, and many incarnations, and it may be the site of the oldest Delhi of them all. The fort's

[14] In fact, just as the swastika only recently became a symbol of anti-Semitism, the Star of David, or Seal of Solomon or hexagram has only over the last century become widely regarded as a sign of Judaism. In some Islamic legends, Solomon (or Suleiman) had a magic ring with a hexagram seal that gave him power over genies or djinns. The use of the hexagram at Purana Qila and other Islamic monuments appears to be ornamental. The Raelian cult had a combined swastika/Star of David symbol until 1991, when it was dropped following objections by some Jews. The Raelians were founded in the 1970s by a former motoring journalist, Claude Vorhilion, who says that he was visited by a four-foot-tall extra-terrestrial with almond-shaped eyes and a sense of humour. The Raelians claim 60,000 members in eighty countries. On his website, rael.org Vorhilion declares himself to be a prophet, an atheist, a committed nudist and a supporter of the former US Presidential candidate John Kerry. I have been unable to locate any Raelians in Delhi.

foundations were laid less than five hundred years ago in 1533, by Humayun, India's second Mughal Emperor, who was then chased out by a usurper. He managed to return to power in Delhi fifteen years later, and was punished for his persistence by tumbling to his death down the stone steps of his own library. The small octagonal library building still stands, but the steps have been bricked up, and I was unable to relive his final moments.

There is a legend that this place is much older, that the fort was built on the site of Indraprastha, 'a city as beautiful as a new heaven' according to the Hindu epic, the Mahabharata, one of the five great cities built by the five Pandava brothers. And there is some evidence to connect Indraprastha with the fort. Until the early twentieth century Purana Qila contained a village with a remarkably similar name, Inderpat, and archaeologists have found pottery (some, incidentally, marked with spirals and swastikas) that may date from three thousand years ago, making a connection with the Mahabharata possible. But as with so much remote history, it has become more a matter of faith. Inside the fort, carefully hidden behind a grove of ashoka trees, unnoticed by me on previous visits, is a testament to that faith, a Hindu temple, adorned with swastikas and dedicated to Kunti, mother of three of the Pandavas. A stone plaque outside records that the temple was rebuilt in 1915, but we are commanded to believe that it marks the site of Indraprastha. The priest, his wife and son are today the only permanent residents of the fort. At night, security guards let them in and out; the son is a student, the wife a teacher, all trying to conduct normal lives from this most abnormal of abodes. It is a quiet place at night, the priest admitted. There had been an evening 'sound and light' show a few years ago, but most tourists preferred a rival event at the more famous Red Fort two miles to the north. In his father's time, he told me, for a few months, at the time of partition, the Purana Qila had been the busiest, most densely populated place in all of Delhi.

Mahatma Gandhi visited Purana Qila in September 1947 when it was a temporary home for tens of thousands of desperate Muslims. The violence of partition had spread to Old Delhi, and many Muslim families fled to the safety and discomfort of the Old Fort, as other camps were set up for Hindu refugees from Pakistan. In the Purana Qila there was little food and filthy stagnant water, and cholera began to spread. Gandhi, who was used to visiting some pretty wretched places, was appalled. He told the prayer meeting later that day at Birla House, 'I have not seen the like of the squalor I found in that camp.' Aid did then get through to the camp, with the notables of Delhi, including Indira Gandhi, joining in the relief work. Most of the Muslim refugees went to Pakistan, and were replaced by Hindus and Sikhs who escaped from violence of the Partition in Pakistani Punjab. Eventually they were housed in resettlement colonies in Delhi and Purana Qila was empty again, with the priest and his family as the sole residents. It is today a place of solitude, where one can sit for hours undisturbed. The northern end of the fort has been closed for major building work. A small group of workers are playing cards. They tell me the rebuilding will take six years. I look aghast, but they are delighted—guaranteed work for that long is hard to come by. They are happy with their Rs 110 a day. One of them offers to show me around, guiding me through the area of the fort that is officially closed to the public. I am shown a back route that enables me to climb high up the north bastion for an uninterrupted 360-degree view of Delhi. I look west, retracing my spiral back towards bungalow land. I saw it suddenly in a new light, as a thick green carpet, an oasis in this perpetual city, the bungalows themselves invisible beneath the trees. Beyond was Rashtrapati Bhavan and the Ridge, and to the north-west I could see the revolving restaurant and the familiar high-rise offices of Connaught Place, shrunken by distance, more pleasing in outline than in close-up.

But down below me, perhaps a five-second hang-glider ride away, are some of the strangest buildings of them all, a series of giant space-age egg-boxes, built in 1972, the year of the last Apollo missions to the Moon. The space age now seems to belong to the past, and the buildings, which are known collectively as the Pragati Maidan exhibition centre, are beginning to look a little whiskery. But with the sun in your eyes and from a distance, it's still impressive.

It took me thirty minutes to descend from the northern bastion, return through Purana Qila, out of the Star of David gates, along the fitness trail, past the swan-shaped boats, and cross a busy arterial road—before I could see Pragati Maidan close up. I had been there once before in the early 1990s, with a camera crew, to take pictures of men locked up in large cages who were making piles out of small pieces of paper. They were government officials counting votes. It was presumed that they would be safe from intimidation if they were behind bars. Today there is electronic voting in Delhi, so Pragati Maidan can host exhibitions without political interruption.

I wandered past some gossiping security guards and found myself in a hall the size of an aircraft hangar, the home for 'Printpack India'. I pick up a brochure:

'PRINTPACK INDIA is for Graphic Arts Industry, what Olympic Games are to athletes. Every four years, crème de la crème of the Indian Graphic Arts Industry is showcased at Pragati Maidan.'

The rest of the text was also in English, but contained a collection of entirely incomprehensible nouns: CtPositives, platen punchers, substrates and AlcoZaps. I looked around; there were hundreds of cubicles, like a school fair, and a lot of men in sharp suits talking on mobile phones, Indians and foreigners.

'I'm dead meat if I'm not in Korea by tomorrow evening—latest. Route me via Timbuktu if you have to.'

'The fucking machine is fucked. And unless you get here in fifteen minutes, you're fucked.'

'Please, please, please, please. Please help me out . . . . Oh, piss off, then . . . Wanker.'

I wander around, unnoticed, just another foreigner, though less smartly dressed than the rest of them. A strong stench of printer fluid and glue pervades the hall; the kind of place where solvent abuse is compulsory. I meandered between the stalls. There were delightfully hypnotic machines where a man fed a piece of cardboard in at one end, and it was crimped and folded and stamped and shaped, and a perfect little box came out at the other end. I moved on to a huge printer, at least ten feet long, like a high-tech mangle, which was printing a brightly coloured plastic map of the world. The company was called Gandinnovations. My eyes lit up; perhaps this had something to do with Gandhi, socially responsible printing perhaps? I asked a depressed-looking young woman sitting next to the printer how her company got its name.

'No idea[15],' she said gloomily, handing me a brochure, without even looking at me. I was beginning to feel a little woozy, and sat down next to her. She gave me a brief, toothy, professional smile and immediately sank back into a semi-coma. I turned to her and said, my mouth a few inches from her ear, 'I think these printer fumes are getting to me.'

She twisted round to look at my face, and gave me a long, hard, interested stare, as if I might be human after all. She then gave me an unprofessional, genuine smile and offered me some Sprite.

'How you can stand it here?' I asked, after swilling the caustic-sweet liquid around the back of my throat.

'It's a job. I need a job. But it does give me a headache, being in here all day.'

'But what do you actually do here?'

'I hand out leaflets, and some business cards. They want someone who looks smart and speaks English.'

'And someone who can stand this frightful smell.'

She gave me another hard look, 'You don't look well,' she said, 'you've gone . . . er . . . green. Here, you'd better have some more Sprite.' A wave of nausea swept through my body.

'Sorry, I've got to go.' I left as quickly as I could, my brief encounter abruptly ended, convinced I was going to vomit on Gandinnovations printer or all over my new acquaintance. Either way it would probably would have cost her her job.

I returned a few days later, fully recovered, to resume my journey, and entered the same hall and was foolishly surprised to see a completely different exhibition underway. PRINTPACK INDIA had been replaced by 'SUPERCOMM—India's largest focussed Telecom event.' It was a lot classier, and the hall had been fumigated. There were lots of famous companies: Sony, Microsoft, Ericsson. I immediately fell into the arms of an old friend, KN, once a gossip columnist, now running a PR company and wearing an extremely broad double-breasted jacket and a bright yellow tie. He was very excited.

[15] I later discover that Gandinnovations has nothing to do with Mahatma Gandhi. It is a Canadian printing company named after its founder, James Gandy.

'You know that Dr Irwin Jacobs has just got here.' I looked at KN blankly.

'He's the ninth richest man in the world. I think that's right, and he's the keynote speaker. He came in his own jet. He owns Qualcomm. Come on—you must have heard of Qualcomm.' He waved imperiously at the big Qualcomm logos all over the exhibition hall. 'They're the ones behind see-dee-em-ay,' he said, as if I would now suddenly become as excited as him. Instead, I began to feel a bit stupid. So I nodded, feigning comprehension.

'Oh, yes. See-dee-em-ay[16],' I said, as if these four syllables had suddenly enabled me to join in his excitement at the mysterious presence of Dr Irwin Jacobs.

'Let's go outside, I need a smoke,' he said, and continued talking. 'The point is, Sam, these big international businesses aren't interested in the likes of me any more, the English-speaking types. They want numbers. They want volumes. They want to reach the masses, because that's where the really big money is. They've realized that India is going to be the biggest market in the world— and it's ordinary people, poor people in cities like Delhi, who are going to buy his mobile phone technology.'

I was slowly beginning to understand what KN was talking about. He lit his cigarette.

'So one of the world's richest men is coming to India to sell phones to some of the world's poorest people?'

'Yes, that's right. That's how much the world has changed and it shows just how much India matters in the world now. And it's not his first trip here; you just saw in there how all the big names in international telecoms have got stalls here. India is already a pretty important player, and it's going to be even bigger, perhaps the biggest, in twenty or thirty years. It's amazing, really, if you think about it.' KN swooned at his own words, as if they had come to him as a revelation from outer space. Silent and then distracted, he stood up. 'Keep in touch,' he

---

[16] CDMA. Code Division Multiple Access is a wireless technology, developed originally for military purposes, which, I am assured, chops your live conversation up into little bits, encodes it, sends it along lots of different wireless routes, collects them together, and decodes it so you can hear it without any delay. Other technologies do similarly magical and arguably pointless things, but according to the website www.fool.com (to which I am indebted) CDMA is cheaper and uses less battery power.

said, crushing his cigarette stub beneath his heel. He sped back inside Pragati Maidan, as if he was worried he would miss the next revelation.

I headed north, searching for refreshment and after a few hundred metres reached a dhaba, and sat down to some scalding tea. I asked the dhaba owner what he thought of Pragati Maidan. 'It's not for me, or ordinary people, just for VIPs,' he said, spitting out the English acronym. 'They don't care about people like us.' I told him, rather insensitively in retrospect, that the ninth richest man in the world was in Pragati Maidan right now and that he had come in his own jet. He began spitting his words out again.

'Do you see those people?' He pointed at some docile workmen sleepily digging at the nearby road with pickaxes. 'They are going to destroy my home.' Fortunately, I did not know the Hindi word for paranoid and kept quiet, blowing on my tea, and sipping it gingerly. 'They're from the Metro,' he continued, 'and they're going to build the new railway on top of my dhaba. My family has been here for one hundred years, when this road . . .' he pointed at a four-lane highway, which a group of suicidal pedestrians was trying to cross 'was a track.'

'Won't they give you any compensation?'

'Nothing, not a paisa. They say I don't own this land. I'm "unauthorized."' Again he used the English word. (I noticed that the suicidal pedestrians had somehow survived.)

'What will you do?'

'I don't know. What can I do? Go somewhere else. If you don't have much,' he waved in the direction of the small hut where he lived, 'It's easy to move.'

'But you must have some kind of plan.'

'No, nothing. Come here in a month and I'll be gone.' As I paid my Rs 3, a phone rang. I thought it was my mobile, as I am usually unable to recognize my own ring-tone. It was the dhaba owner's. He jumped to attention, and answered the phone. Wrong number. But more money in the pocket of Dr Jacobs.

Ahead is Bahadur Shah Zafar Marg, named after the last Mughal Emperor[17], but too close to the previous leg of my spiral for comfort,

[17] He was deposed by the British and sent into exile in Burma after the 1857 Uprising, known by the victors as the Indian Mutiny.

so I head east to Indraprastha Marg, better known as ITO, the acronym for Delhi's sprawling Income Tax Office. Down a side street are men in little booths crouched over manual typewriters, composing affidavits and notarizations on pre-purchased stamp paper. On the opposite corner is one of Delhi's crummiest modern buildings, the School of Planning and Architecture, with moulting plaster and exposed electricity cables. Students have nicknamed it the WC, not only because of its derelict condition, but because of its shape—an oval auditorium like a toilet bowl, and the neighbouring main building rectilinear and upright like a cistern. I wander in to the courtyard to the left of the toilet bowl, where students are eating and smoking and giggling. A group of second-year girl students laugh exhaustingly as I try to talk to them. 'Yes, the building is terrible, but it's the coolest college in Delhi [two-second giggle] . . . and everything's fab [five-second giggle] . . . and the boys are . . .um . . . [two-second giggle] hot [ten-second giggle followed by five seconds of smirks and another ten-second giggle] . . . but the food is . . . um . . . shit [three-second giggle].' They collapse into a huddle and start whispering to each other. They point to an older man, with a goatee beard whom they clearly do not think is hot. 'He's our professor . . . You should really talk to him.' And so I went over, and introduced myself to Professor SR as someone interested in the future of Delhi. Professor SR looked at me suspiciously, but gradually opened up. He painted a gloomy picture of the future of Delhi, in which there were no natural limits to the city's growth. I told him the tale of the 'unauthorized' dhaba-owner, whom I had just met. He was unmoved. Every few years, he told me, the city authorizes some settlements, mainly to please a politician, and it just encourages more migration.

'But,' I argued, 'what about those who have been here decades.'

'That's not the point,' he said, 'we can't reward illegal squatters.

Some of them just become professional squatters, and then get compensation by moving to another place which the authorities are about to acquire.'

'But surely that can't be true of very many of them.'

'Maybe not, but there's a way in which everyone in Delhi thinks they can get away with not obeying the law. I believe in a law-and-order solution to most of these problems and that includes traffic offenders and illegal settlers and politicians and their relatives.'

The SPA is a corner building, and I left it from an exit on the Inner Ring Road, officially Mahatma Gandhi Marg. This is land that was reclaimed from the Yamuna, now invisible, hidden behind the Indira Gandhi Indoor Sports Stadium, and a series of embankments that hold back the monsoon floods. As I walked past a series of institutional buildings, with four-wheel-drive cars parked outside and little gaggles of chauffeurs gossiping or playing cards, I reflected on what Professor SR had said, continuing the conversation in my mind. He was certainly right to demand that the rich and the powerful should obey the law. But is it realistic, let alone fair, to enforce the law against those millions of poor people who have no title to the land on which they live? Shouldn't they be given the right to own the land they occupy? I tried to imagine Professor SR's response to this, tripping gently on a loose paving stone and then falling on to my knees as if preparing to pray. No damage to my bad knee, and I sat down, relieved, on a tree stump. I closed my eyes, tried to block out the sound of the traffic, and could hear the professor's carefully modulated reply, 'Not only would it mean rewarding criminals who have indulged in land theft, but it would encourage many more people to come to Delhi, if they thought they could get land for free.' It was a spiral of a different kind. 'There are no natural limits to the growth of this city,' I remembered him saying, and so, it followed logically, if you improve the city, make it a better place to live, still more people will come; and if more come it will be a worse place.

As I considered these multiple paradoxes, I gazed down from my tree stump throne, scratching at my itchy right leg through my muddied trousers, to see a great convoy of ants, busily carrying small bits of vegetation, building a great city under the soil, perhaps with more ants than the human population of Delhi. My eyes followed one thinner column of ants which was heading past my right shoe and then disappearing from view; migrants, I decided, heading off for another city. And then I realized why my leg was itchy. I jumped up. An entire cohort of ants was ascending my right leg. They were migrating to me. I pulled up my trouser leg, brushing the ants off. I loosened my belt, and scooped inside with my hand and upper arm, crushing the vanguard against my lower thigh. I danced about, spinning around like a dervish, and trampling their ant-hill, destroying their great city, beneath my feet. I saw a young man in torn clothes watching me as if I were mad. *Chinta*, I said, distracted from my discomfort by my delight at being able to use the Hindi word for ant, which I had learnt one day earlier. *'Chinta-chinta,'* I repeated playfully, pointing at the ground, my shoes and then my ant-afflicted leg. He shook his head sorrowfully from side to side, before loping off. A few seconds later I realized that I had used the wrong word. *Chinta* means worry or anxiety; the word for ant is *cheenti*. I looked ahead and the man who I had so embarrassingly misled as to the nature of my affliction was still there in the distance, way ahead of me. So I went tearing after him, thinking I could catch him up and explain what I had really meant. I soon thought better of this plan, slowing down to catch my breath, to protect my knee, and to save myself from further embarrassment.

To my left I gazed over the crumbling walls of a fourteenth-century citadel that once overlooked the Yamuna, and was the first of several forts to be built alongside the river. It was more like a collage of the ages of Delhi. I was now standing on an ancient river-bed, transformed into a ring road. From the remains of the citadel's elegant multi-storeyed palace sprouts a forty-two-foot sandstone pillar, a priapic monolith in the midday sun, inscribed with the edicts of Emperor Ashoka who died more than two hundred years before Christ. Behind the pillar, loom two sluggish dinosaur-cranes, gently stalking the sky, the star players in the rebuilding of a cricket stadium. Nowadays if you mention the citadel's name, Feroz Shah Kotla, most Indians will understand you to be referring to a cricket match[18]. Anywhere else in the world Feroz Shah Kotla would be a major tourist attraction,

[18] The Feroze Shah Kotla stadium is best remembered for a match against Pakistan in February 1999 in which the unassuming Indian spin bowler Anil Kumble was transformed into a national hero by becoming only the second player in international cricket history to take all ten wickets in an innings.

but Delhi has so many forts that this one, stranded midway between the two larger Mughal forts, is all but forgotten[19].

Just beyond the citadel is a second and larger Gandhi memorial museum. Here, in contrast to the striking lack of Gandhi's possessions at Birla House, is a vast reliquary, a collection of objects that Gandhi once used, once touched: a microscope through which he examined leprosy germs, a plastic bowl (which appears to have come from a 1960s Tupperware set), an ivory toothpick and ear-cleaner, a fountain pen, a pin cushion, a spittoon. There are some human remains—two teeth extracted by Dr Barreto in Nagpur in 1936. And in a separate sanctuary, the blood-stained clothing Gandhi was wearing at the time of his death is displayed, alongside two of the bullets that killed him. Most bizarrely, there is, as there also is at the Birla House museum, the watch that Gandhi was wearing at the time of death, the one that fell to the ground and stopped at seventeen minutes past five. I tried to joke with the curator about it. Perhaps, I suggested, Gandhi was wearing two watches that both fell and both stopped at 5.17, or maybe the watch spends half the week here and half the week at Birla House[20]. He was not amused, and sent me off towards the postage stamps gallery, where I discovered that seventy-two different countries have issued stamps bearing pictures of Gandhi. And then another gallery, for what might loosely be termed artwork. There are dozens of images of Gandhi in a wider range of media than I could have imagined: wire on wood, embroidered silk, watercolour on peepul leaf, mosaic of groundnut shell, and two rather lifelike paintings of Gandhi in human blood.

[19] Feroze Shah Kotla was built in 1354 by Sultan Feroze Shah of the Tughlaq dynasty. He had the pillar removed from its ancient location, Topra, north of Delhi, wrapped in silk cotton, and transported by boat to his new palace. The meaning of the inscription was lost until the nineteenth century—and Feroze Shah's courtiers told him it contained a prophecy saying that no one but a great king called Feroze would be able to move the pillar. The seventeenth-century British traveller and long-distance walker, Thomas Coryate, was told that the pillar was erected by a fellow European, Alexander the Great, after his victory over the Indian king Porus.

[20] The two watches are not identical; the one at Birla House has two smaller inner dials, and Arabic numbers. The one in the bigger museum has one inner dial and Roman numbers, and on my return the time had been changed to twelve minutes past five. I have also been unable to locate the well-travelled gun that killed Gandhi, a 9mm Beretta, manufactured in Italy. It was taken to Abyssinia by an Italian soldier in the late 1930s, and later brought to India by a soldier serving in the British army.

A Fourth Intermission

ONCE OR TWICE a year, a major Western pop star comes to Delhi. Usually they're just a little past their prime. My first Delhi pop concert was Sting in 2004, who cut his first hit single, *Roxanne*, back in 1978, when he was already twenty-seven years old (and when I was a record-buying sixteen-year-old who thought *Roxanne*, a love-song to a prostitute, both profound and haunting). For many members of the English-speaking elite of South Delhi these are major events in the social calendar, at which it is important to be present, regardless of any interest in the music or the performer. Normally these concerts are held in Jawaharlal Nehru Stadium, a short car journey away from all of South Delhi. However at the time of Sting's visit to India, the stadium was in use as storage space for Republic Day floats and paraphernalia. Sting was therefore performing in the Delhi's back-up outdoor venue in Pitampura, a part of the capital which most South Delhi dwellers had never heard of.

And so on a rainy Sunday afternoon, Mahatma Gandhi Marg, better known as the Inner Ring Road, witnessed a convoy of plush SUVs, four-wheel drives, Mercs, and a few smart saloons bearing the CD number plates that identify the diplomatic community of Delhi. Suddenly the Delhi elite found themselves in unfamiliar west Delhi districts, where poorer Punjabi migrants had settled after partition. In fact, in West Delhi, the Inner Ring Road is an almost unbroken series of American-style, modern flyovers, except for one terrible bottleneck. Here, at Naraina, shops and houses and temples had been built too close to the road, and in the previous two weeks the municipal bulldozers had been hard at work. They had removed precisely five metres of buildings on either side of the road, regardless of the overall size or purpose of the building. So there was a series of half-buildings, with their façades torn off, and yet with the interiors of the rooms, sometimes with furniture still there, open to the elements. In one former living-room, I saw a man collecting some belongings and placing them in a sack, stepping perilously close to the cliff-edge that marked the limit of the bulldozer's destruction, and behaving as if the wall were still there and he was invisible to the outside world, and the passing convoy. The inhabitants have been told that their houses were illegal encroachments and were being removed as part of a project to consign the Naraina bottleneck to history.

On and on the convoy went, reaching Pitampura as the rain cleared and dusk set in. And inside they went, full of surprised admiration for this huge concert venue in the most unexpectedly modern of settings. Just to the north, loomed Delhi's tallest structure, a elegant tapering TV tower, narrowing to a red-flashing light; and to the south, noiselessly curving its way round the venue, the Metro, here elevated high above ground, which clearly most people in the audience had never seen. I wandered through the crowd, eavesdropping.

'Look, it's amazing. Have you seen those trains—they're really modern.'

'Wow, it's better than London.'

'It's like Bangkok.'

Someone had been to Pitampura last year for another concert.

Tall man: 'I came here to see Shaggy.'

Short man: 'What Shaggy from Scooby-Doo?'

Tall man: 'No, you bloody fool. Shaggy the singer. The one who has sex with that girl on the bathroom floor. Mr Boombastic.'

Short man: 'Oh. I don't know him.'

Sting appeared, on time. He made the traditional Indian greeting of placing his palms together in front of him. '*Namaste*, Delhi' he announced, his first and last words of Hindi, and the crowd just adored him. They danced and hopped and swayed and clapped. He boomed out, 'I dedicate this one to India because it's about sex and religion. It's called *Sacred Love*.' Some in the audience looked slightly embarrassed.

In his newspaper interviews, Sting talked, in the best tradition of Western pop stars in India, of yoga and of karma, of Hindu spirituality. Almost four decades earlier the Beatles had come to India, briefly passing through Delhi, on a spiritual pilgrimage, enhanced or diminished by the effect of narcotics. They had become friends of the Indian sitar player Ravi Shankar (whose daughter Anoushka played the sitar on a recent Sting album). I was reminded of the woman in my old office in London, who, when she discovered I was moving to India, said, 'Is it a very spiritual country?' Her question reminded me of the scene in *The Householder* where the young Indian teacher,

Prem, first meets his American friend Ernest at Jantar Mantar. Ernest is leaping around a huge stone edifice designed to measure the azimuth of the sun, when he sees Prem and stops. They have an English-language conversation in which they both entirely fail to understand what each other is saying, but they still end up as friends:

Ernest: Hi, do you know what I'm doing? I'm becoming. I'm merging. See, this is the sky and this is the earth. And this is I. I'm in all things, and all things are in me. Feel me. Just feel. Here. *(He takes Prem's hand and puts in on his chest. Prem looks bemused.)* Get it? That's cosmic energy. Terrific. I mean, where are such ideas born? Only in India . . . India is always pointing a finger into eternity. Sort of. What a country. What wisdom. What patience.

Prem: It is true. We have taken great strides in our national development.

Ernest: Development of the soul that's the important thing. And you've known it all along.

Prem: We have our five-year plans which greatly enhance our material progress.

Ernest: "Material." You've said the word. Materialism, that's what's wrong with the world today. That's what we've got in the West.

Prem: We have our steel projects which will rapidly enhance the growth of our country . . . *(The film cuts from Jantar Mantar, to a leafy New Delhi avenue, but the same conversation is continuing)* In our country the agriculture is blossoming forth.

Ernest: Yeah, but I don't know. Everything seems to be growing here. And I know I'll find what I'm looking for because, well, you grow souls here. The way we grow skyscrapers or . . . or sweet potatoes, you grow souls.

Prem: Our steel output will be the basis of . . . of great industrial expansion

Ernest: You've got the soul and we've got the flesh . . . By the way I'm Ernest Castaldo.

© *Merchant-Ivory Productions*

(Ernest places his palms together to make a traditional Indian 'Namaste' greeting; while Prem proffers his open palm for a Western-style handshake.)

The screenplay for *The Householder* was written more than forty years ago, but its description of western attitudes to India, and Indian attitudes to the West feels contemporary. Modern Delhi still has many western visitors who, like Ernest, come to India believing they will find themselves and their souls, and meet the 'happy poor', untroubled by their poverty. And Delhi is, more than ever, full of people who see the West as a model for 'progress', who covet luxury cars and European holidays, or crave an American college education for their kids, or just simply want a reliable water and electricity supply.

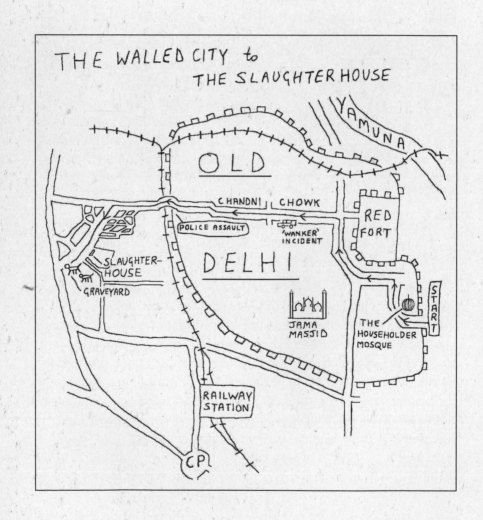

Chapter Five: In which the Author discovers a celluloid wardrobe, is described as a wanker and meets some bestial shoe-cleaners

I WAS STANDING on the roof of a three-storey tenement block in Old Delhi, with my new laptop open, propped up precariously on a heap of broken bricks and tiles. A teenage boy was next to me—my self-appointed guide. We were watching a black-and-white movie on the laptop. Both of us were doing the same thing, looking up at the view from the rooftop and down at the screen of the laptop, up and down, again and again. We'd already had one minor skirmish, when he tried to touch the keyboard, but he'd let me resume control. With my finger on the laptop's touchpad, I was able to fast forward, rewind, and then, frame by frame, search for the right shot . . . and then, finally, I had it. My guide gurgled and pointed excitedly. Triumphantly, I pressed the pause button on an image of a striking eighteenth-century building, with a man and a woman arguing in the foreground. My guide and I smiled at each other as if we had discovered hidden treasure.

Some days earlier, I had crossed from Rajghat, Delhi's memorial to its most recent rulers[1] , in a driving February hailstorm; I could make out for the first time on my spiral the city walls of Old Delhi. And peeping out above the walls, between the swaying trees, was an old red stone mosque. I instantly recognized its three distinctive striped domes. I had seen them, many years ago, before I ever set foot in India, as a celluloid image, which I had then stored away somewhere in my memory. A small mystery had been solved. I had finally tracked down those three onion domes with their thick black and white stripes, each stripe apparently bigger than its nearest neighbour of the same colour, like some ancient optical illusion.

[1] Rajghat is a long stretch of parkland, reclaimed from the floodplain of the Yamuna. It contains the open-air memorials to Mahatma Gandhi, Jawaharlal Nehru, Indira Gandhi and her two sons, and several other important political figures from the post-independence period.

These mesmerising domes had first entered my consciousness when I watched *The Householder* (the same film which had such starkly memorable images of the Jantar Mantar). The quarrelling newly wedded couple live next door to the mosque—and, in one poignant, post-argument scene, the young wife goes to the roof of their building. She is incandescent, shaking with irritation, biting her tongue. Her husband has just accused her of being disrespectful to him. She starts snatching her clothes from the washing line, and on doing so begins to uncover a tantalizing partial view of one of the striped domes of the mosque. Her husband is following her, keen to continue the argument, and gets an accidental slap from the airborne arm of a newly washed blouse as she pulls it angrily from the clothes line. He is now upset that her petticoat is showing, and he bends down to tug, dangerously, at the hem of her sari. For a moment, it as if he will disrobe her in public. But she marches on, head high and sari intact. And in the midst of this domestic dispute, unnoticed by the protagonists, but unmissable for the viewers, the gorgeous domes of the mosque are gradually revealed in all their zebra-striped glory.

As the rains stopped, I went inside the Zeenat mosque, which was, I learned from a signboard, named after the Mughal emperor's daughter who commissioned it[2]. I left my shoes, as is the custom, close to the line of taps where worshippers wash themselves before praying. I wanted to identify where that scene in *The Householder* had taken place and would need to get onto the roof of the mosque in order to be able to identify the right building. Apart from its rain-glistening striped domes, the mosque is simple and austere, adorned only by the green parakeets which shelter and frolic in the eaves, decorating the ground below with their beige droppings. Inside, the mosque was deserted, except for a man asleep on a straw mat, who had wound himself up in a sheet as if it were a shroud and he were a corpse. I began inspecting the mosque, looking for a route on to the roof. And then suddenly the rains returned: heavier and less vertical than before, with great swooping gusts of wind. A blustery squall began to attack the shroud, causing it to flap and

[2] Built by Emperor Aurangzeb's daughter and also known as the Ghata Masjid. It was converted into a bakery by the the British after the 1857 Uprising.

© *Merchant-Ivory Productions*

© *Merchant-Ivory Productions*

billow and loosen in the wind. The man inside was gradually uncovered; a skullcap and a red-dyed beard were revealed. He turned, opening his eyes and staring in my direction as if I were part of his dream, a devil perhaps, from the startled and distrustful look he gave me.

'How can I get on to the roof of the mosque?' I asked, after some brusque conversational foreplay.

'You can't.'

'Why not?'

'Because it is broken.'

'It looks fine to me.'

'You can only see that it is broken when you're on the roof.'

'So you've been on the roof.'

'No, nobody is allowed on the roof.'

'But how do you know the roof is broken, then?'

'Well, if it wasn't broken I'd be allowed on the roof.' It was clear from his decisive tone and the look of satisfaction on his face that the conversation was over, and that he had won. I left. My shoes, waiting for me forlornly on the steps of the mosque, were sodden with rain. I poured half a cup of water out of each clammy shoe, and squelched off home.

I went back to look for the house three days later, armed with an umbrella and a laptop I planned to use as a portable DVD player. I found my way past a cattle byre into a narrow paved street, made even narrower by a huge tree that stood sentry, blocking any vehicle wider than a bicycle. I went through a narrow doorway, which led to an open-air courtyard surrounded on four sides by doors and rooms, stacked three storeys high. I asked a teenage boy if he knew how I could reach the roof of the building opposite the mosque. The boy's neck was bent leftwards at an angle of about twenty degrees to the perpendicular; and he had what appeared to be a nervous tic, which twisted his whole head about its near-vertical axis, every five or six seconds. He responded to my question with a guttural noise, a growling that seemed to emanate from deep in his larynx. He was unable to speak. He pointed at his right ear, signing with his hands, and I realized that he was deaf as well. Still I persisted, pointing upwards, and lifting my legs in an exaggerated, bent-kneed way, miming the action of going upstairs. He smiled (pleased, I imagined, that I had not given up on him), and beckoned me through an archway. Up we went, out onto a rooftop, and immediately I could see we had come to the right place, the domes were visible and at the right angle to the building. I started up my laptop, and began scanning through the film for the argument scene. My guide was bemused at first, but very quickly understood what I was trying to do. My audible excitement at finding the place from where the scene had been shot brought other curious residents up onto the roof.

One of them, a college student, dented my pleasure by pointing out that another floor had been built since the film had been shot, and that most of the rooftop with the clothes line was now a room. I went into the room—now occupied by his television and a computer. And then I was taken on a guided tour of the whole complex of flats, mentally ticking off scenes from *The Householder*. Finally, an old man, unshaven and reeking of cigarette smoke, appeared. He told me his brother used to own the entire building and that he'd been staying there when *The Householder* was shot. He gushingly remembered the lead actress, Leela Naidu[3]. 'She was so beautiful, the most beautiful of them all. Miss India 1961, you know. And there she was, in this house, talking with me; I was just a trainee customs officer.' He sighed theatrically and took me to what passed for his room. He had clearly fallen on hard times; he slept on a sofa in a rooftop shed that used to be the kitchen in *The Householder*. His wife and daughter no longer lived with him. The room was unventilated, with a smell of decay, alcohol and cigarettes. It was full of old metal trunks, newspapers, and layer upon layer of dust. And there at the back was a distinctive mirror, with a double curve on its upper half, set into a wardrobe door. I caught sight of the two of us in the mirror, both contemplating

[3] Leela Naidu has had several avatars, and acted in too few films. She was, in chronological order, a swimming champion, Miss India, the wife of India's best-known hotelier, a film star, the travelling companion and wife of the poet/biographer/travel writer Dom Moraes, and is now a recluse in Bombay.

the past, both unshaven and wild of hair. And then suddenly I realized that I had seen this mirror before. In *The Householder*, the luminescent Leela Naidu would pull silly faces in a mirror identical to this, trying to make herself look grotesque and failing miserably. I pointed at the wardrobe and its mirror, silently, and turned to the old man. 'Yes,' he said. 'Well spotted. It's the same one. It's all that's left, really.'

The deaf-mute boy accompanied me out of the house of *The Householder*; refusing my offer of some rupees, but pleased to have an old pen of mine. And so I headed on, past a deserted building whose signboard promised computer training for girls, past tiny wayside mosques and shrines, a pastel-coloured building with high prison-like walls that proclaimed itself 'The Happy School and the Happy Teachers Training Centre', cycle rickshaws overburdened with children. I stopped outside a huge shop with red and yellow signboards. 'House of Bhandaris. The old and original shop for homeopathic medicine. German and Indian. Est. 1930. Healing Touch Clinic.' Cures are promised for almost every imaginable ailment, using 'approved German homoeopathic special preparations.' *Damiaplant*, I read, will cure 'insufficient libido, impotence, lack of vitality, and weakness'[4].

I was now deep inside Old Delhi, a city of many names: *purani dilli*, the walled city, Shahjahanabad, all of it now a minuscule part of this ever-expanding megalopolis. In my post-millennial, 191-page *Eicher* map of Delhi, it fills the equivalent of just a single page, a reminder of quite how much urban growth there has been in recent times. A century ago, the walled city enclosed almost all of Delhi.

[4] An Internet search for damiaplant led me to that most unusual of Google outcomes, zero results. However, Herodotus describes Damia as a goddess of fertility, and there is shrub called damiana that grows in parts of central America whose Latin name *Turnera aphrodisiaca* suggests that it might indeed enhance one's libido. Dried Damiana is available for $15.66 for 250 grams at globalherbalsupplies.com. I have not tried it.

Today, it is the kind of place that gets referred to in guidebooks as an ancient warren, a maze of streets, a labyrinth, a tangled web. In fact, Old Delhi is not some antediluvian casbah, but, by the standards of this city, carefully planned and relatively recent[5]. The city's founder, Emperor Shah Jahan, who had also commissioned the Taj Mahal in memory of his wife, was deeply interested in architecture and urban planning. He decided in the 1630s to move the capital of the Mughal Empire from Agra back to Delhi. At the time it was built, his new city was seen as the height of modernity[6]. The two main streets run east-west and north-south, intersecting in front of the Red Fort, a city-within-the-city, and the location for Shah Jahan's palace. Most of the elements of Shah Jahan's city are still visible.

I was able to trace much of my route through the old city, not on my modern map, in which the smaller lanes are little more than red smudges, but on a large-scale reproduction of a map of the walled city from 1842. It is still probably the most accurate guide to the layout of Shahjahanabad. The moat, tinted blue, may have been filled in, and a series of railway lines driven through the city, but most of the tiny curves and twists of the back streets are unchanged. Only the area between Red Fort and the Jama Masjid, India's most imposing mosque, is dramatically different, and these changes date back to just sixteen years after the publication of my map. The British, once they had exiled the last Mughal emperor in the aftermath of the 1857 Uprising, levelled most of the buildings around (and inside) the Red Fort. The Fort itself was used for the trial of the emperor, and then as barracks by the British army and, until very recently, the army of independent India.

The walled city's main east-west drag is Chandni Chowk, still Delhi's best-known shopping street. It begins opposite the Red Fort, with a Jain Temple and bird hospital, where pigeons and parakeets have torn wings splinted and bandaged, and sit in rows of small cages (at least four hundred in all), more patient than their human equivalents, awaiting recovery or death. Outside is the fabled congestion of the

---

[5] Less than half as old as the eleventh-century walls of Lalkot in south Delhi.
[6] Shahjahanabad was built on what modern city planners like to call a greenfield site. There were a few mosques and tombs from previous dynasties which were carefully integrated into the new city. As recently as 1902, a guide refers to what we now know as Old Delhi as 'the City of Modern Delhi.' It began to be known as Old Delhi in the 1920s as Lutyens' New Delhi began to emerge from the scrubland around Raisina Hill.

guidebooks: handcarts and porters' trolleys, bullock carts, pedestrians, and cycle rickshaws, all sashaying and pirouetting in search of space and the possibility of forward movement. Cars and taxis and trucks are outclassed here. They are stationary; one optimistic taxi driver keeps his engine on, trying to edge forward, gently kissing the handcart crossing in front of him. No one seems to mind. There is one out-of-place new white saloon car, air-conditioning on, its unoccupied back seat still wrapped in plastic. The driver is a young Indian woman power-dressed in Western clothes, the padded shoulders of her pink jacket turning her into a cartoon of impatience and desperation. She palms her own forehead, as if to say, 'I should have listened. What a fool I am for coming here.' I catch her eye, she smoulders, a look of resigned irritation; I smile at her, and she smiles back. And then a flirtatious gesture, uncommon among Delhi women; she sticks her tongue out at me, as if to say, 'You may be travelling faster than me, but at least I'm in comfort.' I laugh theatrically. She rolls down her window and I wonder if she is going to invite me in. She speaks, and her voice shatters my preconceptions. She is British.

'Hey you, do you know how to get out of here?'

'Where do you want to go?'

'I want to go home.'

'Where's that?'

'Luton . . . but I'm staying near the Imperial. I thought I'd drive my cousin's car around Delhi. But this is a total and utter nightmare.' She sounded her horn. I tried to think of something to say.

'I think you're stuck here for a bit. What are you doing in Delhi? Are you on holiday?'

'Kind of. A family wedding. Mum and Dad thought I should meet the relatives. I think they really want me to find a husband. I like the place, but the men . . .' She trailed off, and took her right hand from the steering wheel. She touched her thumb to her index finger, shaking her entire lower arm up and down to make the internationally recognized symbol for devotees of sexual self-gratification.

'Wankers . . .' she mouthed, almost inaudibly. 'So can you get me out of here? Come on, get in and take the wheel.' She moved her pink iPod off the passenger seat onto the dashboard and gathered her skirt in preparation to shuffling herself over through the gap between the steering wheel and gear-stick. I put up a cautionary hand.

'I don't drive. And, well, I really want to walk.' She gave me a sneer of disbelief.

'Oh fuck, wouldn't you just know it. I don't believe this. Another wanker.' She shook her head, curled her upper lip, and repeated my words back to me in the prissiest of voices 'I really want to walk.' I was silent, frozen to the spot, not quite believing my ears. She was silent for a few seconds, and then apologized to me in a most unapologetic manner. 'I'm sorry. Maybe I'd come and fucking join you, but where would I stick this stupid fucking useless car.' She slammed her hands against the steering wheel, sounding the horn. I stood there, silent, feeling a little unchivalrous, waiting to be dismissed.

'Oh well. Forget it. Get on with your walk, then. You're not my type anyway.' She glared at me, trying to think of another insult. 'And that stupid fucking hat you're wearing . . . idiot.' She sneered a final sneer, rolled up her window, snatched her iPod, wrestled the earpieces into her ear and stared ahead at the unmoving traffic, tapping in time to the music on the steering-wheel.

I retreated from Chandni Chowk, thinking how fortunate I was that chivalry had not got the better of me. I climbed up some stairs on to what appeared to be a marble viewing platform overlooking Chandni Chowk. A watchman told me this was part of the Sunehri Masjid, the Golden Mosque. By accident, I had found refuge in the place where, more than a quarter of a millennium ago, the invading Persian Emperor, Nadir Shah[7], sat up through the night watching as his troops carried out one of the bloodiest slaughters the world has ever seen. A contemporary historian recorded that 'for a long time the streets remained strewn with corpses, as the walks of garden with dead flowers and leaves'. Down below, examining the same streets, I took some pleasure in seeing it strewn with stationary vehicles including the car of my angry, cursing Lutonian that had

---

[7] According to one contemporary, a hundred and twenty thousand residents of Delhi were killed on the night of 11 March 1737. Nadir Shah was apparently furious that an attempt had been made on his life. As well as killing a large proportion of the people of Delhi, Nadir Shah took with him back to Persia the Kohinoor diamond and Peacock Throne of the Mughals. The jewel-encrusted Peacock Throne was broken up soon after the death of Nadir Shah in 1747. The Kohinoor changed hands several times, and is now part of the British Crown Jewels. A number of Indian MPs have demanded that it be returned to India, though there have also been claims the diamond really belongs to Iran, to Afghanistan and to Pakistan.

progressed no further than ten yards in the previous five minutes. Walkers will win out in the end. There are new plans to pedestrianize Chandni Chowk, with broad, raised walkways, and perhaps a monorail for those who want to make a quick exit.

At the western end of Chandni Chowk, the road bifurcates at another mosque. On the right is the road that leads out of the old walled city, but I turned left and down a slope towards the railway. These railway lines mark the site of the old western wall of Shahjahanabad, and its sidings and culverts are home to an itinerant population of street children, drug addicts and rickshaw-pullers. As I arrived, a small group of children had gathered to watch what seemed to be a street play. Two actors dressed in the khaki uniform of the Delhi police were rather theatrically beating up a dazed-looking young man in a blue denim shirt. The younger, fatter policeman had twisted the man's arm behind his back and forced him to bend over. The older, calmer policeman then used his lower thighs and knees to pincer the man's head. The younger policeman raised a bamboo stick high above his head and brought it down across the man's buttocks. I could hear the sound of the stick crunching against cloth and flesh and bone. I shivered and then froze, suddenly realizing the obvious; they were not acting. Two policemen were beating up a member of the public. The fat one hit the young man, with gusto and a look of

pleasure, at least a dozen times, as if this were his daily muscle-burning work-out. The crowd however had turned to look at me, unconsciously clicking away with my camera. And then the violent policemen saw me too; and looked mildly embarrassed. He gave his victim two more, rather theatrically gentle, strokes of his cane, almost as if these might reverse the effect of his previous actions and soothe the pain he had already caused. Their victim was then pulled upright. I walked up and asked the policemen why they were hitting him. The violent one spoke:

'He was selling drugs to children.'

'But why were you beating him up?'

'So that everyone around here knows that we will not allow drug dealing.'

'But surely you can't just beat him up.'

'He was trying to escape.'

'No, he wasn't.'

'Yes, he was. Before you came. Wasn't he?' He turned to his older companion for moral support, who nodded his head and scratched his nose, and wouldn't look up, not willing to catch my eye.

I turned to the drug dealer and asked him his name. He would not or could not speak; he looked at me as if I were an apparition, his eyes glazed and bulging. He opened his mouth slightly and tried to lick his lips. His tongue was engorged and purple. The violent policeman slapped him across the face. He recoiled in slow motion, his shoulder hunching up as if waiting for the next blow. Instead, the policemen began emptying his pockets. A piece of string, some tinfoil, some matches, a few coins, and what looked like a tightly folded empty crisp packet, secured with a rubber band. 'Evidence,' said the violent policeman, speaking a word of English for the first time, as he placed the little package in his pocket without opening it. And then his second word of English, just a little threateningly, a word of closure and command: 'Goodbye,' he said and waved me away.

I had been shaken by this encounter. Sitting down on a low wall, I tried to collect my thoughts. I was upset by my powerlessness. But also confused by my own reactions to what I had just witnessed. First, there was my laughable foolishness in thinking that the protagonists were actors. Second, there was the bored, arrogant self-confidence of the policemen. Third, the image of that smug sadistic look of satisfaction on the face of the younger policeman as he used all his strength to injure and humiliate his victim. Fourth, why did the victim or drug dealer, or whatever he may have been, not speak to me? Was he too drugged-up, or too scared to talk? And why was his tongue so swollen and discoloured? And then fifth, there was the crowd of watching children who had stopped, sullenly, to look at this piece of theatre-*vérité*, as if they'd seen it all before, and instead, when I appeared, they stared at me, the interloper, the new, different element in an act of everyday violence. And finally, and this was the most troubling of all my reactions, was a feeling that perhaps the public beating of a drug dealer might just act as a deterrence; and that possibly, the end might justify the means. But I also realized that everyone present, including myself, had been brutalized by this event. Otherwise, how could I begin to think of the beating as a good thing? I later told a journalist friend about this incident and she accused me of being totally naïve, of missing the most likely interpretation of what I had seen. She said that the Delhi police themselves are sometimes drug dealers and that the policemen were probably beating up the man I photographed for not paying them protection money.

This strange event turned out to be no more than an aperitif for another extraordinary scene of cruelty that I would witness one day later. I resumed my walk the following morning from the spot where I had been waved away by the imperious policemen. I marched over the railway bridge, its walls draped with white bedsheets and multi-coloured saris drying in the morning sun; as if Christo, the Bulgarian artist who enveloped Paris' *Pont Neuf* in shimmering nylon, had appeared overnight in Delhi. I was now leaving Shah Jahan's city and entering its oldest suburb, Sadar Bazaar, less well-planned, but as full of life as Chandni Chowk. The market was just opening, and traders were laying out their produce, or looking at me for their first sale of the day. They beckoned me with their pink guavas, plastic combs, perfume bottles, petticoats, blank DVDs, gun-shaped cigarette lighters; live chickens; padlocks and cheap Chinese radios. I stopped to look at what looked like a pile of backless plastic photograph frames. 'No sir,' I was told, 'these are remote control protectors.' I turned one over and over, dubiously. And then I recalled a recent stay at a cheap hotel, where the TV remote control had been encased in a plastic frame that was tied to the wall. The previous day this man, with his cartful of plastic, had sold more than two hundred remote control protectors. I marched on, accompanied now, to my disbelief and to the delight of the traders, by a cow which was matching me step-for-step, which stopped when I stopped, and started

118

when I started. I went down a side lane, followed by my new friend, who eventually ditched me in favour of a plastic bag full of rotting food. These were narrow lanes, with tall buildings, a series of residential neighbourhoods. At first all the residents, by the evidence of the nameplates and swastikas on their doorway, and the small well-tended shrines, were Hindus. Then at the end of one street, I entered a totally Muslim area, where many of the men wore white skull-caps and the women covered their hair in scarves; the nameplates were in Urdu and the streets were narrower. I had lost my way. My modern map was not detailed enough, My old map did not cover this area. I could not even work out which direction I was going in because the buildings were too high for me to see the rising sun.

I was about to ask for help when I noticed the raptors. Large, proud hook-nosed hawks, at least a dozen of them; they hovered above me and then swooped, disappearing from view, and then reappeared soaring up and out of sight or sitting, tearing at and chewing something on a roof-eave. Then I saw a wooden handcart, carrying a mass of small, dark objects that looked from a distance like fir-cones. Two hawks were circling over the cart—and the cart-puller would lazily wave his stick to scare them away. As I got closer, the fir-cones appeared to be hairy, like rotten rambutans or blackened tufts of grass. I saw what I thought were tiny patches of pinkish flesh, and that the objects were vaguely bowl-shaped. I peered at the cart closely. And then I recognized them for what they were. Ears. Hundreds of them. Freshly cut, I presumed, noticing that the purple-red blood had not yet congealed. I gagged, and a strange noise of disgust came from my throat. The cart-puller laughed out loud. I pulled myself together and spoke to him.

'Cattle ears,' I guessed.

'Yes,' he mumbled, nodding vigorously, revealing himself as man who didn't like to say much, but delighted in gestures.

'Where are you taking them?'

'Factory', he said, using the English word.

'Why?'

'It's work, isn't it,' he said, gesturing at his stomach at the same time. For a moment, we both misunderstood each other. I had ignored his words and mistook his action as implying that he or someone else would eat the ears; conjuring up the image of a rather nice stock, ear soup perhaps. But I realized that he was simply indicating that his earnings from selling the ears would enable him to buy food. But what could a 'factory', which in India can mean a tiny home-based workshop or business, possibly want with these ears.

'No, that's not what I meant', I explained, 'What exactly are the ears used for?'

'Don't know,' he said, almost too quickly, as if he were hiding some terrible secret.

I gestured to ask his permission to take a photograph, but he lifted his stave and shook his head.

'And where did you get the ears?' He pointed down a small lane and moved on, pushing his cartful of ears in the opposite direction.

At the end of the lane, I came upon a scene of slaughter the like of which I had never seen before. Now, I have always loved walking through markets, even Middle Eastern meat markets, and am used to the sight of flesh and offal, heads and trotters; eyeballs and bladders. But I was not prepared for this. After my first shocking glimpse, I looked down and shut my eyes as if not quite believing what I had seen. The air was suffocatingly heavy with the smell of fresh meat. Beneath my shoes, the street was sticky from the blood and viscera of cattle. I looked up a little, and a small river of blood was running past me, into a drain and the sewers of Delhi. I drew breath and lifted my head to take in properly the tableau before me.

I had wandered into an open-air slaughterhouse. It was a scene of cruelty and comradeship, a giant courtyard of death and laughter. The human beings were mainly young men: noisy, showing off, shouting instructions, hurrying each other up, telling stories. Two schoolgirls, with ponytails peeping out from under their headscarves and with brown leather satchels on their backs, wandered through their midst, and the men leapt apart to let them through. An old man was hunched over his steaming tea, as if unaware of the series of human and animal dramas being enacted around him. And everywhere there were cattle in different states of life and death and incompleteness. The living cattle were silent and dignified. They were being unloaded, almost unpacked, from small trucks, and then led into what looked like garages, open-fronted, where they were lined up in rows, all of them facing in the same direction. The young men started at the front, with the buffalo nearest the street. One of them grabbed it by the tail,

120

the other by the head, and forced it to lie on the ground. It looked up in my direction, plaintively, I imagined, a drool of gelatinous saliva escaping from its half-open mouth. With one upward stroke with his knife, the butcher cut the throat of the buffalo. Its body moved slightly, a gentle rattle of its rib-cage. Its eyes remained open, gradually glazing over, as it bled to death. And then the butcher moved on to the next one, which was standing, waiting and watching, with apparent equanimity. And so the killing was repeated ten times in this one building. Then another young man appeared and began removing the skin, the leather of the first buffalo, with a series of light knife cuts, and some tugging; he removed its skin as if it had been wearing an all-in-one wetsuit. Within minutes, the cattle had been cut up into pieces and sorted into neat piles. Skin, ears, hooves and intestines on one side. Tongues, flesh and offal on the other.

I had begun to realize that I was not particularly welcome here. I saw one man in the near-distance using his knife to point me out to his friend. I waved cheerily at them. They glared back at me with frozen eyes. A group of six young men came up; they pushed one of them closer to me. He asked, in broken English, what I was doing there. 'Just looking, just going for a walk,' I replied, as nonchalantly as one could, when surrounded by several unfriendly knife-wielding butchers. No photos, he said, grabbing at the digital camera that hung by a strap from my arm. He turned my camera over in his hand. The review screen clearly showed a picture I had just taken, of five cattle heads all in a row stripped clean of skin (and ears) by an expert butcher. He said 'No. No photos.' I took charge of the camera, theatrically switched the display off, hoping to convince him that I had destroyed the picture. He held out his hand, and demanded the film. I switched to Hindi, trying to explain that digital cameras didn't really have a film, opening up the camera to show him the battery compartment. He let me walk on, surprised more by my linguistic skills than convinced by my explanation.

I soon came upon another group of young men, over-excited and showing off. They were taking it in turns to demonstrate their technique for removing cattle from a small vehicle the size of a rickshaw. Here the live cattle had actually been packed on top of each other, only their rumps visible when the tailgate of the vehicle was opened. A young man would grab the tail of a buffalo, twisting and pulling at it at the same time, until it slipped out backwards and thudded onto the ground. A gentle prod with the toe of his boot in the haunches soon brought the cow to his feet. This group of butchers was more friendly, I thought. They wouldn't let me use my camera (five thousand rupees for each photo, they said), but would talk to me, and agreed to answer my questions. They were playfully untruthful. I asked them, trying to make conversation, how old the animals were. *Paintees.* Thirty-five, I was assured. And they all laughed. I asked them their names? Mohammed—they each said in turn. Louder laughter. Do they enjoy their jobs? It is not a job, it is our pleasure. Raucous hilarity. One of them, with cavernous eyes, put his bloody hand on mine and led me into the space where they had just killed a least a dozen cattle. The piles were less neat here, and I had to wade through entrails. They showed me, with an invisible, imaginary buffalo, how they killed and skinned and butchered. One of them said, 'Let's show him properly'. And they all laughed again.

I thought they were going to fetch in one of the cattle they had just unloaded. I was wrong. They advanced on me, a little more hostile, still laughing. One of them put his hand on my shoulder and lifted his knife. He brought the knife to within half an inch of my throat, and with a great venomous sneer, he then cut through the air as if he were ending my life. I was surrounded by neat piles of cattle meat, and it briefly flashed through my mind that they could turn me into small cubes of flesh within minutes. But also I knew, somehow, that they wouldn't harm me. Why would they? I lifted my hands and said 'No more. Please.' They laughed. I think they were pleased that I was scared. 'I'm not going to hurt you,' said the knife-bearer, taking his hand off my shoulder. 'Do you have any more questions?' 'No, No. And I really have to leave now', and I got out my mobile phone. I dialled my wife's number and it was engaged. I pretended to have a long conversation with her, telling her where I was and what I had been doing and that I'd meet her in fifteen minutes. They listened in, giggling to each other as they tried to make sense of my English. Suddenly the hostile butchers seemed like naughty children who had played a trick on an adult. By the time I had finished, they were quiet, almost timid. Each of them shook my hand, before I left in the direction of a mosque I had spotted earlier.

Beyond the mosque was a graveyard, with a stone bench. A mongoose darted in and out between the headstones—looking for prey, a snake or a mouse perhaps. I sat down, still shaking with disgust and fear and anger. I tried to think about everything I had just witnessed. I could not work out what had upset me more—the sight of such slaughter, or the hostility of the slaughterers. I could not find the language to express what I felt. The word 'inhuman' kept popping up, but it seemed doubly inappropriate, since the non-humans were so gentle and serene, and the humans were so raucous and violent. I sank into gloom. I noticed two black puppies which were chasing each other around the headstones; they were large enough not to be threatened by the manic mongoose. I chirruped at the puppies, and they came sidling up, nervous at first, ears erect. I put my hand down to stroke them, and one of them licked me, looking up at me with big golden brown eyes. The other tried to clamber on his back and they both fell over, wrestling and gambolling in the dust. Both of them came back to me and ran in and out between my legs, rubbing themselves against me, licking my shoes, jumping up to lick my hands. And suddenly my mood lifted. Tears welled, and I smiled to myself, and felt a sense of relief at being reminded that all was not ugly in this world. I was comforted by the puppies' playful affection, their trust in me.

For a brief saccharine moment, it was as if the puppies had been heaven-sent to restore my faith in nature. And then, as suddenly as my mood had lifted, it plunged again. I had suddenly realized what was actually happening, and why these two puppies were quite so friendly. I shuddered. They were having a meal. They were cleaning my hands, my trouser legs, my shoes of all the detritus, the fresh blood and guts, from the slaughterhouse. They were eating the remains of freshly slaughtered buffalo. I tried to push the puppies away, disgusted once more, noticing the blood on their lips and fur. But the puppies thought I was playing with them. And they were hungry, and persisted, not understanding my change of mood. It then occurred to me that at some time in the past, the leather of my shoes had, once before, been cleaned of the flesh and blood of a cow. Then it was by a butcher who had stripped a cow of its skin, perhaps one of the butchers who had terrified me only fifteen minutes earlier. And suddenly it did not seem so objectionable or stomach-curdling to let the puppies lick my shoes. And so I sat there, as they licked and licked until my shoes sparkled and shone with the glistening drool of puppy saliva.

A Fifth Intermission

I AM A Person of Indian Origin. I have a slate-grey passport-like document issued by the Indian government that says so. But I'm not really. I was not born or brought up here, and I do not have a single direct ancestor who, as far as I know, ever lived in India. I have become the proud possessor of a Person of Indian Origin card because I am married to an Indian citizen. But the actual card was not easy to come by.

It involved a total of seventeen visits to three separate ministries and five different offices. It took up at least four full days of my life. I was interviewed twice, the second time at home with my wife, Shireen. The first time was at the offices of the Foreigners Division, Ministry of Home Affairs, in a large, unventilated, very public room, brimming with non-Indians from every continent. I reached the head of the queue after two hours of eavesdropping on other peoples' immigration problems (a bald Canadian Buddhist woman in a maroon gown who wanted to live in a Tibetan refugee camp; an Afghan man who wanted a residence visa for his fully veiled third wife; an elderly widowed man who had left India for Pakistan at partition almost sixty years earlier and now hoped return to live with his sister in Delhi). I was asked, among other more prosaic questions, to explain why I had married an Indian woman ('Love,' I said, monosyllabically), and then, with a leer and a twinkle, whether I had had many Indian girlfriends. 'N-no,' I eventually stuttered. My hesitant response did not reflect either uncertainty or mendacity on my part, but my surprise at the question and my growing irritation with the questioner. The interview ended abruptly. He wrote 'Refer for further enquiry' on my residence permit and explained that I would receive a home visit. 'We need to be sure that marriages to Indian citizens are genuine.'

One Friday afternoon, several weeks later, at five p.m., I received a call on my mobile phone as I was spiralling my way through central Delhi. The investigators from the Home Ministry would be at my home at five-thirty. I explained that I could not get back by then. Never mind—they would wait. As I travelled home, images of *Mr and Mrs,* a television programme of my childhood, flashed through my mind. A gormless husband would be placed in a soundproof booth, while his bright-as-a-button wife would stand on the stage. She would be asked semi-intimate question about their life together: what was the first present she gave him when they were dating? What colour nightclothes was she wearing yesterday? And so on. The husband was then released from the booth, and would invariably get the answer wrong, to his embarrassment and everyone else's amusement. It was gentle viewing—a mild celebration of female omniscience and male autism. But now I was going to take part in a real-life version of *Mr and Mrs,* and my precious PIO card, and perhaps my right to stay in India, would depend on it. And, suddenly I could not, for the life of me, remember the colour of Shireen's toothbrush, or the name of her favourite Hindi movie, or her shoe size. My mind had gone blank. Fifteen years of marriage had been erased from my memory. As I sat in an autorickshaw, panicking, a few of her preferences, her quiddities, came back to me, and I began to compile a mental list. She prefers Alfonsos to all other mangos. She also likes Al Pacino, knows every song from *Evita* and hates emptying rubbish bins. She has splendidly tapering fingers, a very long second toe on both feet and can become indignant at the bat of an eyelid—but surely they weren't going to be interested in all that. What would they ask? What might they have asked Shireen already? A few trick questions, perhaps. I was sweating with nerves by the time I reached home.

Two men were seated on the edge of the sofa, looking even more nervous than me, untouched glasses of water in front of them. Shireen was questioning them about their professional qualifications—which were not very extensive. I gave her a self-conscious kiss on the cheek and sat down opposite them. At that point, our children burst into the room, a dancing duet of carefree excitement at their just-concluded Internet Messenger conversation with their London cousins. 'Guess what, Tashi's got a boyfriend,' they said, referring to my eight-year-old niece. Then they stopped, only slightly subdued by the presence of strangers, and skipped away into the kitchen to tease the cook.

'What are these children?' asked the chief investigator.

'They're ours,' Shireen responded with a slight chill in her voice.

'Children of both of you? They are very old.'

'Yes, both of us. They're twelve and eleven.'

'How do you have children if you are just married?' I had not prepared for this baffling line of questioning—and was later reprimanded for just sitting there with my mouth open. Shireen, on the other hand, delivered a crushing blow.

'Ridiculous *(sotto voce)* . . . this is all totally ridiculous *(out loud)* . . . we've been married for fifteen years.'

I nodded eagerly.

The two men looked at each other, aghast, and then started scrabbling through the cardboard file they had brought with them. They spoke to each other in a whisper. It became clear that they normally interviewed newly married couples.

'Can we see your marriage certificate?' I showed it to them and was asked for a copy. I explained that I didn't have a photocopier but that I could take a photo of the certificate with my camera, download it on to my computer and print it out. And so, as they endured a further interrogation at the hands of Shireen, I printed out a photograph of the certificate. They then got up and left—abruptly ending my brief cameo on *Mr and Mrs*—having promised a decision within two weeks.

The following evening, a Saturday, our cook, Pan Singh, told me one of the men who had come yesterday was at the gate, asking for a *lifafa*, the Hindi word for envelope. I asked him to invite the man in. Pan Singh returned, a little sheepish, saying the man refused to come in, but just wanted a *lifafa*—with our marriage certificate. And so, slightly puzzled, I printed out another copy.

Later that evening, I told a friend this story. 'He wanted a bribe, you idiot. A *lifafa* is what you put the bribe in. Nowadays, *lifafa* means bribe. You'll never get your PIO card now, and he'd have been perfectly happy with 100 rupees.'

Each Indian I meet has a corruption story—of bribing a policeman to file a case, of paying a school principal for admission to a state school, of kickbacks to the local municipality to build an awning over a shop-front. Corruption is pretty normal. As long as the amount demanded is not unusually exorbitant, most just accept it as part of life. It even gets justified as a way for officials to supplement their very low government salaries. It is perhaps another advantage (or a drawback when I can't get something done) of being a foreigner in Delhi that no one has ever directly asked me for a bribe.

Three weeks later I went to the Foreigners Regional Registration Office to hear the good news, and the bad. 'Your application for a PIO has successfully passed the enquiry stage,' the official informed me without looking up. 'But unfortunately, Mr Miller, all your documentation has gone astray and you will need to resubmit.' I looked heavenwards and brought my hand down rather heavily on the table. 'I'm sorry. We're not computerized yet, and some of our agents are a little careless.' It may have been my imagination, but I'm sure I detected the trace of a wink in her left eye. 'Probably best to apply next time you're in London,' she told me cheerfully. I walked away presuming, but unable to prove, that my papers had been deliberately lost because I had not paid a small bribe.

I took her advice. Three weeks after putting in my application to the Indian High Commission in London (no interview necessary), I finally had my precious PIO card—together with a fifteen-year visa, the right to buy property in India, and, to my amusement, the ability to join the diplomats' queue at immigration at Delhi airport. This is of no practical use, because I still have to wait just as long for my luggage, but I do get childishly gleeful as I saunter past the first-class passengers.

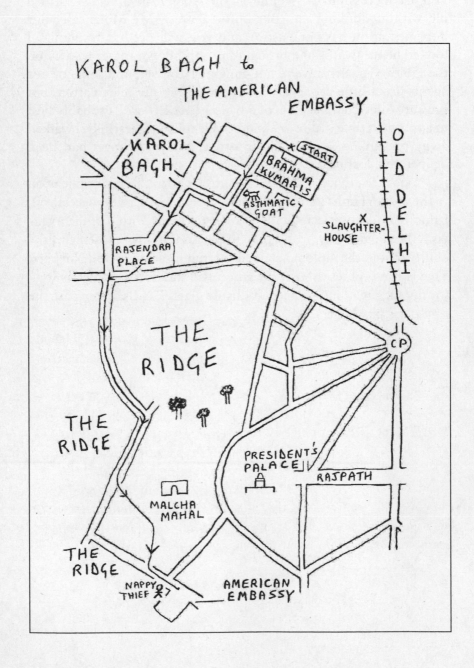

Chapter Six: In which the Author expectorates a carrot, meets an asthmatic goat and identifies a nappy thief

TWO HOURS AFTER leaving the bloody-mouthed pups, I was eating an ostentatiously unostentatious vegan meal. Perturbed and nauseous as a result of my latest adventure, I had walked and walked, in a mini-spiral of waywardness, hardly aware of my surroundings, neglecting the basic tenets of psychogeography, vaguely contemplating my vegetarian  future, when I was called to a sudden halt by a large sign on the other side of a furiously busy road enticing me to enter the promisingly named International Centre for World Renewal. I began crossing over, dodging juggernauts and autorickshaws heading towards Connaught Place and the heart of Delhi. I squeezed between the twisted railings of what was once a road-divider, a major casualty of a serious accident, which had managed to billow out the railings into the shape of the front of the vehicle which had hit them. The traffic in the other direction was less hectic, but I looked down to see the tarmac pock-marked with ochre stains—congealed blood I imagined, in my disoriented state. I finally reached the pavement on the other side, and beside the entrance to the International Centre for World Renewal were several smaller similarly hyperbolic signboards, this one a little obscure but strangely seductive:

Health, Wealth, Happiness for
21 Births is your God-Fatherly Birth Right.
NOW OR NEVER

Those last three words were painted in scarlet, each letter eight inches high. I was in the mood to give 'now' a chance. I headed in, passing through a dust-choked courtyard and entered a square room, whose four walls were covered with dazzling cartoon-strip murals. No one was there. In the centre of the room was an armchair. I sat down and looked around me at the swirl of colours and caricatures. The head of a man, a comic-book Tintinesque villain with x-ray vision and a magnificently oiled handlebar moustache, was leering at a woman in a scarlet sari. And next to him, written in English: 'Sex-Lust'. Underneath was written the Hindi word काम (*kaam*), or sexual desire[1]. I began to look at the other murals—all depicting acts of destruction or depravity. These were scenes from nightmares: a hanged man, a nuclear war, a stabbing, a race riot; like Hieronymus Bosch with clothes on.

As I gawped at the murals, two men carried a small table into the room, and placed it in front of me. I greeted them; they bowed their heads slightly and withdrew—returning minutes later with several foldaway plastic chairs. I got up and began a closer examination of one tableau displaying five sins, arrayed vertically: lust, anger, greed, attachment and pride. In Hinduism, there are usually five sins rather than the Christian seven[2]; and for sinners it

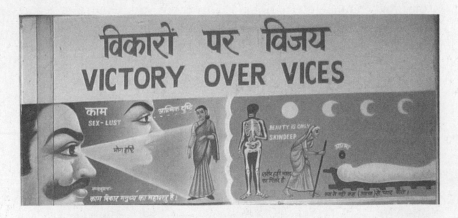

[1] काम or *kaam* is cognate with Kama in Kama Sutra, where Kama means eroticism. Kaam also means work.

[2] The seven deadly sins of Christian tradition are: pride, envy, anger, sloth, greed, gluttony and lust. These are not canonical and there are several variant lists. The five sins or vices of Hindu tradition are: Kaam (lust), Krodh (anger), Lobh (greed), Moh (personal attachment), Ahankar (pride).

is not hellfire that awaits, but rebirth as a lesser creature, an ant, perhaps. I felt my brow furrow as I looked more closely at the 'Sin of Attachment'. A father was crying as his young son lay on his deathbed. Amongst the other portrayals of the

sin of attachment was a grief-stricken adult monkey carrying the corpse of a baby monkey, and a (human) mother gazing lovingly into the eyes of a young child resting on her lap. I turned back— and was startled to see an Indian woman in a white sari ensconced in the armchair I had just vacated.

'Do you have any questions?' she asked me in English.

'No . . . I mean, yes. Lots.' I gabbled, caught off guard by her ethereal appearance, hypnotized by her angelic gaze and gently confident manner.

'Sit.' She commanded, pointing across the table, at the chair opposite her. I sat.

'Where am I?'

'This is a place of peace and meditation. We are Brahma Kumaris and you are welcome to join us.'

I had met Brahma Kumaris[3] before; western women, dressed in white, members of a Hindu sect of the same name. I knew that they had a pilgrimage centre in the hills of southern Rajasthan, at a place called Mount Abu, and the only other thing I could remember was that, like Jains, they didn't eat garlic.

'What do you believe?'

'We don't believe. We know.' There was heavy, deeply meaningful emphasis on the word 'know'.

---

[3] The Brahma Kumaris were founded in the 1930s by Dada Lekhraj, a diamond merchant from Hyderabad, now in Pakistan. He moved the organization to India after partition. It claims—and probably has—several hundred thousand members around the world. In some ways, its ideas and practices prefigured many of the New Age sects that emerged in the 1960s, and which derived their philosophy from a largely Hindu tradition.

'What do you know?'

She looked at me a little quizzically, as if she were not sure whether I was a total fool or just teasing her.

'The Truth. It is not a matter of words. You must come and join us.'

'That would be very nice . . . I was just looking at the paintings on your wall.' I was beginning to regain my investigative poise. I pointed to the tableau of the five sins and cut to the chase. 'Why is attachment a sin? What is wrong with that man crying over the death of his son?' She drew a deep breath, and looked straight into my eyes, a half smile creeping over her lips.

'You have a son?'

'Yes, and a daughter.'

'It will be hard for you overcome attachment.'

'But why should I?'

'It will take some time for you to know the answer to that question' She looked deep into my eyes again, as if searching for something inscribed on the back of my eyeballs. 'There is only one object of love. The *Paramatma*. The Supreme Soul. Earthly attachments are of no value. I am a soul . . . the body is only a costume.' And then she added, as a hesitant afterthought. 'You are also a soul.'

A man came in with a tin plate covered in food and interrupted our staccato discussion. In the centre was a small steel bowl filled with boiled whole lentils, and around this was a patchwork of cooked and raw vegetables, dominated by the humble carrot in several avatars.

'Eat,' she commanded. I began eating, my blood-instigated nausea having subsided.

'What is your name?' I asked; non-controversially, I thought.

'My name is Brahma Kumari.'

'Eh? I don't understand. Surely you're a member of the Brahma Kumaris. You must have a name, a family.'

'Now my name is Brahma Kumari.'

I opened a new line of conversation.

'This food is very tasty,' I said with only a soupçon of hyperbole. She almost scowled—the trace of furrow just visible in an otherwise inscrutably mellow face. She got up and walked up to one of the

132

murals, and pointed, silently, to some words in English written on the wall. She encouraged me to read out loud, moving her index finger from word to word. Obediently, through the debris of half-chewed carrot floating in saliva, I spluttered the chiastic epigram, 'We eat to live. We should not live to eat.' A small piece of carrot flew out of my mouth. It landed in the bowl of lentils. I quickly picked it out, and secreted it in my trouser pocket. She said nothing, but had clearly seen it all. I felt I had been disgraced.

Three middle-aged western women entered the room carrying light day-packs. They greeted 'Brahma Kumari' warmly, and sat down at the table with her. One of them began chanting 'Om Shanti' underneath her breath, while the other two discussed something, train timetables I think, in quick-fire Italian. Then 'Brahma Kumari' joined them. I carried on, solemnly finishing off the carrots, trying to be as inconspicuous as I could be. They all began discussing the future, the impending destruction that would engulf the world. Only a few would make it to the Satyuga, the coming Golden Age. They began talking about Baba, the founder of the movement, and of people they knew, and I heard the name Dawn Griggs mentioned in an undertone. The name was vaguely familiar. Suddenly, 'Brahma Kumari' turned to me and asked me if I had any more questions. I asked her about the 21 Births referred to on the signboard outside. 'Ah, that would take me a long time to explain.' One of the Italian women giggled softly. 'But come', she with a soft firmness, 'I will show you our small bookshop'. And so I left, a little unwillingly—feeling I'd been uncovered as a soulless time-waster. I was led away to an outhouse with a collection of exorbitantly priced Brahma Kumari pamphlets: a place, I felt, where the less spiritually inclined are sent to spend the proceeds of their materialism. I felt obliged to purchase, and walked off with a Brahma Kumari 'Thought for the Day' calendar, full of more cute-and-clumsy chiastic platitudes[4], feeling only a little wiser and wondering why I knew the name Dawn Griggs.

[4] Among the more contrived aphorisms were: 'Even though you cannot change time, realize it is time for you to change'; 'If you want to advance in life, make sure that your wants don't advance'; 'It is better to make use of a chance to change rather than try to change your chances.'

When I returned home later that day, an Internet search for Dawn Griggs came up with an old BBC news story

> Wednesday, 17 March, 2004, 18:23 GMT
>
> ### Arriving tourist killed in Delhi
>
> **An Australian woman was stabbed in the face and killed after arriving at Delhi airport and taking a taxi, Indian police said.**
>
> The woman was named as 59-year-old Dawn Griggs, who had arrived on a plane from Hong Kong at 1.30am on Wednesday. A 24-year-old taxi driver was arrested after a body was found in a forest close to the airport at around noon.

It was a particularly brutal murder, covered in graphic detail by the Indian press, and one in a series of attacks on Indian and western women that have gained Delhi the reputation of being India's least safe city. Dawn Griggs was in fact no ordinary tourist: she was a Brahma Kumari who was heading from the airport to the building I had just visited, when she was killed with a screwdriver. There's a website, realearning.com.au, celebrating that very human sin-or-virtue of attachment, by commemorating Dawn Griggs' life, in tributes and photos, as well as a prose-poem full of Brahma Kumari imagery.

> she died alone
> in the wee hours of the morning
> in an eerie forest near Delhi where no one heard her cries
> fighting off the young thief who bore the sign of death
> her light suddenly transformed into the eternal
> her bones a metaphysic of love
> the song of spirit and now of memory[5]

Although the Brahma Kumari movement was founded by a man, most of its senior officials are women, and its beliefs and practices have proved particularly attractive to middle-aged western women, who can be seen in large numbers at Mount Abu. For many ordinary members of the sect, meditation, chastity and the search for spiritual

[5]In August 2008, two taxi drivers were convicted of Dawn Griggs' murder and sentenced to death.

peace are the most important features of the Brahma Kumaris, and the movement's very strong millenarian beliefs are underplayed. They have good reason—18 January 1977 was predicted as the end of the world—and when this did not happen many believers left the fold. The Brahma Kumaris do continue to believe that the world as we know it is coming to an end, probably in 2036—and a new Golden Era will begin in which an elite of Golden Souls will rule the world[6].

I drifted out of the Brahma Kumari centre onto the pavement and asked a passer-by for the name of the street. It was the New Rohtak Road—a famously congested way of leaving Delhi at a very slow speed. This area, Karol Bagh, became a refugee settlement for Hindus and Sikhs fleeing from what had become the Pakistani province of Punjab. Most of those families stayed on, building permanent homes. Those who were successful tended to leave, usually for South Delhi. But Karol Bagh developed into a thriving, lively colony with the chaotic feel of many of India's smaller cities. Vehicles, animals, rubbish dumps, small shops, pedestrians, all vie for space on the pavements and street; above, there are cobwebs of cables bringing telephone, satellite TV, electricity and Internet connections to its residents. I again attracted the interest of an animal, a goat with asthma, who rubbed against my leg in an amatory manner as I tried to take a photograph of a man selling computer parts from the back of an old wooden pushcart. The goat was coughing, a terrible rasping cough from deep in its throat and looked up at me with plaintive, almost tearful eyes. I touched it, tentatively, between the ears, stroking softly. It coughed once more, a deeper, even more violent rasp, and

[6] The Brahma Kumaris are both secretive and hierarchical in relation to organizational and teleological matters. However, 'cult-busters' have given them a relatively clean bill of health, and I have not traced any accusations of ritualized brainwashing, abuse or misappropriation of funds. Ex-members of the organization remain fairly supportive—see xbkchat.com—and though there were well-documented claims that a child was sexually abused in a hostel next to the building that I visited in Delhi, it was not suggested that this was condoned by the Brahma Kumaris. However, the organization has had its fair share of space cadets, quite literally. In 1998, on the Spanish island of Tenerife, Heide Fittkau-Garthe, the leader of a breakaway Brahma Kumari faction, encouraged 32 of her followers to kill themselves on top of Mount Teide, telling them that a spacecraft was coming that would take their souls and their lifeless bodies to another planet. Fortunately, the police got there in time, and Fittkau-Garthe was sent to prison.

vomited out a large piece of what had clearly once been a blue plastic bag. We parted company—the goat sidling down a lane of shops towards a jewellery emporium, as I watched and walked, bumping into a man who was naked from the waist up. He had taken his shirt off so that it could be pressed right there in front of him, by a tiny, ancient woman with a coal-iron using a large slab of stone as a surface. They both turned to me with big smiles as I blundered on towards Rajendra Place and the Ridge.

Rajendra Place is a decrepit shopping mall that only dates back to the 1990s, crumbling as if it were a fourteenth-century pre-Mughal caravanserai. It is a failed attempt to bring commercial life to a run-down area of the city. This is Delhi at its most mediocre. Walkways and staircases are turning to rubble, steel reinforcements protrude dangerously, huge malarial puddles wait to be evaporated by the sun, blue wall paint can be pulled off in sharp-edged sheets. Above, precarious pieces of concrete are destined to crash to earth. A watchman told me that cheapskate builders had used the wrong cement mix. For no obvious reason, Rajendra Place appears to be very popular with accountants. Further on is an entirely empty McDonalds, an un-air-conditioned cybercafé, a large hotel in the middle of a building site—and the new Metro line, towering high above the fractured pavement. A passing accountant tells me that the Metro will bring new life to the area; *sotto voce*, I suggest that a few controlled explosions might be just as effective.

Just beyond Rajendra Place, I re-encountered the arid rocky forest-lands of the two-thousand-acre central Ridge, whose innermost edge I had touched earlier on Mandir Marg, and whose antiquity now seemed entirely self-evident. I was still close to the centre of one of the largest cities in the world—and yet apart from the road down which I was marching, an occasional vehicle and the odd wisp of rusted barbed wire, there was no sign that *homo sapiens* had ever existed. The Ridge is one hundred thousand times as old as this one-thousand-year-old city; India's capital is suddenly little more than a slightly suppurating pimple on the face of history. The Ridge is a lung and a mask to Delhi, and the trees of the Ridge extract air pollutants and produce oxygen, and from here the city is invisible, inaudible.

The Ridge is uninhabited, almost. Hidden away in the midst of a thick jungle of *keekar* and *babul* trees are two very different buildings, just twenty metres apart. A satellite ground station next to a ruined medieval hunting-lodge. The former is bristling with modernity, large satellite dishes, CCTV and high security defences. The inhabitants of the decrepit Malcha Mahal take their security even more seriously. Next to a footpath leading up to the building is a rusted metal signboard which declares

ENTRY RESTRICTED. CAUTIOUS OF HOUND DOGS. PROCLAMATION. INTRUDERS SHALL BE GUNDOWN.

Malcha Mahal is occupied by unambiguously unwelcoming members of the former royal family of Oudh, whose rule ended in the 1850s. They fell on hard times, living at one point in the 1980s in a waiting-room at New Delhi Railway Station before hiding themselves away from the world on the Ridge. They have not shot anyone, to my knowledge, though they have let loose their non-vegetarian Doberman Pinchers on those who have gone beyond the signpost.[7]

The end of the Ridge and the re-emergence of urban Delhi are marked by an unlikely presence: a larger-than-life tribute to the 'liberator' of no less than six countries, none of them within nine thousand miles of India. A double-sized head-and-shoulders bronze statue of Simon Bolivar rests on a stone plinth. He is overdressed, gaunt and frowning, as if the Delhi sun has got the better of him, so far from his multiple South American homelands. A hagiographic plaque reveals that he'd only been there since 10 March 2004, and gives no particular reason for his recent appearance, except that 'the

[7] This story has become the fall-back, stand-by, silly-season, stock-in-trade, timeless filler for almost every Delhi-based foreign correspondent. I first attempted to visit Malcha Mahal in 1991, as a young reporter for the BBC. On that occasion a liveried servant, whose once-white uniform was muddied and torn, appeared with an angry black dog on a tight leash. He carried a silver-coloured tray, on which I placed my business card and a letter asking for an audience. Ten minutes later, I received a letter informing me that my request had been turned down, but that I was welcome to ask again.

Doubts have been raised by other members of the Oudh royal family about the real identity of the inhabitants of Malcha Marg. See oudh.tripod.com/bhm/hoax

Oudh (also known as Avadh) was an important principality in northern India—with Lucknow as its capital. The last Nawab of Oudh, Wajid Ali Shah, was deposed by the British in 1856—shortly before the Uprising. This event was the backdrop to a famous Prem Chand short story, *The Chess Players*, which was then turned into a film by Satyajit Ray.

fruits of his ideas and actions place him amongst the most illustrious historical figures of all times.' This point also marks the start of Delhi's diplomatic quarter, and I decide that Bolivar must have been chosen for this spot as the person who is a national hero to the largest number of countries[8].

The diplomatic enclave, named Chanakyapuri after a famously wily Indian politician[9], who predated Bolivar by some two thousand years, was laid out in the 1950s and 60s on flat arid scrubland sandwiched between New Delhi and the Ridge. The streets are disconcertingly wide and under-used; the plots are rectilinear, some of them huge. The largest of them, as I headed away from the Ridge, is a mini-America spread over almost thirty acres, where the security is even more intimidating than at Malcha Mahal. First comes the American Embassy School (which admits all but Indians[10] at the cost of some $15,000 per annum for ninth-graders and above)—fully air-conditioned with 'a 350-seat theater, two libraries filled with 53,000 books and full Internet access, two gyms, two swimming pools and a diving pool, five tennis courts, two soccer fields, two outdoor basketball

---

[8] Simon Bolivar (1783–1830) played a major role in the liberation from European rule of Venezuela, Colombia, Bolivia, Ecuador, Peru and Panama. He also had a cigar and a country named after him. The official name of the road on which his statue has been installed is Simon Bolivar Marg. I later came upon an adjacent road named after Bolivar's contemporary, José San Martin, who played a major role in the liberation of only three South American countries: Argentina, Chile and Peru.

[9] Chanakya was a political strategist of the fourth century BC, whom Nehru described as the Indian Machiavelli, and who is reputed to have united the Indian forces against the army of Alexander the Great. He is also famous for his *bon mots*, such as 'A woman is four times as shy, six times as brave and eight times as libidinous as a man.'

[10] See http://aes.ac.in/aes for more details .The admissions policy excludes Indians not by name but by declaring that 'Eligibility for all other [non-American] nationalities is limited to children whose parents or legal guardians are temporarily relocated to India for employment purposes and are resident in Delhi.'

courts, two climbing walls, a small skate park and a fitness room with a full range of Life Fitness equipment.'

And just a little further down the road is, as far as I can discover, India's only baseball diamond. I have walked and driven past these walls many times, and been puzzled by the floodlight towers that surround a small part of the American Embassy compound, as if it were a concentration camp. It was only recently, when I discovered Google Earth satellite photographs of every part of the world, that I was able to make out that the floodlights belonged to an undersized baseball field, the pitcher's mound, denuded of grass, clearly visible. But the security guards would not let me in.

Outside the entrance to the US compound closest to the baseball diamond, I came upon a large number of smartly dressed Indian men and women lolling about on a grassed-over sidewalk. There were at least thirty women, many in western clothes, their hair tied up in neat buns and ponytails, most of them sitting on their heels, waiting for something and barely talking to each other; and far fewer men, strutting up and down, some wearing jackets and ties. I heard a tannoy announcement and one of the women leapt up, smiling back at the others as she skipped towards the compound. I went up to the group she had left behind.

'Are you waiting for visas?'

'No, we are trying to get work.'

'What kind of work.'

'Household work—housekeepers and maids. And the men are mainly drivers.'

'But why do you come here?'

'Because this is where foreigners come to get servants.'

'So you prefer to work for foreigners.'

'Usually. They pay better and give us more time off.'

Another woman butted in—'But some of them are totally mad. Ha-ha-ha.'

I went up to the door and was asked for my passport. Non-Indians only. I entered into a small enclave within the US Embassy, called the Domestic Staff Registry, operated, I read on a notice-board, by the American Women's Association or AWA. I was welcomed by a small, hyperactively welcoming, wire-haired American woman who told me not to be shy, but did not give me a chance to open my

mouth. 'Come in here and register and then you can go through the files. Show me your passport. A Brit—uh-huh. Now sit yourself down with these files. When there's someone you want to see, to interview—just say, and I'll tell you what I know and call her in. You want a housekeeper, I suppose. Most men who come here do. But don't be fooled by looks (she screwed up her eyes and scrutinized me; clearly I was a possible fool)—the attractive ones are the worst. That's my experience. Some servants want to trap you into marriage—but I can see (she nodded extravagantly at the wedding band on my ring finger) that they'll have to forget about that with you. There's a Mrs Miller to contend with. Ha-ha-ha. Anyway, get reading.' I had not spoken a full word—and had managed to have a discussion about my marital status with just a few nods and grunts of affirmation. I sat down with a pile of brown folders, from which I could partially reconstruct the life stories of those women crouched on the pavement outside, hoping and waiting to be called inside, for their chance to work for a foreigner.

The files contained CVs of each job-seeker, medical test results (smears and stools), letters of recommendation, and, overwritten in pencil, comments from members of the AWA who had been checking up with previous employers. There were many sorry stories, full of gossip and sadness, and I read and read, entering a world of pain and pathos. One woman, Annette, 'was a very good worker. She is clean, trustworthy and bathes regularly. But her husband beats her, and she missed work because of that several times. He is an alcoholic and asked us for money.' A would-be maid, Rosy, 'is not literate. It is best not to crowd her memory with complex instructions'. Another, Shireen, '. . . had very good references. Unfortunately I found her to be very difficult and argumentative; she was very moody and unable to accept constructive criticism. She has a massive chip on her shoulder.' A driver, Krishnan, was 'let go because of his grumpy disposition'. After a while I began to realize that I was learning more about the former employers, through their often deeply prejudiced accounts of how their employees smelled or were incorrigibly uninterested in ironing to the standard expected of them. Many were described in terms more appropriate to a household pet. The saddest tale of them all was about Sonu, a maid, who had been shown up as a liar and a thief. Initially, I read, she had denied doing anything wrong, but later 'when shown the evidence' she owned up and was dismissed. Her offence, I read further down the page, was that 'she used an imported nappy as a sanitary towel.' 'Imported' had been underlined twice. In the eyes of her former employee she had clearly committed a great crime, and one which was displayed in embarrassing and permanent detail on her file. And yet this was clearly an incomplete story. We did not learn how exactly this Sherlock Holmes of an employer found poor Sonu out, or what was her version of these events. And yet just outside, sitting on her haunches like the other women, was Sonu, hoping that I or some other foreigner might give her work, presumably unaware of what her previous employer had written about her.

The American woman returned, ticking me off for not calling any of the women for interview. I lacked the courage or commitment to social re-engineering to get Sonu tannoyed and tell her what was on her file. And, after all, I did not need a housekeeper. I apologized and left, looking over my shoulder at the women, Sonu included, sitting outside. I headed firmly southwards towards Delhi's most distinguished slum.

A Sixth Intermission

'DO YOU KNOW Moses?' she asked, fixing me with a wildly intense glare. I must have looked puzzled.

'The Mount Sinai Moses,' she clarified, clearly exasperated by having to talk to such a simpleton, 'in the Bible.'

My mind nervously wandered to the only other people with the name Moses whom I could think of, Ed and Grandma[1], before I found myself saying, 'Not personally, but I've certainly heard of him.' A chortling tremor ran through my body, as if I was about to be overcome by a fit of giggles. I lowered my head, so as not to catch her eye, as she continued,

'We are descended from the Pharaohs. Do you know what I am saying?'

She squinted at me through the beam of sunlight that separated us, specks of diamantine dust dancing through the air, each of us seated beside the crumbling column of a fourteenth-century hunting lodge. Was this a test? Could I keep a straight face? I felt my cheekbones begin to quiver. I could not control them. More than anything else, I must not laugh. A pigeon swept down, close enough for its wingbeats to fan cool air onto my cheeks. I shuddered, looked around at the bare stone walls of the Malcha Mahal and my mood became suitably dark again. I nodded mournfully in the direction of my interlocutor, and was able to remain po-faced through the rest of a theatrical twenty-minute oration on the sorrows of the royal house of Oudh. It was a breathtakingly bravura performance that ended with a declaration that seemed to give a clue to the speaker's hidden tragedy, 'Ordinariness is not just a crime. It is a sin. A sin.' These words would later ring in my ears.

---

[1] Edwin Moses is probably the greatest hurdler of all time, and double Olympic gold medalist. Grandma Moses was a fantastically popular American painter, who only took up painting in her seventies and lived to the age of 101. The other Moses, the Mount Sinai one, was the adopted grandson of a Pharaoh. The Egyptian historian Ahmed Osman argues that Moses and the monotheistic Pharaoh Akhenaten were actually the same person. Other esotericists have argued, with even less evidence, that Moses was buried in India. See Gene Matlock: *Jesus and Moses Are Buried in India, Birthplace of Abraham and the Hebrews* iUniverse Publishers (2000).

Two weeks earlier, I had just finished writing about my previous failure to gain access to Malcha Mahal, when a friend, MS, a full-time Hank Williams devotee and a part-time Delhi resident, told me he had an appointment to meet the Prince and Princess of Oudh. He invited me along. And so one Friday afternoon, we drove through the forests of the Ridge up to the signboard bearing the threat that intruders would be 'gundown'. We were met by a silent manservant in tattered blue livery and a gold-tipped turban who ushered us up a rocky path to the weather-scarred hilltop hunting lodge. There were no doors or windows. Out of an arch emerged Prince Cyrus, dapper and jaunty, wearing blue suede shoes, and more than welcoming. From the shadows of a column stepped his older sister, Princess Sakina, proud and gaunt, eagle-eyed, wild of hair, old before her time, deep trenches in her face, as if etched by terrible tears of sorrow. She was less than welcoming.

I had brought a bouquet of blue flowers. They were placed on a table next to a crystal decanter that contained the ashes of their mother. Princess Vilayat Mahal had, I was told, killed herself by swallowing crushed diamonds—clearly, I was led to believe, a very regal way of dying[2]. Sakina has not left the building since that day. She says she never will. She spoke of betrayal, of servants who had robbed and deserted her, of journalists who had misquoted her, of government officials who had broken their promises. She spoke of a former prime minister[3], who had deliberately stopped her mother from getting an allowance, and refused to allow the hunting lodge to be repaired. 'He came to see us, you know. But we turned him away. Shoo, shoo, shoo.' Cyrus laughed, and I saw the faintest of

[2] The Holy Roman Emperor Frederick II and the Ottoman Sultan Beyazid II were both said to have been poisoned with diamond dust. The fictional Nawab Sahib, in the Hindi film *Chaudvin Ka Chand*, set in Lucknow, the capital of Oudh, used it to kill himself. Recent scientific research, based on feeding crushed diamonds to animals, suggest that the dangers of such a practice have been exaggerated (for a fuller discussion see www.nanomedicine.com/NMIIA/15.1.1). Diamond miners have 'stolen' diamonds from their employers by swallowing them, and have not been harmed..

[3] PV Narasimha Rao who was home minister at the time of their move from a waiting-room at New Delhi railway station in 1985 where they had lived since the mid-1970s. Princess Sakina showed me a letter from Narasimha Rao's private secretary, Ramu Damodaran, which referred to the 'repairs' to Malcha Mahal that the home minister had sanctioned.

smile on the lips of Sakina. 'We can't trust anyone except our dogs. Dogs cannot be deceitful'. She pointed out through an arch, where I saw a huge black Great Dane, regal, gorgeous and terrifying, looking in at me. 'We don't call them dogs. They are Anubis. It is humans who are dogs.'

A sad softness comes over her. She talks a little about the past, of Lucknow where the old Oudh palaces, confiscated by the British at the time of the mutiny, are crumbling. She remembers a Jewish governess whom she clearly adored, and who had taught her that ordinariness was a sin; and Zita, the last Austro-Hungarian empress, who had written to her mother. Cyrus told us of the beautiful silver cutlery that he'd had to sell, and that he had an old General Electric Fridge that he now uses as a wardrobe. There is no electricity at Malcha Mahal, no running water, though Cyrus has now managed to get a telephone connection.

I climbed up on the roof, overgrown with shrubs and weeds, and, standing on a fractured stone parapet, gazed beneath me. All around lay a carpet of green, the treetops of an ancient forest, the distant towers of commercial Delhi like a mirage in the November haze, the stately domes of India's British interregnum poking through the undergrowth like toys on an unmowed lawn. I, quite truthfully, told Cyrus that that I had never seen such a spectacular view of Delhi. He said he would like people to come and stay at Malcha Mahal—

writers or painters, perhaps, who would appreciate the view from this rooftop. A heritage guesthouse perhaps, bringing in a small income. They would need to do some basic work on the property—put in some rooms, doors, windows, furniture, electricity, water, toilets—but apart from that he seemed optimistic about the guesthouse, though he didn't seem so sure that his sister could cope, or the dogs.

Back downstairs, I found the courage to ask Sakina if I could take some photographs. There was a slight nod of coyness; yes, I would be allowed. She offered me an apple, and then another one when I had gobbled down the first. There was no sign of any other food for Cyrus and Sakina (or of a kitchen), so I did not take a second apple. I did take a series of photos of Sakina standing in front of the entrance arch to Malcha Mahal. She had stopped trying to be intimidating and extraordinary; she was almost posing for the camera. She waved, slightly embarrassed, as we left. We walked back through the forest towards the car, a jackal casually strolling alongside the road. I was left thinking about the things I wished I'd said, *l'esprit d'escalier*. I wished I'd told Sakina that being ordinary might not be such a sin after all, and that in a city of fifteen million people it is quite hard to be other than ordinary, even for those of us who feel we're different. And most of all, I wanted to suggest that the struggle to avoid ordinariness might just drive you mad. I do not suppose she would have heard me out.

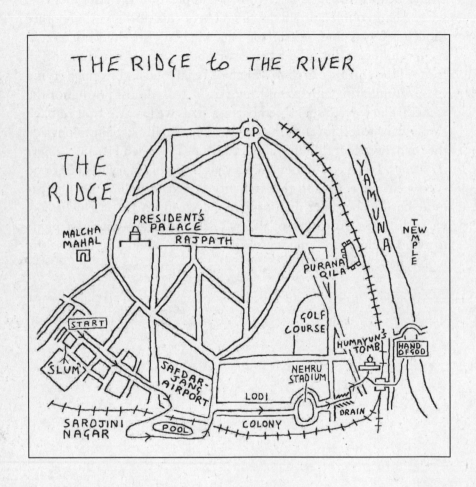

Chapter Seven: *In which the Author rediscovers Tintin, prepares for the Olympics and locates the Hand of God*

VIVEKANANDA CAMP IS an 'unauthorized settlement' sandwiched between a series of high walls marking the territory of the American Embassy School, the British School, the Russian Trade Mission, and the Austrian, Swiss and Swedish Embassies. About three hundred families live here on a plot of land slightly smaller than a full-sized baseball diamond. Its proximity to the Delhi of the diplomats has made it a place of interest to foreign visitors who wish to get a sense of 'real India'. And indeed here are outdoor water pumps; huts with tarpaulin sheet roofs; large families living, cooking, eating, sleeping, giving birth, having sex and dying in single-room homes. It is, like many slums, very well looked after by its inhabitants, clean and spruce, with neat piles of sorted rubbish—even if the area around has been used as a dump. At the back of the settlement I find an unexpected building, a single-storey brick hut with three yellow steel squares padlocked to its outer wall—as if Matisse had been asked to decorate a Delhi slum. Closer up I find a metal plaque, glinting in the midday sun, declaring this strange apparition to be a 'Free Computer Kiosk For Children', and in minuscule writing below, that the kiosk was 'supported' by the American Embassy School and

the American Women's Association of Delhi. One of the yellow squares had been prised loose and I could just make out the screen and keyboard of a computer, securely welded to the window frame.

I realized that I had come across three 'hole-in-the-wall' computers. I had read about these, and their evangelical inventors. They were aimed at providing poor children with access to computers, bridging 'the digital divide' with a downmarket, open-air cybercafé. I asked an old man smoking a hookah beside the hut why the computers were padlocked. 'Broken. Someone tried to steal one of them. Look. It's loose.' He got up, stiff-limbed, and shook the yellow cover of the computer nearest to him. 'But they didn't get anything.' The red metal cage had defeated the thief.

I introduce myself to a man who has a perfect view of the hole-in-the-wall computers from his bed. Sushil is normally an office assistant, a peon[1], but an encounter with an autorickshaw has left him with a broken leg and he's been bedridden for six weeks. He stays in a room only a little larger than a ping-pong table, with his brother, his sister-in-law and three children, a large television set and hi-fi and a small cooking range. He tells me that the computers were very popular with the children, they loved playing games on them, but there's no guard or supervisor, and some kids from outside had vandalized the kiosk. It hasn't been working for more than a week, and no one knew when it would be reopened; apparently someone from the American Embassy School had the keys to the padlock. He told me proudly how the President of Afghanistan, Hamid Karzai, had been a recent visitor to the kiosk[2]. There is, in every person I speak to here, an almost embarrassed pride in the success of this small community drawn from all over the country and from several religions. They are the elite of slum-dwellers, and they know it. The diplomatic community depends on them for cleaners, drivers, gardeners and cooks and in return they get designer-label cast-offs, above average salaries, VIP visitors and (by Delhi standards) a good supply of electricity. The day I was there the American Embassy School was paying for a street party for the kids, and (normally)

---

[1] Peon—in Indian English a widely used word for office boy or assistant, originally from a Portuguese word meaning footman or pedestrian. It is cognate with the English word 'pawn'—when it has the meaning of a minor but numerous chess piece.

[2] Vivekananda Camp has had visits from two Presidents—Karzai of Afghanistan and Wolfowitz of the World Bank, both of them parachuted into office by President George Bush. They came, separately, to Vivekananda to be shown the hole-in-the-wall computers. A third visitor was a possible future President—the Democratic Governor of Virginia, Mark Warner, the insiders' tip for the 2012 US elections.

those children have regular free access to the computer kiosk[3]. But there is no running water in the houses, there are no private toilets, and the population per square foot of floor space is as high as anywhere in the city.

All around is Delhi at its most sparse. The Ridge, empty except for jackals and peacocks and the princely siblings; Chanakyapuri, home to a few disoriented diplomats and deserted after dusk; to the east, Nehru Park, with landscaped lawns where foreigners jog and sweat off their party paunches; a nine-hole golf course, and a polo ground—only used in season. Beyond that is Delhi's least-visited large open space, a huge expanse of tarmac and grass that is going to seed, and the scene of two dramatically different airport accidents.

It was as Willingdon Airport that this tract of land entered my childhood consciousness. I was a youthful admirer of the twentieth century's most famous Belgian: Tintin, a teenage journalist with a quiff[4], whose cartoon escapades I can still recall in embarrassingly accurate detail. Near the start of *Tintin in Tibet*, the most visually evocative of all his adventures, the eponymous hack, accompanied by his dog Snowy and his alcoholic, blaspheming collaborator, Captain Haddock, spends three eventful hours in Delhi. And they nearly miss their flight from Willingdon airport to Nepal. They sprint desperately across the runway towards the Air India plane, but Haddock, blinded by a

---

[3] A week later two of the three computers were working again. And groups of extremely excited children had gathered around them—one of them was drawing a picture of a European style house—front door, four windows, chimney stack, fenced flower garden and wicker gate. The other group were playing 'Who wants to be a millionaire?'—and kept getting stuck on the second question.

[4] I like to think that Tintin inspired me to become a journalist, although he never seemed troubled by deadlines and demanding editors. Tintin's creator Hergé never travelled to Delhi, as is obvious from the rather unlikely route that Tintin took through the city. They start at the international airport and end at Willingdon and travel by taxi, foot and on the back of cow via the Qutb Minar, Red Fort and Tughlaqabad, inscribing a zigzag across the face of Delhi, This has been interpreted as a piece of ambulant signmaking. See tintinologist.org. It is more likely that Hergé did not use a map, or did not realize that his picture of Ghiyasuddin Tughlaq's tomb (which he did not name, unlike the other places) was so obviously recognizable. He did correct the spelling mistakes in the first French-language edition, where he wrote Dehli and Ghandi, but didn't correct other errors such as the maroon-coloured taxi with a West Bengal number-plate. Tintin did make two other visits to India, in *The Blue Lotus* and *The Cigars of the Pharaoh*, to the fictional princely state of Gaipajama (cow's pyjamas).

149

Three hours have passed ...

We still haven't seen the Jama Masjid and the Rajghat, the memorial to Mahatma Gandhi ...

Yes, but aren't you forgetting the time?

INDIA GUIDE to DELHI

mote, runs up the wrong airplane staircase, and plunges to the tarmac. He is—and here we enter the realms of airline fantasy—still allowed to board the plane. An Air India stewardess patches up his wounds with sticking plasters as the flight leaves Willingdon for the Himalayas and a series of perilous adventures with an abominable snowman, levitating Tibetan monks, and a lost Chinese boy called Chang.

On a summer's day in 1980, twenty years after the publication of *Tintin in Tibet*, the second accident happened. It was the start of a family tragedy, a story scarcely more credible than one of Tintin's escapades. By then renamed Safdarjang, after the nearby tomb of an eighteenth-century potentate, and no longer a commercial airport, it became forever linked with an event that some people believe changed the course of Indian history. Sanjay Gandhi, 33 years old, amateur pilot, would-be dictator and heir apparent to Prime Minister Indira Gandhi, was flying a stunt plane from the Delhi Flying Club at Safdarjang—he and his co-pilot plunged to earth and were killed on impact[6]. Sanjay Gandhi's mantle was taken by Rajiv, his older, gentler brother, a professional pilot with Indian Airlines. Within a dozen years, Sanjay's mother and brother had also died violently.

After the September 11 attacks on New York, Safdarjang airport was closed to private aircraft. The prime minister's helicopter occasionally uses the airstrip and it remains a high-security zone. But it all has a sleepy air, a contrast with the hurried hubbub of the airport I had imagined; drainage ditches were being cleaned, small-time farmers had planted crops near the approach road, a policeman slept in a sentry hut, workmen were playing cards. I accidentally wandered through a high-security zone without being stopped. When I attempted to leave by another exit there was a brief embarrassed commotion as a senior police officer attempted to find out who had let me through.

Safdarjang airport is still the official home of the Delhi Flying Club but its members have to drive to Karnal, more than two-and-a-half hours away, to fly a plane.

'We still do theory classes here,' I was informed by Narender, the keen-to-please receptionist, who clearly has to spend a lot of time apologizing to would-be aviators.

'And you can sit in a plane in the hangar, and see the controls—but it is strictly forbidden to take the plane onto the runway.'

'You can't be getting many new members.'

He shrugged, disconsolately, glancing in the direction of the empty clubrooms. 'What to do?'

I heard screeching sirens from the direction of the runway and looked out to see two fire engines racing each other.

'They are bored. They have nothing else to do. Sometimes a VIP lands but it's very quiet most of the time. Very quiet. I don't think there's much of a future here.'

Narender didn't know it, but the real estate sharks are circling. The land occupied by this non-airport is enormously valuable, and there aren't many modern multi-storey air-conditioned shopping malls in this part of Delhi.

But there is no shortage of places to shop in affluent South Delhi.

---

[6] Sanjay Gandhi played a leading, though unofficial, role in ruling India during the Emergency period of the mid-1970s. Indira Gandhi's cousin BK Nehru, who was also a diplomat and civil servant, later said Sanjay's death may have been 'the best thing that could happen to India'.

A shopper's dream, I was told the other day by an expert in such matters. And just to the south of Safdarjang airport is Sarojini Nagar market, the professional shopper's preferred destination for both price and range. For saris and pickpockets, I am also advised, it is unsurpassed. The market is set in a residential neighbourhood, purpose-built for low-ranking white-collar government workers, and consists of a series of street stalls, small hole-in-the-wall shops, and some larger neon-lit brightly decorated air-conditioned stores. There are second-hand snow-suits for children, export-quality shirts rejected because of a misaligned button, a special offer on Fair and Handsome, a new face cream for men that promises to make your skin less dark[7].

On 29 October 2005, three days before Diwali, and six days before Eid, when the markets are at their busiest, a bomb went off next to a juice stall in Sarojini Nagar market, killing 43 people and maiming many more. I asked one T-shirt seller about the explosion. At first, he was monosyllabically taciturn. Then suddenly, as if a switch had been flicked, he became lyrically intense, telling me of flames and dust and shards of metal flying through the air, of a woman on fire, of bits of paper falling to the ground and strange split-seconds of silence interrupted by screams. He then suddenly fell silent himself and shuddered, as if shaking off the demons of the past. Now everything's normal, he told me, almost too quickly, and turned dull-eyed to a paying customer. I looked around. There is no memorial, no remembrance of Delhi's most deadly terrorist attack[8]; the juice stall has been rebuilt, and there is nothing to be seen, but a scoured roughness to the brick pavement where the bomb exploded.

I drift through the rest of Sarojini Nagar, along a road that runs parallel to Delhi's under-used circular railway—which has just 11 passenger trains a day, but is kept busy by freight traffic, and past a community centre belonging to the 'Slum Wing' of the Municipal

[7] A follow-up product to the controversial, extremely popular face cream for women, Fair and Lovely. The 'fairness cream' business in India in 2005 was worth about nine billion rupees, or two hundred million US dollars.

[8] A few minutes before the Sarojini Nagar bomb, a similar explosion in Paharganj killed at least 16 people. In 1996 about 25 people died in an explosion in Lajpat Nagar in Delhi. In 2001, 12 people were killed in an attack on Parliament. Further bombings in September 2008 killed at least 24 people. According to the Indian authorities, Islamic militants with possible Pakistani backing, were responsible for all these incidents.

Corporation, and reach the 'Sanjay Gandhi Lake-Park'. Opened in 1982 on the second anniversary of his death, by his brother, Rajiv, the Lake-Park has a Dada-esque quality to it. The 'Lake' part of the memorial, a curvaceously serpentine pool, lined with blue tiles, is empty and as dry as a desert, while the 'Park' part of the memorial is very wet; in fact the lawns are totally sodden, as if some giant watering-can robot had got its wires crossed. The only positive aspect to all this is that an impressively large puddle is probably extensive enough to prevent any children from reaching a damaged slide which has a jagged hole the size of a child's fist in its fibreglass structure, with a frayed edge sharp enough to remove a chunk of flesh from a sliding toddler. There is also a separate outdoor swimming-pool hidden behind high walls, with an eleven-point list of rules and regulations; Point 10 (d) says: 'Spitting and flowing nose in the pool is strictly prohibited.' The pool however is closed for repairs, and, I am told by a glum watchman, is as dry as the lake.

Beyond and above the Lake-Park is one of Delhi's first flyovers, with a magnificent wide-angle view over the gloomy emptiness of Safdarjung airport. On the other side of the flyover are civil aviation ministry offices and a small Shia enclave known as Karbala—after the Iraqi city where, in the seventh century, the Prophet Mohammed's grandson Hussein was killed. Two small eighteenth-century mosques contain relics of his parents, Ali and Fatima: the impression of a single footprint in marble for the Prophet's son-in-law, and a circular grindstone for his daughter. For grinding wheat, I was told by my self-appointed guide. Until the 1940s this area was surrounded by jungle, but at the time of partition in 1947 Hindu refugees from Pakistan were allotted land around the enclave. Now there are only eight Shia families left. One man told me that Hindus have encroached on religious land, and that they were trying to get it back. But he didn't hold out much hope. There were no inter-communal problems here, he said, but after a moment's thought, added that the other residents liked to pretend that Karbala didn't exist. 'We are invisible to them.'

This part of the Indian capital has a series of housing estates that were built for government workers in the middle of the last century, a crescent of utilitarian colonies that curve around what was then the southern border of Delhi. There are no curves to be seen inside the estates, however, and most of them have been laid out in grid

153

formation with lettered and numbered street names. They reflect the carefully graduated hierarchy of the Indian civil service, and the need to house those cohorts of low-ranking white-collar workers for which the Indian bureaucracy is infamous. Originally, there were eight types of housing, numbered I-VIII, (sweepers will normally live in Type-1 toilet-less cubby-holes, while the only a few of the most senior civil servants—and government ministers—live in Type-VIII bungalows), but the middle types have been subdivided, and there are now 11 official gradations, and a total of seventeen semi-official ones. Normally a promotion will mean a slightly bigger home in a marginally grander location[9]. All government servants are entitled to accommodation, and as the bureaucracy grew, so did the number of low-cost, low-density housing projects—in way that had a major impact on the way Delhi grew so rapidly southwards in the years after independence.

The majority of these government estates are faceless and run-down, and often reviled by their inhabitants and visitors. But they

do also have their aficionados. Lodi Colony, for instance, just beyond Karbala, has been the unlikely subject of a 2001 essay-portrait by Ranjana Sengupta. It is a persuasive essay—in which she savages those who are only interested in Delhi's past, and forcefully reminds us that 'somewhere between the exotic and the kitsch is real Delhi'. And Lodi Colony, her case study, is, she says, 'unlike Delhi's more

[9] For the delightfully byzantine rules governing the allotment and use of official accommodation see http://estates.nic.in/ Civil servants do not pay rent, but there is instead a small licence fee, up to a maximum of 10 per cent of income. In 2007, the Estates Department of the Ministry of Urban Development and Poverty Alleviation was responsible for 63,745 residences in Delhi. Among changes introduced recently was one that reduced the percentage of the cost that allottees had to pay for converting an Indian-style WC to a European style WC from one hundred per cent to ten per cent. An extraordinary amount of detailed information about the operations of the Indian administrative service and the careers of senior Indian civil servants is openly available on the Internet—if one is able to decipher the Edwardian bureaucratic jargon that is still in wide use.

celebrated locations, still alive and kicking.' And she has a point: this under-loved housing estate, frayed at the edges, has a seductive sense of serenity and permanence and space, with little green courtyards, washing lines, and disassembled motor-bikes. None of the buildings are higher than three storeys and all of the flats are built to the same basic specification; but the estate is full of enough functionless arches and minor design peccadilloes to make it a lot more architecturally intriguing than its sister estates. But this is not the future, and Lodi Colony is not really 'kicking'. Delhi no longer feels like the civil servant city it once was, and Lodi Colony is beginning to feel like just another monolithic souvenir of one of Delhi's previous incarnations.

It's possible to date Delhi's emergence into modernity to 1982. This was the year of the Asian Games, which was the spur to the construction of many of the city's flyovers and five-star hotels. And the centrepiece of the Games was the Nehru stadium, built between three minor medieval tombs to the east of Lodi Colony. The stadium is Delhi's largest, with a capacity of seventy-five thousand, but it has rarely seen a capacity crowd, and is, in practice, outranked by the National Stadium at the end of Rajpath, and by the cricket Valhalla at the Kotla ground. The list of tenants outside the Nehru stadium betrays the obscurity or unexpectedness of some of the activities within. It is home to the Wushu Association of India, the National Project for the Eradication of Rinderpest, Fibcom (India), and the

National Hydrogen Energy Board (Ministry for Non-Conventional Energy Sources). I wandered around the stadium, followed by an affable Sikh watchman in a turquoise turban. The all-weather russet track had seen better days and more serious runners. I briefly ran at full pace, breasting the finishing line as if I had won the 100 metres at the Olympics that Delhi hopes to hold in 2020. As I slowed, pumping the

air with my fist, I caught my left foot on the misaligned metal of the track. I jarred my good knee, and came to a sudden halt. I fell to the track and rolled up my trouser leg, looking, with the excitement of a hypochondriac, for signs of swelling.

The watchman knelt beside me, and silently and studiously examined my knee, before helping me back to my feet. 'I'm Milkha Singh,' I told him, and he laughed. I had guessed the name of his hero, 'the Flying Sikh' who came fourth in the 400 metres at the 1960 Rome Olympics—still the best performance by an Indian track and field athlete[10]. I hobbled out of the stadium—scrambling over a barbed-wire fence into a car park and on past the SCOPE Complex, a ten-storey modern home to dozens of state-owned enterprises, hosting a conference on 'The Dissemination of Trenchless Technology', and reached an oppressively pungent open sewer, housing Delhi's most insanitary slum.

On the south side of what is officially the Khushak drain, a long, narrow park with tall trees protects the well-heeled neighbourhood of Jangpura from the worst of the sights and smells of Delhi shit that flows sluggishly past its homes. The contrast with the other bank of the sewer is dramatic. For on the north side, garishly advertised by its multicoloured polythene roofing sheets, is a settlement of one thousand Muslim families, some of whom actually live on the bed of the sewer. The drain is about twenty metres wide, and so, except during the monsoon when the area is flooded, it is possible to stay in temporary structures built of wood and polythene without faeces actually floating in while you sleep. During the monsoon, it is a lot less sanitary, and the residents of this unauthorized settlement, Punj Peeran, will cram into the huts of people staying slightly higher up the sewer bank. But on the fresh December morning when I passed through, the black stream of sewage was at its narrowest, only three metres wide. Some women were using grassed-over parts of the sewer-bed to sort scraps of coloured fabric for recycling and resale. As I walked up to them I felt the ground give beneath my feet. Wetness seeped into my left

[10] PT Usha fans will dispute this point. She missed out on a medal in the 400 hurdles at Los Angeles in 1984 by only 0.01 seconds, but Milkha Singh in getting his fourth place, also managed to go faster than the old world record.

shoe. I had stepped into a minor tributary of the sewer. I cursed. A young man gave me a wry smile, and making his knowledgeable way from tussock to tussock, he guided me to dry land. Atiq was unusually welcoming, even by Delhi standards. He told me that he'd never seen a foreigner in Punj Peeran before. He introduced me proudly, as his new friend, to a growing crowd of fellow residents.

Atiq was full of unexpected contentment. From a distance, Punj Peeran looked like an inner circle of hell. Close up, it didn't look much better. But Atiq told me that things had improved a lot, and they wouldn't want to move. He had part-time work nearby as a builder. The police had stopped harassing them, demanding money for not evicting them, or accusing them of being illegal immigrants and threatening them with deportation. There was usually water once a day, early in the morning, from a single pipe that ran the length of the settlement—and when there wasn't, they'd make a hole in the nearby over-ground water-main and place buckets under the leak. They had a more dangerous solution to their electricity problems. No one would give them a connection, so they just took it, by stringing an electric cable from the pylons supplying Jangpura on the other side of the sewer[11]. And yes, most of the children went to school, but the classes were a bit crowded. There is a large permanent community of Muslims in nearby Nizamuddin and they felt reasonably safe. The settlement had been there for at least fifteen years, and while this is quite the most pitiable of places, Atiq did not want pity.

I asked him where the people in Punj Peeran came from and Atiq's mood changed suddenly. He became vague and evasive and defensive. 'We come from here and there, everywhere'. I asked him whether they were all Bengali-speakers. 'Yes, we are . . . most of us. But we're from Kolkata, from Assam, from Bihar . . . we may be Bengalis but we are not', he insisted without prompting and with an embarrassed gleam in his eye, 'from Bangladesh'. This is where they almost certainly do come from. But to admit to being Bangladeshi in Delhi would be to risk deportation as an illegal migrant.[12] In the 1990s,

[11] This practice, known as 'hooking', is widely used in Delhi.
[12] Bengali is the main language of Bangladesh, the Indian state of West Bengal and an important language in several other Indian states. Bengali accents differ

there were numerous attempts to round up suspected Bangladeshis, who were then transported more than one thousand kilometres to the border and 'pushed' by the security forces across the unfenced border. Most of them were then, more willingly, pushed back by Bangladesh, who said they were Indians. No one knows how many Bangladeshis there are in Delhi, and there's no easy way of distinguishing them from Indian Bengalis[13].

The sewer veers off southwards on a long detour before dumping its untreated contents into the Yamuna river. But I would reach the river much more quickly by following my spiral through Nizamuddin, home to Delhi syncretism in the form of a Muslim shrine visited by people of all religions. Nizamuddin was also my first home in Delhi, and a source of excellent kebabs, rumali rotis and Sufi music. But for the first time, the geometric growth of my spiral meant that I was going to miss out on visiting somewhere in Delhi that I knew and loved. I vacillated. I remembered my many afternoon wanders around that most gorgeous of Mughal monuments, the impossibly perfect tomb of the Emperor Humayun. (I would never have such feelings for that flashy jewel-encrusted latecomer, the Taj Mahal) In those days I disliked Delhi, and Humayun's Tomb was my place of consolation and escape. I was once ill for two months, and I measured my gradual improvement with longer and longer walks inside the labyrinthine tomb complex. I had sworn not to write about Delhi as if the past were more important than the present, as so many had done before me. But Humayun's Tomb is my only place of nostalgia in Delhi and so I made the detour.

Humayun's Tomb had changed and so had I. In truth, I had occasionally been back since my illness, usually ferrying first-time visitors around the sights of Delhi. I would take photographs and my sense of the place was mediated through my camera lens, and the

---

markedly and most Indian Bengalis say they can tell a Bangladeshi by their accent. However, many Hindu Bengali families actually migrated to Delhi at the time of partition from what is now Bangladesh, and was then East Pakistan. In the social hierarchy of Delhi, illegal Muslim Bangladeshi migrants are at the bottom. And yet more still come and their story remains largely untold, in part because they are too terrified to own up to their country of origin.

[13] The settlement at Punj Peeran 'disappeared' in 2007. There was a fire, possibly started deliberately, and the residents of the settlement were moved out.

opinions of my companions. I'd say unthinkingly that the restoration of the wildly overgrown Mughal gardens and the reconstruction of its hydraulically-complex water system were marvellous things. Alone, I had to look at it through my own eyes. The place is now busy, full of tourists, clean and tidy, with nicely mowed lawns—and yet

when I saw it like this I became inconsolable, bereft. I could feel my brow furl in recognition of my own irrationality and bewilderment. It had been my secret special place, now it is for everyone. It was wild, and now it is pretty. 'As good as new', I imagined someone telling me. I longed to see it again as I remembered it. But that is nostalgia. And now Humayun's Tomb, restored and pristine, is part of a confident new international city, provisionally ranked, after the Red Fort, at number two on most tourists' sightseeing list.

It is one of the many paradoxes of this prospective candidate for the world's largest urban conglomeration in the world that it is very green. Delhi has not only the vast unvisited forests of the Ridge, but also a large agricultural enclave. Beyond Nizamuddin, beyond Humayun's Tomb, across the Ring Road, and on the other side of a mysterious mountain of newly excavated mud, are fields of green. This is rural Delhi, fertile farmland on the floodplain of the Yamuna river—a great swathe of flatland that splits the city into two unequal parts, separating the smaller eastern part of the city, (known as trans-Yamuna) from the rest of the metropolis. Here farmers, in their own little universe, rent their fields from the Delhi authorities, or occupy it until someone bothers to throw them off—and they grow more than twenty different crops. I was able to vanish into a grove of sugarcane, buy some ruby-red carrots that I pulled from the ground, and sit talking to a farmer in a field of wheat, who then presented me with a liquorice-purple baby aubergine so shiny that I could see on its surface the reflection of a small shaving cut on my upper lip. This is not the Delhi I am used to. There are no permanent buildings allowed here, just small temporary wooden shacks, with the city skyline in the mid-distance. One farmer, Ram Lal, told me how his younger son is doing a computer studies course at a Delhi college, and his other son works with him in the fields and they all stay in one room in a small village that is at the foot of the nearest bridge. His wife and daughters stay in their original village some 200 kilometres away, where the three men return once a year during the rains. This land is cheap to rent, but it's not worth improving because, he says, one day soon, the city will take it over. He points to the massive mound of mud. 'That's from the Metro, they dug it out of Connaught Place. And next to it they're building a power station. And look at that.' He pointed in the distance across the river. 'That's the new temple'. And there in the far distance I could just make out, through a dusty haze, the faraway curves and pinnacles of the Akshardham temple complex, Delhi's most controversial new building. I meandered on down to the river bank past more sugarcane fields, guided by a gentle whiff of ordure.

The Yamuna river is Delhi's shameful, rancid secret. This city would not exist but for the river, and for most of its thousand-year history the Yamuna has played a major role as a source of water and a means of transport. But it has now become one of the world's largest open sewers, with more than two billion litres of untreated household and industrial waste flowing into it every day. In the other great inland cities of the world—Paris, London, Vienna, Cairo, Moscow—the river is the centre of urban life, it is the most important landmark, its banks are lined with many of the city's most impressive buildings. In Delhi, I've come across people living here for years who say they've never seen the Yamuna. In fact, they probably *have*, while crossing to trans-Yamuna by bridge, but never realized that this huge noxious drain was Delhi's sacred and ancient river. In Delhi, it is a struggle even to get near the river, and you may regret it when you do. From close up, it is as black as pitch, with a grey-green scum where its viscose waters lap stodgily against the river bank, and a fog of minuscule midges flutter and hover above the filth. But with a little imagination, and if you don't look too close, and while the wind is blowing eastwards, my stroll along the Yamuna seems rather beautiful, and the place seems, momentarily, to have been transformed into an unlikely pre-urban pastoral idyll. But the moment the wind changed direction, the stench of shit became hard to stomach. The farmers did not seem to mind. One of them was using a small diesel pump to bring water from the Yamuna to his field. I asked him if the water wouldn't poison his crops. 'Not at all,' he said, 'it's a very good fertilizer—as long it's mixed with fresh water from the bore-well.'

Apart from midges and crows, and the gently fading throb of the diesel engine all is quiet. There are no ferry boats, no fishermen, and clearly swimming would be suicidal. There used to be 'a bridge of boats' just south of here, a kind of pontoon crossing, still marked on my 2001 map. But that was taken apart three years ago and I'd have to walk over the nearest iron-and-concrete road bridge half a mile upstream. And so I wandered along the bank looking into the blackened waters for signs of life—and of death.

I had been told to keep an eye out for half-burnt human corpses floating down the river or caught up in the reeds. Most Hindus burn the bodies of the dead before immersing the ashes, but for some the cost of sufficient wood is too much and the bodies are dispatched into the river without having been fully burned. I scoured the water and the bank—relieved not to see a corpse, and not quite sure why I had been so keen to see one. I trundled on towards the bridge, paying less attention to the river banks, trying to intimidate, physically and verbally, my newly broken digital camera into showing signs of life. I looked up, and saw something in the reeds that seemed to be pointing across the river at the new temple. Then, I realized just what I had seen and froze, squeamishly stunned to have actually found what I had been looking for. I had spotted a disembodied arm in the bullrushes. It was tawny brown and standing up as if in imitation of the Statue of Liberty or the Lady of the Lake. There was something wrong, though. I could not work out how it had become upright—someone must have placed it there. But that seemed too macabre. And how did it become that colour, and why were its fingers so indistinct and tightly clenched? I edged closer, pulling up a long branch, almost my height, which had been

161

planted in the mud as a field-marker. I poked at the arm and to my consternation the end of the branch slid without resistance into the flesh and out through the other side. I pulled the branch back and swung it through the air and the hand broke off. And I knew. It was the hand of God, made of straw. It was nothing more than an effigy of a Hindu deity, one of thousands brought down to the river banks at religious festivals. I laughed, and wondered what I might have done if I had found a real arm.

A Seventh Intermission

'DELHI, YOU SEE . . .' a young woman informed me the other day, '. . . . is a brutal city.' She paused, her fists curled up with rage and frustration. 'Women . . .' she spat the word, '. . . are nothing here.' We were sitting at adjacent computer terminals at a Delhi cyber-café. She had been pawed by a fellow bus traveller while on her way to work. For Indian women who have grown up in most other parts of the country, Delhi is a shock. Men stare carnivorously at women on public transport. Harsh or angry words are rarely enough to break those stares. And then there is the touching. In crowded places, men will rub their bodies against women, pinching and groping at leisure. But many of them also consider themselves the guardians of female morality. Men will hiss at women who they consider underdressed. Female legs are rarely to be seen in Delhi, although navels, thanks to the sari, are widely visible.

The local Delhi pages of the newspapers are full of eve-teasings, molestations, rapes, forced marriages and dowry-deaths. Women in this society are of distinctly lower value. And do not think this is for lack of role models. The most powerful of all India's prime ministers, Indira Gandhi, lived in Delhi for most of her life. As I write, the most influential figure in Indian politics is Indira's daughter-in-law Sonia, much more powerful than the (male) prime minister she nominated. And Delhi's chief minister for more than nine years, Sheila Dikshit, the person behind many of the recent improvements this city has seen, is also a woman.

But it is the story of the 'missing girls' that demonstrates the true value that many Delhi-ites, male and female, place on women. Government statistics reveal that every year in Delhi more than 24,000 foetuses are aborted, for the simple reason that they are girls. The sex ratio has become seriously skewed. For every one thousand boys who are born in Delhi, there are less than 820 new-born girls[1].

---

[1] Municipal Corporation of Delhi figures for the first six months of 2004 showed the sex ratio at birth had dipped to 819. In fact, there is not an identical biological chance of a boy or girl being born. The 'normal' ratio at birth is about 955 girls to 1000 boys.

Many have been surprised to discover that the sex-ratio is even more unbalanced in the affluent parts of the city. This is because modern technology, in the form of amniocentesis and ultrasound, allows the pre-natal identification of girl babies and give easy access to female foeticide for the well-off. All of this is illegal, of course, but notoriously hard to control. Every ante-natal and abortion clinic in Delhi is supposed to have a large notice declaring that 'Here pre-natal sex determination (boy or girl before birth) is not done. It is a punishable act.' But prosecutions are very rare.

The consequences of this may be enormous. Political scientists and psychologists have warned of the emergence of an underclass of tens of millions of 'surplus' males in India and China who have little prospects of finding a life partner, and who, it is claimed, will turn to crime and militaristic nationalism[2]. Some economists argue that as women become scarcer and therefore more valuable, female foeticide will stop. There are already tales of Delhi men buying brides from other parts of India, replacing the customary (but illegal) dowry with a bride-price. But in all this young women remain commodities. An attempt has been made by the Delhi government to monetize the different values placed on boy and girls. Five thousand rupees will now be deposited in a bank account in the name of each new-born girl—but it can only be encashed (with interest), eighteen years later, if the girl has had at least ten years of education. It's a genuine and imaginative attempt to tackle several importance issues at once, including high female infant mortality and high levels of female illiteracy. But given that an abortion will often cost more than five thousand rupees, this measure seems unlikely to act as a major disincentive to female foeticide.

There are other, more radical ways to encourage serious debate about the status and image of women. A bisexual Scottish-American performance artist and self-proclaimed 'drag king' came to Delhi recently. And one Tuesday evening in South Delhi, in the tiny back room of the Khoj arts centre, over tea and samosas, Diane Torr described her work to a small group of gob-smacked Delhiwallahs. Ms Torr first presented a slide-show of photographs; a performance

[2] See Valerie Hudson and Andrea den Boer, *Bare Branches: The Security Implications of Asia's Surplus Male Population*, MIT Press 2005.

artist with snakes crawling over her naked body; a woman who had strapped a huge green plastic clitoris around her pelvis. She then told us about a fellow performer whose stage act consisted of putting yams up her own backside. Fortunately there was no photograph of the yam-woman, and we were never told just what she'd been attempting to achieve or illustrate with her yams[3]. Diane Torr then showed a short film about her women-only drag-king workshops in which she teaches women how to become men. She shows them how to bind their breasts, glue on a false moustache, insert and position a flaccid penis created from a tubular bandage stuffed with cotton wool, before putting on male clothing. But more important, her students learn to behave like men—eating with their mouths wide open, the food spilling out; sitting with their legs splayed out as if the hugeness of their genitalia prevented their knees from touching; and staring in a shameless and lascivious manner. The aim is that that they go out in public and experience the public side of what it is to be like a man for a day, or an hour, and 'assume the sense of privilege and entitlement that goes along with the male gender.' At the end she asked the glassy-eyed audience for questions. There were none. Female emancipation has a long way to go in the Indian capital.

[3] An Internet search for yam + anus reveals that the yam-woman was American performance artist, Karen Finley. Her purpose was to illustrate the act of anal rape. The yam was not raw, but soft and came from a can.

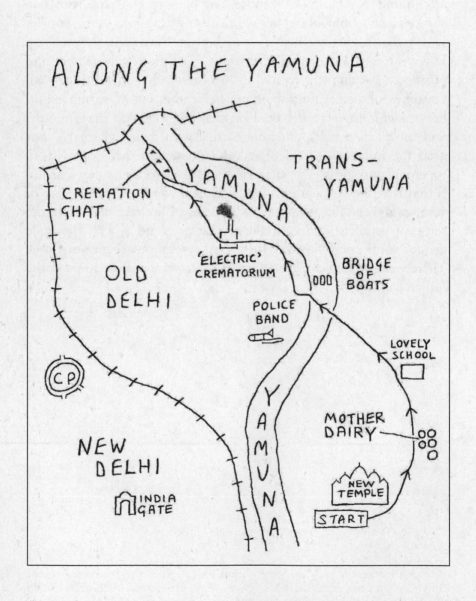

Chapter Eight: In which the Author is accused of queue-jumping, delivers a discourse on Mozart and considers the best way of disposing of a dead body

THE EXTREMELY CONSPICUOUS Akshardham temple complex is in the process of becoming one of the city's most distinctive landmarks. Its fortress-like walls, and its cluster of off-white domes, are visible from incoming aircraft, and from the high-rises of central Delhi. It has been hailed as a kind of Hindu Disneyland, a place of fun and pilgrimage. Opened in November 2005, it also quickly became a place of hyperbole—the Eighth Wonder of the World, according to some of its own publicity literature. The temple became controversial for two reasons. It was, for a while, a symbol of the resurgent Hindu chauvinism whose supporters were then in power in India—and it was the first large-scale post-millennial encroachment on the farmlands of the Yamuna floodplain[1].

[1] Until 2004, the mainly Hindu BJP was at the head of a coalition government in India, which gave its blessing to a programme of temple-building. But by the time Akshardham was completed a Congress government was in power; and the main guests at the opening ceremony were a Muslim (President Abdul Kalam) and a Sikh (Prime Minister Manmohan Singh). There was considerable litigation in relation to temple in the early years of the millennium, with accusations that it violated land-use regulations, and would be environmentally damaging. The Supreme Court finally ruled in the temple's favour in early 2005.

The security is very tight; no phones, cameras or tiffin boxes. I was asked to remove my belt and wallet for separate inspection, and my copy of a biography of Jimi Hendrix was carefully examined and refused entry. 'No books' was the impromptu explanation. It wasn't worth arguing. Akshardham's sister temple in the state of Gujarat was attacked by gunmen in 2002, for reasons that remain unclear, and more than thirty people were killed. The visitor is welcomed by a large signboard announcing the temple's first attraction: 'An arena of Ten Gates, symbolising the Ten Directions. May Goodness and Auspiciousness flow into us from all Directions.' I was still a little peeved by the confiscation of my Hendrix and decided that I would pass through each gate as a way of bringing me a bit of inner peace. As I approached, I realized that this would mean getting very wet. In an impressive display of hydrotechnics, each intricately carved gate had been transformed into a shimmying curtain of flowing water. I poked my finger into the curtain, and got a firm spray of water in my face. I moved to the next signboard, from which the words INCREDIBLE and AMAZING screamed out at passing visitors. Akshardham does not undersell itself. 'Incredible', I read, were '148 lifelike stone elephants each weighing three tons' and 'Amazing' were 'authentic stone carvings hand-carved by 11,000 craftsmen and volunteers offering 300 million man-hours of service.'

The intricate interior of the main temple is carved out of imported Italian marble and its ceiling shows an attention to detail that is visually stunning and awesomely intricate, and made me feel a little giddy. The Hindu gods around the walls however are slightly less impressive, perhaps because one can examine them close-up, and there seem be a few too many malformed toes and visible slips of the chisel (were these the work of the volunteer hand-carvers?) At the heart of the temple is a lusciously golden statue of

Swaminarayan[2] the nineteenth-century man-god in whose name Akshardham was constructed. The exterior includes (as promised) 148 stone-carved statues of half-sized elephants protruding from and rubbing against a wall-frieze. Each elephant is different, with an array of accompanying gods, animals and humans, including a half-size photographer using a 1960s-style SLR camera, with a long zoom—all chiselled out of sandstone.

The main attractions, though, are not the temple, or the elephant carvings, or the vegetarian snacks, or the 108 water spouts, or the lotus garden, or even the musical fountains, but the three-in-one high-tech religio-tainment variety performances to which the southern part of the temple complex is dedicated. First, I discovered, were the 'diorama animatronics' in the Hall of Values. I didn't quite know what to expect. We were made to wait for forty minutes, in a snaking queue of increasingly agitated Swaminarayan devotees—and me—who united to drive back a group of teenage queue-jumpers. I felt like giving up, and began chatting disconsolately to a group of American Gujaratis who were making their first trip to Delhi, and were unhappy about the lack of sidewalks. I regretted the confiscation of my Hendrix and I stared into space, trying to imagine what Gandhi might have made of this temple. Finally, we were led inside and the mysteries of diorama animatronics were revealed. In fifteen separate rooms—we were witness to 3-D theatrical episodes from the life of Swaminarayan, in which the hero and some of his disciples spoke and moved. The humans were played by androids whose arthritic movements seemed to be those of a human imitating a robot, rather

[2]Swaminarayan was born Ghanshyam Maharaj in 1781 in northern India, and among his many achievements is that he walked more than twelve thousand kilometres across India. There are three significant Hindu sects which see themselves as followers of Swaminarayan. The best-known, BAPS (nothing to do with the Scottish buns of that name, is actually short for the tongue-twisting Bochasanwasi Shri Akshar Purushottam Swaminarayan Sanstha) is responsible for a large number of Akshardham temples around the world including a huge one in Neasden, London. Kids.swaminarayan.org is the most accessible of guides to BAPS. At number 45 on the Swaminarayan kids website section on 'Things to know' section is the question '*What should we use the internet for?* Answer: The internet can be very helpful, but at the same time it can be very harmful . . . we should only use the internet for *satsang* (in the service of god) and if we need it for a school assignment/project to research.'

than the other way round. The hip and knee movements were smooth, better than mine, in fact, but the arm and facial movements were staccato and stilted. In the first three rooms, the audience clapped at end of each performance, but by the tenth room exhaustion had set in, and the non-stop goodness on display seemed to have become a little tiresome. We were now racing against each other to get to the next room, and eventually, three hours after I entered the Akshardham complex, I had completed the first stage of the religio-tainment extravaganza. Only two more stages to go—but I had an appointment with a knee doctor, and so, picking up my Hendrix from the security officials, I hailed an autorickshaw and returned to South Delhi.

A week later, encouraged by the doctor to keep on walking, I went back to Akshardham. Chekhov's short stories were permitted entry, and so I would have something to read as I queued for India's largest IMAX cinema, showing a 45-minute film about the life of Swaminarayan, and the 12-minute subterranean boat-ride through 10,000 years of India's history (7.2 seconds per century). An officious ticket-seller with a Swaminarayan baseball cap and a sleepy left eye said that I would have to buy a ticket for the diorama animatronics as well as the IMAX and the boat-ride. I readily assented—but said that I would skip straight to the film. 'No,' I was told. I would have to see the diorama animatronics. I explained that I had already seen it, last time I had visited—and it had taken an hour, and it was very good, but I didn't want to see it again.

'No, that is not allowed.'

'But I've already seen it.'

'No queue-jumping', I was told firmly and just a little unfairly.

A smiling young Indian woman, a fellow visitor, told me it would be good for me to see the diorama animatronics again. 'It is very soulful', she said with the kind of look normally reserved for the mentally ill. I cracked, losing my cool, slamming my Chekhov down on the ticket counter and began muttering about incompetence and intolerance. I think I lived up to their expectations of me, a difficult foreigner with no patience, and, probably, no soul, and, just possibly, a little mad. I marched off and feeling a little ashamed. And I would probably never see the 45,000 extras in the IMAX film, or learn about the 'rishi-scientists' of ancient India, while floating on a boat through an underground tunnel.

Outside Akshardham I made for the nearest field of cauliflowers on the Yamuna floodplain, destined, according to a large signboard, to become the site for the Commonwealth Games village in 2010 . There was another smaller yellow signboard strung from a tree at the far end of the field, above a straw hut. The sign read PCO—or public call office. I  approached. Outside the hut was a formica-topped desk, with a seated woman in a sari talking in Bengali on the phone. An older man was standing at the other end of the table, watching the digital rupee counter display that told him how much money he would make from this call. I said that this was the most unusual place I had seen a PCO, in the open-air between a field of cauliflowers, and a field of spinach. He laughed.

'How did you get the connection?' I asked, well aware of how the complex issue of getting a landline in Delhi is a matter of public humour.

He pointed at an inconspicuous six-inch plastic and steel contraption clamped to the table-top. 'Wireless,' he said, using the English word. It was a transmitter. I was amazed. Wireless technology had reached this small piece of rural India in the heart of one of the largest cities in the world. The wireless telephone kit had cost him Rs 10,000, and he'd made that money back in 4 months.

'We farmers can't afford mobile phones like you rich people. So we need PCOs to call our villages—and now with wireless we can have them anywhere. The trouble is now my profits are down, because someone else realized that this is easy money. Better than farming, at least.' He pointed over to another hut, two fields away, and there was another yellow PCO sign. It turned out that this small agricultural community had three PCOs, each using wireless technology. And their huts had been waterproofed with plastic street banners advertising mobile phone companies (SMS @ 5 paise a week—Limited period offer) which had been removed from the nearby streets of trans-Yamuna. Such were the unexpected benefits of new technology for one marginal community.

After crossing a dual-carriage highway, and a putrid rubbish-clogged sewer I reached a busy market street in the first of dozens of sprawling trans-Yamuna colonies, rarely visited by the denizens of other parts of Delhi, and my first foray into this part of the city. It reminded me of the older, smaller Delhi I used to know when I first lived here in the early 1990s, and indeed felt like any large northern Indian town. There were three men dragging a metal cart full of rubbish along the main street, alternately smiling and grunting, oblivious to the frustration of an impatient car-driver behind them. A dog, with bald patches on its back, lay on top of the cart licking its testicles. A group of men played cards and drank tea, served by a woman who went unthanked, unnoticed. There was no obvious distinction between the roads and the pavements, people waved cheerily at me for no reason, children asked for pencils, and women stitched clothes by hand in open doorways. And yet it was also a warren of electronic activity. There was a 'cybercafé': at Rs 10 an hour the cheapest I had found in Delhi, with just a single dial-up computer and a half re-upholstered chair, and a queue of three waiting to use it. There were mobile phone shops and small business centres; signboards promising service of dubious legality ('all DVDs and software copied here') and doubtful utility ('typing and scaning [sic] here'). My Eicher map seemed to place this area in a blurred no-man's-land between several localities. I asked a pomegranate-seller where I was.

'Ganesh Nagar Mother Dairy,' came the reply.

'Is that its real name?'

'No, it's really just Ganesh Nagar, but no one's heard of that. So everyone calls it Mother Dairy as well. That's the Mother Dairy factory just up there', he said, pointing at a series of huge cylindrical milk-white storage vats on the horizon.

From above, and with the help of Google Earth, which shows the vats as five neat round white circles, it is clear that the Mother Dairy factory is even larger than the Akshardham complex, with a two-kilometre perimeter. From the ground, prying eyes are kept out by a whitewashed boundary wall, topped with spiralling military-style barbed wire. On a signboard along the wall—the general public is informed in English and in Hindi that Mother Dairy is committed to following 'food safety management systems and apply[ing] HACCP (Hazard Analysis Critical Control Points) principles to provide safe products to customers'. This is, in its obscurity, intended to be reassuring. Mother Dairy is a multi-billion-rupee milk business, a major local employer, and critical to the economy of this part of Delhi. It is also a proselytizing co-operative that is particularly proud of environment-friendly policies for which it has won several awards[3].

Built into the boundary wall is one of Delhi's 636 Mother Dairy kiosks—familiar to almost all the city's residents—where you can fill the jug you brought from home with fresh milk from a dispenser, using a token purchased from the counter. If you are jugless you can buy a small plastic pyramid of milk, which will try to jump from your hands as the milk sloshes around inside, and seems designed to defeat any attempt to open it without spilling its contents. These milk kiosks have come to play an important role in city life.

They have become an urban substitute for the village well. In rural India, around the village well, women exchange information (gossip, according to the men), sort out problems (normally, say the women, caused by the men) and often run a parallel, more effective, village administration than the official male-run one. In cities, only the poor have buffaloes and cows for

[3] According to its own literature, Mother Dairy was the first industry in the country to implement ISO-14031(Environment Performance Evaluation) which is a technical standard based on the more accessible-sounding (even blindingly obvious) 'Plan-Do-Check-Act' model of business improvement. It also uses solar power for heating; and 'water harvesting and recuperation' to cut its water consumption. It has introduced the Japanese Kaizen productivity management system (also known more prosaically as learn-by-doing, or continual improvement) which is widely seen as a key factor behind Japan's post-war economic miracle.

milking, and almost everyone else needs to get milk from a kiosk once a day, more often in the summer when the milk will sour quickly. And so the Mother Dairy booths, and the rival kiosks of the Delhi Milk Scheme, have become a regular meeting-place where people come to buy milk (and yoghurt and cheese and fruit), but seem quickly to forget their original purpose, and stand around in groups, chatting, networking, sharing useful knowledge about the city. The area around these kiosks has become public space with a purpose. But the kiosk outside the Mother Dairy factory is an exception, it is deserted. A newspaper seller told me that it's little used. Locals have to cross a busy road to get to it; there is nowhere to stand around and chat; it is really a show-kiosk; the man in charge of the kiosk is fast asleep, slumped forward on his counter, his head to one side.

I continue with my brief wander through the hyperactive streets of Trans-Yamuna, where every fourth building is either being knocked down or rebuilt. Once these were Mughal hunting-grounds and farmland, but now there is nothing green. The fields became building plots; the old contours of the land are invisible, with streams that have been transformed into sewers as the only trace of the past. This is aspirant Delhi, with signboards and posters that promise overnight computer literacy, fluent English in a

week, a 'guaranteed cure for rough skin', and a beautician's diploma for Rs 500. There are huge billboards outside the Lovely Senior Secondary School with foot-high blown-up passport photographs of its most successful pupils. A grimly-determined Charisma Allangh was, we learn, the Class Ten 'topper' with a 96.4 per cent aggregate. A boy with the broadest of smiles, by the single name of Kshitiz, topped Class Twelve[4]. I try to enter, but the gates are locked. My brief foray into trans-Yamuna was coming to end, and the spiral was forcing me back across the river, knowing I would have to reserve a more complete adventure until I returned for the final twist of my whorl.

I walked back towards the river through quiet residential colonies and found a bedraggled crowd—mainly women and very small children wrapped up in oversized woollens to protect them from the winter cold—gathered outside the main entrance to the gated Taj Enclave housing estate, an up-market mainly Muslim area of East Delhi. One of the women, a sleeping twin in each arm, tells me they're waiting for free food—the meat of a sacrificial goat—because yesterday was the Muslim festival of Bakri Eid[5]. She's a Hindu, but laughs as she tells me she'll be a Muslim for the day if she gets a good meal. She lives close to the river, where her husband works as a labourer on the new Yamuna bridge construction project.

There is an old seasonal pontoon bridge at this part of the river; known as the bridge of boats. It's actually a rather uneven road that's been laid across floating metal pontoons, like giant scuba-diving tanks, bobbing on the waters of the Yamuna. Pontoon bridges have been used on the Yamuna since Mughal times, and now only this one remains. An 1858 print of Delhi shows a bridge of boats, just north of here, with two people riding an elephant into

---

[4] Lovely is both an adjective and a surname—I have been unable to find out why it was used as the name of this school. However, a recent Delhi education minister was called Arvinder Singh Lovely. Charisma is a relatively common, and burdensome, first name—often spelled Karishma, and apparently deriving from the Persian *kirishma*, meaning a 'wonderful deed'. Kshitiz is a relatively uncommon first name from the Hindi for horizon.

[5] Bakri Eid or festival of the goat, is better known in the rest of the Muslim world as Eid al-Adha, or festival of sacrifice. It commemorates the day on which the prophet Ibrahim (the Judeo-Christian Abraham) nearly killed his oldest son, Ismail (Ishmael), for whom God substituted a goat at the last minute. In Jewish and Christian tradition it was Abraham's second son, Isaac, who was about to have his throat cut. In Muslim tradition, all Arabs, and therefore the Prophet Muhammad, were descendants of Ismail. While in the Jewish tradition, the tribes of Israel, and therefore Jesus, were descended from Isaac. There's another less well-known syncretic tradition that Abraham/Ibrahim is actually the same person as the phonetically similar Hindu god Brahma—and that his wife Sarah is Brahma's consort, the goddess Sarasvati.

Shahjahanabad, and a horse-drawn carriage leaving the city[6] . Today, I note with foolish delight, it has become a bridge of goats, as a large herd of survivors of Bakri Eid, with no goatherd to be seen, make their way towards the western bank of the Yamuna. In the midst of the goats, is a man pushing a cycle-rickshaw laden with air-conditioners; from my vantage point on the river bank, the goats seem to be helping him to push his heavy burden across the river, but he is unappreciatively shooing them away.

Next to the bridge of boats are the incomplete concrete piers and columns of the new bridge, and a ferryman taking workmen and equipment across the river. He beckoned me. He had no oars, or punt, or rudder or engine—instead a rope was stretched between the river banks, and passed through a metal ring on the prow of the small boat. I climb in, my clumsiness and body weight causing the ferryman some anxiety. He showed me how to pull on the fraying rope, and I sent us gliding over the malodorous Yamuna, rope-weals swelling on my palms. I stopped the boat half-way, to rest my hands, and leaned over the side to have a closer look at the tar-black water. The boatman misunderstood my movements and shouting, grabbed me by my shoulders. He told me I was mad—and that a few sips of Yamuna water would kill a grown man. I laughed and thanked him for saving my life. I did swirl my index finger into the water, which had the consistency of milkshake and the opacity of liquorice. I had created a little eddy, and the midges danced with excitement, their minuscule wings catching the winter sun, and momentarily transforming the surface of the water into a twinkling of diamonds.

Back on land, I struggled my way through a waterlogged building site, waved on theatrically by hard-hatted construction workers, leaning out precariously from bamboo scaffolding, directing me over tangled piles of steel wire and hillocks of gravel towards the nearest road. As the clanking of metal on metal, and the shouted instructions of the building foreman, began to fade, they segued with an entirely unexpected sound that seemed to be coming from a coppice beside a broad avenue of rutted, fossilized mud. It was, I imagined western classical music, as if a brass band were playing Mozart on the deserted

---

[6] In fact, Delhi was pretty deserted in 1858. In the aftermath of the 1857 rebellion, the British emptied the city.

Yamuna floodplain. How absurd, I told myself. The winter sun was turning my mind. But the music got louder as I neared the coppice, and I thought I recognized it as the opening bars of *The Marriage of Figaro*. Peering over a hedge, into a small sapling-ringed clearing, rubbing my disbelieving eyes, I realized that this was not an illusion or a dream. It was a police brass band in mid-

performance. At least thirty uniformed men sat and stood with their backs to me in a semi-circle, the sunlight dancing off their gleaming golden trombones, trumpets and tubas, and the conductor, on his feet and pacing around, was flamboyantly wagging his baton at them. He spotted me—and distracted, he allowed the tempo to slow, and a trombone broke ranks, squawking out a false note, and the overture was transformed into a cacophony of blustery yowls, and the conductor dropped his baton, smiling accusingly at me.

I went up to him, and learned that the musicians were all serving officers in the Rajasthan police, practising for the National Police Brass Band competition. They were trying out their new set of instruments for the first time. The conductor was delighted that I had recognized *The Marriage of Figaro*—but quickly lost interest when my ignorance about brass bands became obvious. He did not want to talk about anything else. I asked him why the police had chosen this secluded spot for their rehearsals and he muttered that this area was part of a large police camp—but that I would have to speak to a senior officer if I wanted to find out more. He then referred to the area as Yamuna Pushta, or Yamuna Bank, giving me a clue to why this unlikely place had been chosen as the location for a police band to practice. Yamuna Pushta was until recently Delhi's largest slum, home to as many as three hundred thousand people, equivalent to the entire population of Delhi in the 1900s.

In 2004, the shanty towns lining the west bank of the Yamuna closest to Old Delhi were reduced to rubble. There is now little sign that anyone had ever lived here. As late as September 2007, it could still be seen as it was three years earlier, before the bulldozers moved in, on Google Earth, whose satellite photographs were clearly not being updated very regularly. There, in cyberspace, Yamuna Pushta still existed as a densely packed settlement in the heart of Delhi clinging to the contours of the river banks. But it had all gone, most of it returned to agriculture and swamp. An unsurfaced road, six buses wide, which will serve the new bridge, has been driven through the heart of what was the old settlement.

As I strolled along this broad, unfinished muddy avenue, a man pushing a bicycle along its rutted surface drew up beside me. For once, someone else started the conversation. Anil wanted to know why I was there—and I found my tongue in Hindi. I told him I loved to walk, that I was happiest when I walked, and that I had walked many miles that day, and I told him of the brass band and Mozart. He laughed, and then asked who Mozart was, as if he might be a friend of mine, and as if Mozart and I might have something to hide. When I told him that Mozart was dead, he looked at me as if I might have been responsible. Gradually, we set aside our misunderstandings, and Anil should now be able to give a pretty good account of Salzburg's most famous son. He told me how he used to live here in Yamuna Pushta before the bulldozers came, and how he knew that they were coming and had left with all his belongings tied to his bicycle; but others had stayed and had lost everything. He had made friends with the police ('I told them things they wanted to know.' 'What?' 'Just gossip. But they thought I was helping them, that I was their little spy'), and they had let him pass through the area, and he'd dug in the rubble for things to sell. Now he'd just come to see where he used to live; there'd been a rumour that a new settlement had sprung up. But it was a false rumour. Anil told me that the police were camped throughout the area, and pointed over a wall to some large brown tents pitched in neat rows. That's why the brass band was here, there's nothing for the police to do. And he was right. Yamuna Pushta was full of bored, sleepy policemen (and a group of police musicians) defending some government-owned fields and scrubland from being resettled by the poor.

Anil pointed out the almost invisible traces of the Yamuna Pushta

178

settlement. A wall along the northern side of the rutted highway still stood, with roughened painted bricks marking where only two years earlier one home had begun and another one ended. Anil said some of the people who had lived here had been moved to official resettlement colonies in north-west Delhi, but most had drifted to other nearby slums. Life in the resettlement colonies was no better than at Yamuna Pushta and they were all far too far from their jobs and the social networks that made their lives possible. As for their former home, a loosely drawn sketch map inscribed on a tin notice-board, bearing the imprimatur of the Delhi Development Authority, gave a hint as to the future of Yamuna Pushta. The map showed the area I was now walking through as having a huge car park, a food court and a small children's playground.

Anil and I separated, he was heading back across the river to a friend who might get him a job on the Metro. I made my way towards the only nearby solid building, an elegant, single-storey whitewashed, semi-circular concrete-and-glass construction the size of a baseball diamond. I climbed over a pile of Yamuna Pushta rubble and sidled up to a group of men sitting on the lawn, playing cards, with big friendly smiles on their faces. 'My name is Rakesh. Welcome to cream torment,' their blue-shirted spokesman said, elliptically, in English. 'Cream torment?' I repeated back to him, staring at the building which seemed to consist of several large rooms, with a stage and at least fifty plastic chairs screwed to the marble floor. Then I saw a smaller square building, which he pointed at, with three narrow spiral-flanged steel chimneys. I spoke to him in Hindi, and his words of English became clear. I was in a crematorium.

It looked unused. There were no visible bodies, no mourners, no cars in the car park. Several windows were broken. But the lawns were well-tended, and there were enough workers to sustain several card games. Rakesh was keen to show me around

'Where are the corpses?' I asked, coming straight to the point.

'We don't get many. Six or eight a week. It's very slow here. Boring, really.'

'Why so few?'

'People don't like electric crematoria. They are very religious and think you should be burned with wood in the open-air. They say if you are not burnt properly you will become a ghost, and maybe

179

they are right. We only get beggars, foreigners and people who have died in traffic accidents. The MCD[7] sends them. We burn them. Come and look.' He was clearly delighted to have a visitor.

The crematorium, he told me, was built in 1965, and the large building with several rooms with rows of plastic seats, was designed for memorial meetings and prayer ceremonies, but hadn't been used for a long time. The smaller building contained the four furnaces, all in working order and recently refurbished. He led me in past a black marble table, where the funeral bier was placed before cremation. The furnaces themselves were like pizza ovens, with a large tray on wheels that send the corpse on its final journey into the maw of flames. At the back of the furnace is a much smaller opening, where the ashes and bones are collected. Rakesh, as jovial as ever, showed me a series of numbered metal troughs, in which the remains of recently cremated bodies are kept separately, in case they are claimed. Next to them was a larger pile of human bones, vertebrae and smaller bones from the hands and feet clearly recognizable; the larger bones were all broken, with occasional long shards from a femur or tibia, and ball sockets from major limb joints. These are mixed bones, Rakesh told me, from unclaimed corpses. Rakesh took me over to several jute bags packed full of human bones, neatly lined up. 'They'll be sent to Hardwar and put in the Ganges river.'

For a brief period in the post-independence years, electric crematoria were centre-stage in the battle over modernity. Traditionally, Hindus and Sikhs were burnt on a wood pyre in the open-air, usually near a river; the cremation of the dead was a very public occasion, visible to the entire community, part of everyday life. The practice of open-air cremation was criticized by reforming administrators as being primitive, brutal, irrational and environmentally damaging. Electric crematoria were built in most large Indian cities. Many are underused, some are now derelict.

One former bureaucrat told me it all went wrong when Indira Gandhi had her father, Jawaharlal Nehru, cremated in public in a ceremony overseen by Hindu priests. He had said in his will that he did not want his funeral to be religious. Meanwhile, the electric crematoria became the subject of urban myths, of tales of power cuts that left

[7] The Municipal Corporation of Delhi runs this and several other crematoria.

180

half-burnt corpses rotting in the midsummer heat, of mourners who have received cattle bones instead of human remains, of skulls that exploded because of the heat of the furnace. Electric cremations are also very cheap and, therefore, associated with the poorest of the poor, and the friendless. Today, few families will attempt to demonstrate their modernity (or risk their loved ones becoming ghosts) by opting for an electric cremation. There are new, more expensive touchstones of modernity; such as holidays in Europe, a collection of Indian contemporary art or a wide-screen wall-mounted plasma TV.

It is clear that electric crematoria have an image problem. The Delhi authorities have tried to get around this by converting them to natural gas—shortly after Delhi's buses and taxis were also converted—reducing the pollution, avoiding the power cut problem, and, Rakesh assured me, lessening the smell. But the rebranding has failed; they are still known as electric crematoria, and the predicted legions of fresh corpses have not materialized.

Just a few hundred metres away, on the other side of a small sixteenth-century fort[8], is a traditional cremation ground, Nigambodh Ghat, which is always bristling with bodies. The car park was full. Four men were lifting a corpse out of an army truck. The body had been wrapped tightly in a white sheet and tied to a wooden stretcher, and strewn with rose petals and garlands of marigolds. They carried the bier high, above their heads, as they manoeuvred their way between the cars. I decided to follow them from a discreet distance. I realized that the head of the corpse, almost hairless and a mottled yellow, was uncovered, and I could see the sharp tip of a nose as they raised and lowered the stretcher.

I still shiver when I encounter a corpse, even though, working as a journalist, and living in India, I have now seen thousands of them. I grew up in a society where people very rarely see a dead body, where the corporeal consequences of death, confined to a coffin, are left to the imagination. And then one day in May 1991, reporting

---

[8] The fort, Salimgarh, was once an island fortress—but the Mughals built a bridge linking it to the mainland and the Red Fort, while the British turned the river under the bridge into a road, and transformed Salimgarh into little more than a huge traffic island. Even worse, they also drove a railway line through the middle of the fort, and used it as a barracks and a prison for opponents of British rule.

from Bangladesh on the deaths of more than a hundred thousand people in a cyclone, I saw piles of corpses, hundreds and hundreds of people, bloated, white-and-pink, mostly naked, that had been gathered for mass burials. These are images that haunt me to this day, and probably always will, and chill shudders of disbelief shake through my body, and tears well in my eyes, as I write these words. But the images of the living haunt me still more. There was a group of men, wiry and dark, who wore two strips of cloth, one around their loins, the other round their mouth and nose. They were dragging the swollen corpses across the sodden land towards the burial pits. One of them, with the torch-like eyes of a soul-reader, looked at me, who'd just descended, God-like, in a military helicopter, as if to ask 'Do you know what our lives are like?' I'm taken back to that day every time I see a corpse, but in a way that I have learnt not to fear. It was then that I first understood why death was called the great leveller, that I first felt that the search for success and riches could seem almost absurdly irrelevant and futile, and that, most of all, I needed to be able to try to answer the question that I imagined the soul-reading, corpse-carrying Bangladeshi had been asking me.

But in a place of death, my nosiness about other people's lives is tempered by a fear of intruding on the private grief of the mourners— so I try to make myself invisible, which is a little unrealistic for a large white man in an Indian cremation ground. I sat down on a stone bench, watching the four stretcher-bearers briefly rest the bier on a marble table, each of them, in turn, appearing to whisper something into the ear of the corpse. They then covered his head. I look around. I count twenty-six identical tin roofs and beyond that the steps that lead down to the river. Beneath each roof, open to the winds and to the eyes of everyone, is a slightly hollowed-out raised plinth where the cremations take place. There is some kind of activity at eleven of them. The funeral pyre furthest from me has just been lit, a huge pile of wood with the body invisible beneath it, and there is a large crowd of mourners, a woman is wailing and shaking with grief, and being held tight by two younger men. She is behaving as if she wants to climb onto the pyre. Closer to me a white-shrouded body has been laid out on three logs of wood, one underneath the feet, one under the small of the back, one at the back of the neck, the head of the corpse seems to loll awkwardly and a small piece of wood is inserted as a support, as if it might make the process of being burnt a little less uncomfortable. Gradually the body is then covered in a pyramid of wood. To my right, two mourners are sifting through ashes of a recent cremation, pulling out fragments of bone and putting them in a tin bucket; the ashes are being swept up separately and being placed in an iron saucer the size and shape of a hub-cap. It all feels rather democratic (until I spotted the special VIP area); mourners have not dressed up—and it's not always clear who is a member of the public and who works at the cremation ground. No one seems to notice me and I realize what should have been obvious: there is no privacy here, death is a public occasion

To my surprise, the corpse I had been following was not taken to one of the cremation plinths, but carried on towards the river. Here on the blackened western bank of the Yamuna, they deposited the corpse. One of them stayed guard, shooing away some emaciated pi-dogs, while the other three went back into the cremation ground. I walked along the bank a little and found the courage or gall to walk up to the lone mourner. I asked him why this body had been brought to the river bank. He spoke back to me in fluent English and seemed pleased to have living company.

'He will be cremated right here. He's from the hills and Hindus there always to do it next to water.'

'But why are you alone, where have the others gone?'

'The others are arranging the wood. I'm making sure these bloody dogs don't get anywhere near. They look hungry.'

'Is he . . . was he a relative?'

'No, I never even met him. He died last night. Massive heart attack. His cook found him. His sons are in America, you see, and can't get back in time, and they asked me to come. I was at college with one of them. All the relatives here in Delhi are very old, but there's a nephew who said he'll turn up, and the cook's here too. He was an army man years ago—and the army lent a truck and a couple of people.'

'Isn't it very inauspicious if your son can't be at the cremation?'

'Yes. It is. But I don't believe all that. Neither do his sons'

'So why not the electric crematorium?'

'I don't know. Tradition, I suppose. Just in case they're right about the ghosts.' He laughed and turned to me. 'It's still better than burial, isn't it. Sticking them underground with the worms.'

'But you waste so much wood like this.'

'There's a lot of wood in a coffin. And if you look at it like that, maybe we should just leave the dead in the jungle like they used to. You know that in Bombay, Parsees are still left out for the vultures to eat.' I was about to tell him that my wife was a Parsee, and that the Parsees are worried because the vultures are disappearing from Bombay, killed off by medicines injected into cattle, whose dead bodies the vultures then eat[9]. But his fellow mourners were returning, carrying lots of pieces of wood. I slunk off without his name or mobile number, or business card—and those other big-city things that people swap—and was left feeling that our discussion of comparative funeral traditions had been truncated. I moved to another part of the bank and watched the body of the army man disappear beneath a wigwam of wood. I retreated to the half-built VIP section of the cremation ground, watching the dead and the living go by, thinking about what the lone mourner had said, and deciding in the end that the Parsee way of bodily disposal is probably the most environmentally sound, though a lack of urban vultures did seem like a difficult problems to solve.

I wrote notes on our conversation and looked up again to see something that disturbed me deeply. Down on the river bank, entirely alone apart from some foraging dogs, was another corpse, wrapped in white, the shroud tight about the stomach. It was the body of a hugely pregnant woman. I sank into a morbid disbelieving gloom, constructing a series of desolate fantasies. I began to dream up her life story, creating an imaginary lover who had deserted her and a family that had disowned her. Perhaps she had killed herself—and that is why no one had come for her funeral. But then the council would have taken her to the electric crematorium—so who might have brought her here? And what about the baby—had she given birth, or was the foetus still in her, dead I suppose? Hadn't I read somewhere of women who were clinically dead but able to give birth?

---

[9] Parsee Zoroastrians traditionally leave bodies in open-topped buildings called towers of silence, where they are picked clean by vultures. Many Parsees now opt for cremation or burial, but orthodox believers say a dead body should not be allowed to defile the sacred elements, earth and fire. The vultures have been dying of renal failure, caused by the ingestion of residues of the anti-inflammatory drug, Diclofenac, in the bodies of dead cows.

My reveries were interrupted by the sight of a dog approaching the corpse, sniffing the ground. I took a piece of broken brick and threw it at the dog. I missed but the dog still turned away. I took a photograph with the corpse and the dog, and the Metro line across the river as a backdrop. No one would believe me if I didn't take this picture.

A plump man in his fifties came down and peered at the corpse, and tucked the shroud in a bit where the wind had loosened it and went back towards the main cremation ground. I moved quickly to intercept him. I asked in Hindi, pointing at the corpse, 'What happened to the baby?' He looked at me, totally bemused. I repeated my question, even more earnestly, and asked how the woman had died. A smile came upon his face, and he began to laugh gently as he turned away from me and went back towards the corpse where four other mourners—all men—had gathered. He spoke to them, and pointed at me, and they laughed. The laughter became more raucous and audible. One of them, short with an enormous paunch, began stamping his foot with hilarity. Another old man bent over the corpse and patted the stomach as it were a household pet.

The man with the paunch was deputed to go to me, and he told me that the corpse was that of his seventy-seven-year-old brother—whose stomach was even bigger than his own, which he patted proudly. His brother had died in the night, he said, after drinking half a bottle of whisky. 'Not a bad way to go. I wouldn't mind that. He had a good life and now we'll give him a good funeral.' I apologized for my stupidity.

'We all thought it very funny.'

'I could see that.'

'He'd have found it funny too.'

'I'm glad,' I said, allowing myself a foolish smile, remembering how I'd been gulled a few weeks earlier by what I thought was the arm of a human corpse. Nothing in Delhi is, I decided, quite as it seems.

An Eighth Intermission

THE WEATHER IN Delhi is pretty predictable. It is hot in the summer, and cold in the winter, and rainy in the rainy season. There are occasional minor surprises: springtime hailstorms, with vicious pellets of ice; pre-monsoon thunderstorms when rain falls like a guillotine and the trees dance and forks of lightning scar the evening sky. Sometimes the rains are late, or barely come at all. But for the British, used to a climate that changes season several times a day, Delhi's weather is a little boring. However, there is one dramatic event in Delhi's recent meteorological history that has entered folklore.

Delhi University, on the western side of the Northern Ridge, was built on the old British cantonment and laid out with military precision on either side of Probyn Road[1]. It is a huge campus of colleges and hostels and snack bars; the old parade-ground has become a park full of smooching couples, picnicking students, dancing butterflies, sleeping peons and gardeners spraying water over rosebeds with ancient leaking hoses. The area is a peaceful, friendly, somnolent sort of place which was torn apart by a freak of nature in 1978, more unpredictable than an earthquake, and, for its victims, even more terrifying. At least thirty people were killed and several hundred injured on 17 March 1978, when a tornado tore up Probyn Road through the heart of the university, sucking up cars and humans into its funnel-shaped vortex, and spitting them out as if they were the shells of pumpkin seeds. Navtej Sarna, now a novelist and a diplomat, was a student then, who crouched, bewildered and terrified, in a college corridor. He remembers 'a motorcycle on Mall Road being deposited on the roof of Khalsa College; a soft drink kiosk near Delhi University's Arts Faculty was found, battered and bent, nearly 500 metres away. Buses were flung a hundred metres off their

---

[1] Officially Chhatra Marg (literally Student Street), but still known as Probyn Road after a British General. The area around Delhi University has twice been a cantonment area, both before the 1857 Uprising, and at the start of the twentieth century. After 1857, the cantonment shifted temporarily to the Red Fort area, and after the building of New Delhi it moved south-west, in the direction of the international airport. But some military encampments remained north of the University area.

course and the human casualties were horrifying.' Telegraph poles were bent at right angles, trees were twisted and uprooted, walls were flattened. The rest of the city was totally unscathed.

There's never been anything like it in Delhi, before or since. Northern India is not a tornado-prone region, and the events of that day have created their own complex mythologies, which have been espoused by people who are expected to be bulwarks of rationality. First, there was the astrophysics professor who said that a UFO, not a tornado, was responsible for the devastation. And then were some officials at the Indian Defence Ministry who believed that the tornado was an act of revenge by a long-dead Muslim saint.

Professor SK Trikha is retired now, and refuses to meet me. But he will talk, at length, on the telephone from his residence in North Delhi. This former professor in Delhi University's Department of Physics and Astrophysics tells me stories that would have an eavesdropping member of his profession blushing with embarrassment—but he does so in the language of a scientist. He runs through the circumstantial evidence that convinces him that there was no tornado—that witnesses saw a flying saucer, that trees had been cut rather than broken, that telegraph poles had been bent inwards, that the government refused to conduct post-mortems—before delivering his most important finding, that levels of radioactivity in areas affected by the 'tornado' were extremely high. He told me how he walked around the DU Campus on the evening of the devastation with his own Geiger counter, and the highest levels of radioactivity were exactly those which had suffered most damage. He believes this could only have been caused by a nuclear-powered aircraft, spinning on its central axis so as to hover at about ten feet above the ground. Because it was spinning, it created a vacuum which sucked up everything beneath it, and its directional nozzles, he told me, were responsible for slicing off the tops of the trees. It was a

UFO, he said, in the real meaning of the phrase, 'The "U" in UFO,' he pointed out 'stands for unidentified. And, as a scientist, I have not been positively able to positively identify it. Perhaps it came from the USA, or the USSR, perhaps it came from another planet.' But no, he will not meet me; it would not be 'appropriate'. 'Call me tomorrow,' and I call again, and he talks about science and the supernatural, but no meeting transpires. Perhaps he is concerned that he may become an object of derision. It has clearly not been easy for a man of science to admit that he believes in UFOs.

I have not found anyone apart from Professor Trikha who doubts that there was a tornado, but there is some disagreement about what caused it. The official scientific explanation relates to layers of air of different temperature coming into contact with each other, while others seeking a more metaphysical explanation refer to the butterfly effect, the cornerstone of modern chaos theory, usually expressed for non-scientists in the rhetorical question 'Does the flap of a butterfly's wings in Brazil set off a tornado in Texas?'[2] But on a trip to the far northern end of the Probyn Road, just beyond the university, I heard another bizarre tale that provided an alternative explanation of the great North Delhi tornado of 1978. On my Eicher map, the land beyond the University is left blank and unlabelled. This is defence territory, a remnant of the old cantonment and out-of-bounds for most civilians. I was following up a reference to some 'tornado graves' which alluded only obliquely to their precise location or history. Eventually I came upon the well-guarded Centre for Fire, Explosive and Environment Safety, a modern building at the end of a cul-de-sac. I asked about the graves, and was told they were somewhere nearby but no one seemed to know where. I was taken inside the Centre to an office, where a squat Colonel from south India greeted me suspiciously, as if I might be a passing spy, and asked a lot of probing questions about what had brought me here. Once I passed his test—an achievement he celebrated with a wicked smile and an exuberantly parabolic slapping of his thigh—he proceeded to tell me the strange story of Probyn's Horse and the tornado graves.

[2] The notion of the butterfly effect was the creation of the American meteorologist Edward Lorenz who gave a lecture entitled, 'Does the Flap of a Butterfly's Wings in Brazil Set Off a Tornado in Texas?' in 1972.

The Centre for Fire, Explosive and Environment Safety had been build on land previously occupied by the headquarters of a cavalry regiment called Probyn's Horse, formed in the aftermath of the 1857 Uprising, and commanded by the British officer, Dighton Probyn. At partition, in 1947, the regiment, which was largely Muslim, was allotted to

Pakistan, and most of its squadrons and its regimental regalia were taken across the new border. But there was one thing they did not take with them: the grave of the *pir* of Probyn's Horse, a kind of regimental patron saint, who was buried here in North Delhi alongside his wife and son. For three decades the graves were almost forgotten and were disturbed and dug up when construction work began on the current building in the late 1970s. Before the new building was completed, the tornado struck, causing serious damage and destroying the concrete roof. The *pir* of Probyn's Horse had got his revenge, and the graves were rebuilt. The Colonel laughed raucously as he told me this, slapping his thigh again, spelling out the irony of the story: the Indian armed forces' disaster management research institute is itself being protected from disaster by some old graves.

He then led me to an immaculate brick structure with a corrugated iron roof. Inside were three identical tiled graves, a flame burning in an alcove in each headstone, each grave covered in green cloth, with fresh marigolds placed carefully on top. Looking after the graves is a serious business, and the Colonel said he has lots of volunteers— and not only Muslims. And then the Colonel—a south Indian Hindu—bent and touched his head to the floor in front of each grave. Better safe than sorry, I said. He smiled. Even in the army discretion is the better part of valour.

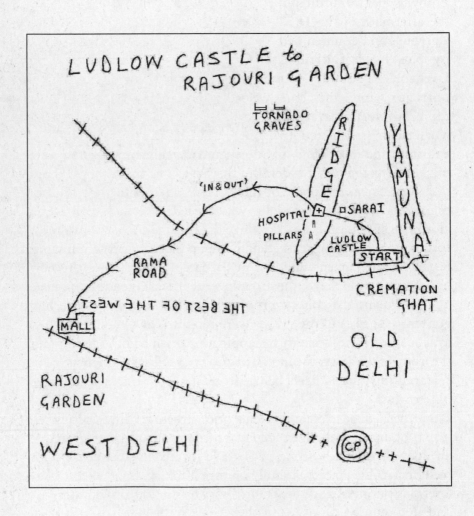

Chapter Nine: In which the Author visits Ludlow Castle, learns the meaning of choledocholithotomy and almost buys a packet of condoms

TOPOGRAPHICALLY, DELHI IS an upturned wedge △, the final slice of a birthday cake—a triangle that narrows to a point in the north, with the Yamuna as its hypotenuse, and the rocky wildernesses of the Ridge forming its other two sides. I was now near the northern tip of this triangle and I began a gentle westwards walk from the river towards the Ridge, through the genteel area known as Civil Lines, with sleepy broad streets and spacious bungalows. It was from the bungalows of Civil Lines that the British ruled Delhi once they'd exiled the Mughal Emperor from his palace in the Red Fort. In the early twentieth century, from the time Delhi was anointed as the new capital, and until the completion of New Delhi in the 1930s, it was the control room of Britain's empire. Its imperial past is still discernible beneath a shabby senescence. This has become a land of educational institutions, and residences for old Delhi families and state government ministers. Modernity in Civil Lines is subterranean. The modest steel and glass of a Metro station entrance poking out from a broad pavement is the only reminder of the speed at which most of this city is changing.

I sought refuge from the sun under the shade of a concrete bus shelter. Painted neatly on the shelter in four-inch-high English and Hindi lettering were the perplexing words 'Ludlow Castle', which I knew as the name of a medieval ruin on the Welsh border of my homeland. I looked around, hoping that a castle-like

building, or some other explanation, would reveal itself. I stopped a young woman, striding purposefully past, and asked where the castle was, using the word '*qila*' which means both fort and castle. She took pity on me and began giving directions to the Red Fort. No, I said, repeating the words 'Ludlow Castle' in a range of accents and pointing to the writing on the shelter. 'There's no castle,' she laughed, using the English word and pointing across the road to a large institutional building. 'That's Ludlow Castle School.' She marched me over to the school, and handed me over to the care of a security guard. He had no idea why the school was called Ludlow Castle, but introduced me to a woman teacher (whose feet passing pupils would bend to touch—out of respect, and, perhaps, fear), who took me to meet the headmaster, Mr Sharma. He in turn set the school secretary to work telephoning retired colleagues who might be able to tell me how the school got its name; another man was sent to find a caretaker who had worked at the school for forty years.

It felt as if a major part of the school's resources had been committed to answering my question. Mr Sharma, proud of what he described as the most prestigious government school in Delhi, admitted that he knew little about its history, because he had not been there long. His predecessor had been transferred to a less well-known school because he'd refused to admit pupils recommended by politicians. Officially, enrolment was only by examination, with 2000 children competing for 150 places, but politicians' nominations would take up at least 25 per cent of them. Despite this, Mr Sharma was very happy because Ludlow Castle, he told me with stomach-puffing pride, had been chosen as 'a lifeline building for retrofitting'. I tried to look suitably impressed, even though I did not know what he was talking about. He was in full flow. 'They chose the police HQ, the divisional commissioner's office, a big hospital, the Delhi secretariat . . . ' and in a theatrical whisper, 'Ludlow Castle School'. He jumped up, waving his hands around. 'And this very room, my office, is the pilot room.' He started rushing round his office, pointing out the red clamps that attached his metal cupboards to the wall, the anti-slip mat for the trophies in the cabinet above his desk. And then he uttered the word 'earthquake' and all was clear.

At 9.20 a.m. on 8 October 2005 I was seated in my Delhi bathroom, reading *The Times of India*, when the earth moved. It was my first earthquake. For more than thirty seconds I was entertained by the tinkling dance of a dozen half-empty bottles of unguents and lotions lined up on the bathroom shelf. Meanwhile, more than 700 kilometres away in Kashmir, at least seventy thousand people were dead or dying. Delhi had been fortunate. A similar earthquake, with an epicentre closer to the Indian capital, would be devastating. The Delhi

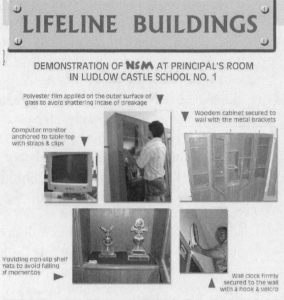

LIFELINE BUILDINGS

DEMONSTRATION OF **NSM** AT PRINCIPAL'S ROOM IN LUDLOW CASTLE SCHOOL NO. 1

Polyester film applied on the outer surface of glass to avoid shattering incase of breakage

Computer monitor anchored to table top with straps & clips

Wooden cabinet secured to wall with the metal brackets

Providing non-slip shelf mats to avoid falling of momentos

Wall clock firmly secured to the wall with a hook & velcro

government, with American technical and financial assistance, is trying to make some of its larger buildings as quake-proof as possible. And so, a Velcro strap has been attached to the wall-clock in Mr Sharma's Ludlow Castle office to ensure that an earthquake will not turn it into a lethal missile. The panes of glass on his trophy cabinet had been covered with shatterproof plastic. 'This is all non-structural mitigation,' he announced, as he led me through the chemistry lab, where beakers of acids were now stored on a tray with an anti-spill rim. In the biology lab, he pointed to a wall-mounted glass case containing a stuffed baby crocodile that still needed 'retrofitting' and then commanded me to sit down. The head of biology had just moved house, the headmaster explained, and so, amid bottles of dissected frogs and worms, and the unretrofitted crocodile, we sat down to a hearty snack of samosas, dhoklas[1], Black Forest gateau and sweet tea.

As I was inserting a third dhokla into my mouth, the school secretary rushed in and whispered at length in the headmaster's ear.

---

[1]Anyone who has not eaten freshly made dhoklas has not truly lived. They are cake-like slices of steamed chickpea flour, a staple snack in Gujarat; and when well-prepared, are tastier by several orders of magnitude than even the best Black Forest gateau.

The headmaster looked at me questioningly. I was concerned that I might perhaps have been mistaken for a VIP, given the warmth of my welcome, only to be revealed as a dhokla-stealing pleb. But the warmth was genuine, and they had been able to find out more about the history of Ludlow Castle. It had been a castle in British times, a huge one, Mr Sharma declared, spreading his arms out wide, with a giant ballroom; and it was built by a doctor called Ludlow hundreds of years ago and demolished in the 1950s. His information was, as I found out later that day, partially correct.

In the basement of a modern building at the foot of the Ridge, ten minutes from the site of Ludlow Castle, are the offices of an organization that calls itself 'Sarai'. Anyone who asks the simple question 'What is Sarai?' may not get such a simple answer. It is a place, but it also an idea. Sarai is Delhi at its most modern, its most virtual. It exists in a series of rooms in Civil Lines, but it also orbits in cyber-space. According to its own publicity literature, Sarai 'encompasses an inter-disciplinary research programme, a platform for critical reflection, a screening space, a convivial context for online and offline conversations and a media lab'. I have known about Sarai for several years, as an unashamed lurker on its e-mail groups—receiving regular updates on a eclectic range of subjects, often about Delhi, ranging from 'the Culture of Telephone Booths', through 'Society and the Soap Factory to 'Locating Sexuality through the eyes of Afghan and Burmese Refugee Women in Delhi'. Many of these discussions are suffused with post-modern jargon, but usually they are worth the effort.

Sarai—the non-virtual part of it—consists of three rooms: a private inner sanctum where individuals have their own workstations; a glass-walled public access computer area (the media lab), and a large meeting room with a café. No one looked up when I walked in and sat down, eavesdropping. There was a three-way discussion about French philosophers (Foucault and de Certeau), a young man was retying his ponytail as he watched cricket on a wall-mounted TV (not quakeproof—a potentially lethal missile, I decided), and a young woman was sitting at a table staring at her coffee mug as if it were an object of worship. I interrupted her to ask for help getting access to the Sarai online archive (I needed to find out more about Ludlow Castle). She gave me a split-second look of exasperation, before getting to her feet and handing me over to the resident computer expert. He took me into the media lab (with only one of the eight computers free), sat me down in front of a terminal and began logging me in. 'Username: guest. Password: guest. You do know Linux and Mozilla Firefox[2], don't you?' 'Er, yes—a little.' I was lying. I suppose I was rather proud of myself for having heard of them, and too embarrassed to admit that I hadn't ever used them. I knew that they were the main software competition to Microsoft, and that they were, in some way that I didn't quite understand, alternative, democratic and trendy. He'd put me on to a local area network where I could now access the archive. I entered 'Ludlow Castle Delhi' in the search box, and the entire screen went white. So did I. My usual solution, 'Ctrl-Alt-Del', had no effect, I panicked. And looking surreptitiously around, knowing I was doing something very naughty, I pressed my finger down hard on the on/off key. With a tell-tale squeak the screen went blank. I looked around again; no one was staring with disdain in my direction. I'd escaped detection, and thirty seconds later I turned the computer on again, to a profusion of messages about how sinful I'd been to turn it off improperly.

I clicked on an icon shaped like the head of a dinosaur, and to my astonished delight I found myself on the Firefox Internet browser. Again, I entered 'Ludlow Castle Delhi' in the search engine, and after a nerve-racking couple of seconds of white-screen uncertainty, I was able to begin piecing together a brief history of the 'Castle'. It was built in the 1820s for Doctor Ludlow, civil surgeon of the British community in Delhi, who added castle as a bit of arcane wordplay on the Welsh Marches' most famous ruin. The Delhi version was never much of castle—more of a sprawling two storeyed mansion, with some modest gap toothed crenellations and a stunted octagonal tower. It became the Residency, the official headquarters of the British Agent in Delhi, the last of whom was killed in the Uprising of 1857, officially referred to in Indian schoolbooks as the First War of Independence. Some of the bloodiest

---

[2] Mozilla Firefox—Netscape's successor and the main rival to Explorer as an Internet browser. A firefox is a red panda still found in India. Mozilla is a contraction of Mosaic Killer (Mosaic was the first widely used Internet browser). Linux is an open-source operating system, invented by Linus Thorvalds, a rival to MS Windows and Apple's Mac OSX.

battles of the Uprising took place amid the bungalows of Civil Lines, and Ludlow Castle itself changed hands several times. In the post-1857 era, Ludlow Castle retreated into a more genteel existence as the very British Delhi Club, a place of bridge and billiards, piano duets and whisky sodas. In 1903, it was the temporary home of the world's richest man, the Nizam of Hyderabad, who paid what was then the astonishing sum of £3000 to stay there while attending the Delhi Durbar marking the coronation of Edward VII as Emperor of India. With the building of New Delhi to the south, Civil Lines began to fade into relative obscurity, and the club was transformed into a school for boys. Eventually the old building was demolished as Ludlow Castle was turned into a model school, co-educational and bilingual. A Bombay blogger who went to the school in the 1950s remembers, 'my favourite perch, for eating my lunch, was a memorial [of the 1857 Uprising] over a solitary grave in our football field. Whenever they dug grounds in school for construction, human bones still turned up'[3]. And in 1984, the school became a place of refuge for thousands of Sikhs fleeing the violence that followed Indira Gandhi's assassination. It became briefly and tragically famous again in November 1997 when a school bus skidded off a bridge across the Yamuna and thirty Ludlow Castle School pupils were drowned. Now the search engine response to 'Ludlow Castle School' relates largely to 'earthquake retrofitting', with cute pictures of white-uniformed schoolgirls doing 'duck and cover' exercises, in which they hide and smile from under their desks.

The road up to Hindu Rao hospital from Sarai and Civil Lines is probably the steepest in Delhi, the only one where single-geared cyclists need to dismount and push. This is the Ridge at its most

[3] See thoughts-n-trivia.blogspot.com for Girish Bhatnagar's comments on Ludlow Castle School. A swimming pool was built in 1972 on the site of his lunch-table grave.

inhospitable, a dry-earth slope of rocks and thorn bushes. At the top, as well as one of Delhi's largest hospitals, are two very different sandstone memorials, each pointing skywards, each with a strong connection to the town of Meerut. Both have stood on the Ridge since the 1860s. The older and

shorter is a wind-polished tapering Ashoka pillar[4], carved more than two thousand years ago and inscribed with advice on how to be virtuous; it was brought to Delhi from the town of Meerut in the fourteenth century, broken into five pieces in an accidental explosion, clumsily reconstructed, and placed in its current setting in 1867. The younger one is the Mutiny Memorial, a Gothic steeple erected in 1863 by the British as a memorial to the soldiers who died defending the Ridge from the Uprising of 1857 that spread from the town of Meerut. Visitors are reminded that this is a partial view of the events that became known as the Mutiny—by a plaque placed on the Memorial in more recent times, as a kind of historical footnote, declaring 'the enemy of the inscriptions on this monument were those who rose against colonial rule and fought bravely for national liberation in 1857'.

The Hindu Rao government hospital has long been the butt of medical jokes, and has a reputation as a place, whether sick or healthy, which it's best to avoid. I first visited Hindu Rao in the early part of the new millennium, and while exploring the oldest part of the building[5] came upon a particularly squalid pile of medical waste in a corridor next to the plastic surgery ward. There were used syringes, soiled bandages and specimen bottles complete with specimens—and

---

[4] See Chapter 4 for Delhi's other Ashoka pillar at Feroze Shah Kotla.
[5] The oldest part of Hindu Rao hospital was built by the British Resident, William Fraser, who was murdered by an Indian nobleman in 1835. The house was bought by a merchant called Hindu Rao, after whom it was renamed. It was later turned into a hospital.

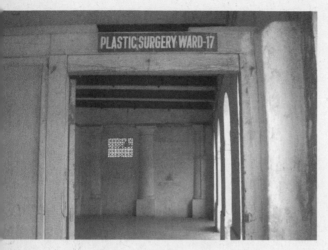

some cockroaches having a feast. Half a decade later, the plastic surgery wards had been emptied, the corridors cleaned and the cockroaches had disappeared. The only medical waste I could find was near the incinerator, neatly stacked in colour-coded heavy-duty plastic bags. Hindu Rao seems to have had a minor makeover. In 2005, it even got its own website as part of the Municipal Corporation of Delhi Hospitals' portal, launched with some fanfare as a new healthcare service to the people of the Indian capital. The site includes a brief history of the Hindu Rao building, clinic opening hours, several paragraphs of tongue-twisting medical obscurity (including references to Choledocholithotomy, Myringotomy and Sialolithiasis[6]) and a shopping list of operations provided by the hospital, including, I do not joke, 'amputation of penis'. It is not quite clear whom the website is targeting.

By my reckoning, I had now reached the highest point above sea level in Delhi. But there was no view of the city because the forests of the Ridge hide Hindu Rao from the rest of Delhi as if it were a Bavarian Schloss, occasionally peeping out from its emerald ruff. And so, to get an unbroken panorama of Delhi, I climbed the steps of the tower block that houses surgical wards, the blood bank and administrative offices, squeezing past a gaggle of jolly smokers— patients, visitors and staff—who have sequestered the final flight of the staircase as an open-air ward for future lung cancer sufferers. I stepped carefully between tidy cairns of cigarette and *bidi* butts and emerged into the sunlight on the roof of the hospital. I was staring down at something that was, momentarily, astonishing. It was a huge city that wasn't Delhi. There was absolutely nothing that I

[6] Choledocholithotomy is a surgical exploration of the bile duct, myringotomy involves an incision in the inner ear, sialolithiasis is caused by stones in the saliva duct.

recognized. I could not see the old walled city, or the river, or Civil Lines or Ludlow Castle School or the Mutiny Memorial or the Ashoka pillar. It was as if the Hindu Rao staircase had teleported me to another city. And then I spotted, in totally the wrong direction, the Gothic spire of the Mutiny Memorial. I realized that I had turned the city upside down, and smiling foolishly to myself, muttered, in an inverted echo of Kipling, that west is east, and east is west. And the city I knew was behind me, and the unknown city, so much larger than I expected, was West Delhi. Suddenly, for the first time, I began to see how Delhi with its low-density housing, its huge tracts of floodplain and forest, might contain a population of more than fifteen million. The city seemed to go on for ever.

I peered more closely at panoramic west Delhi, and with the help of the *Eicher* map could make out below me the late-imperial architecture of Delhi University, built as a temporary British cantonment, and the shrunken parklands which were once Mughal orchards, and two overground Metro lines snaking their way westwards, and in the far distance, the only place in Delhi further from the earth's core than Hindu Rao, the Pitampura TV tower beneath which I once heard Sting sing '*Roxanne*', his reggae-and-tango paean to a prostitute .

Hindu Rao's socio-economic footprint ripples down the western slopes of the Ridge—with small, unkempt buildings which provide homes for junior hospital staff, and house businesses selling an impressive range of surgical and pharmaceutical paraphernalia. And then at the bottom of the Ridge, this medical hinterland crashes into the footprint of another institution, Delhi University. There, on the streets, is a brief intermingling of white coats and T-shirts; of the sick and the stoned; of hypochondria and flirtation. Then, as I continue westwards, the students take over, establishing their own brief dominance with a wave of cybercafés, bargain boutiques and fast food shops. The University Bookshop's window display is plainly the creation of a marketing whiz-kid who has discovered that students aren't really interested in purchasing textbooks. The titles on display are *Creative Loving: An Inspiring Guide to the Art of Making Love*, *Guitar Facts*, *The Hitchhikers Guide to the Galaxy*, *Week-by-week Pregnancy Planner*, *India's Cricket Captains*, *Delhi Nightlife Guide* and *The Street Guide to Flirting*.

A mildly academic flavour spills beyond the University area and well into west Delhi. The Aptima Air Hostess Academy shares a newly whitewashed building with a mobile phone showroom and the British English Academy. A little further was the 'Bright College' which promised coaching classes in 'English Conservation'. I tried not to smile, pinning my lips together—and decided I would offer some corrective advice. But the receptionist showed no interest at all when I pointed out the spelling error, and told me that business was booming. I slunk off, reflecting on a minor dilemma. There are many books written by westerners about India which laugh at Indian ways of speaking and spelling in English, and I'd sworn that I'd not do that. I once laughed out loud at a sign in South Delhi which said 'Adult Litracy Centre' and pointed it out to my wife, who couldn't hold back a smile herself, but then lambasted me for making fun of Indians. The truth, she pointed out, is that many sign painters are illiterate in their mother tongue, and it's barely surprising that they have such trouble with English. 'So would you if you had to copy some words from Japanese.' And since then I have taken a more nuanced view of Indian infelicities in the English language. English is now another Indian language—spoken by more people than in my homeland. And Delhi alone probably has more English speakers than any English city except London. So who am I to tell an Indian how to parse her English noun clauses or that 'prepone'[7] is not a word?

I had earlier spotted a gaggle of African students outside a

___

[7] Prepone means the opposite of postpone—and is widely used in India, in everyday speech and in official documents, in place of the slightly ambiguous British English 'bring forward' or the American English 'move up'. For a full discussion of prepone see www.languagehat.com/archives/000645.php.

cybercafé near Delhi University, but as I trudged through the traffic-heavy, post-independence streets of West Delhi, I realized I was in a foreigner-free zone. It is unmentioned, a black hole, in Delhi's tourism literature. This was also virgin territory for me, and it reeked of doggedly optimistic aspiration. There were dozens of computer training centres, schools for beauticians and air hostesses, with every signboard in English, and, of course, an abundance of English-language academies and colleges. The message is brutally clear. You will be nothing if you don't learn English. Everyone in this part of Delhi speaks Hindi (often in addition to Punjabi) and yet almost all the signboards are in English. Most parents now want to send their children to English-medium schools, even when no one in the family speaks the language, and in spite of evidence that children who start learning in a language that is not their mother tongue do less well at school. The key role of English for the aspirant is to get a good white-collar job, and to raise your social status. Hindi and other languages are for films, family, friends, and, if you are rich and Anglophone, to give orders to your servants.

I soon came upon a petrol station, much like any other in Delhi, with puddles of dirty water and diesel, and angry motorists blocking each others' access. But this one had a bright yellow building next to it, which from a distance looked like a newly inflated bouncy castle. It was a 'convenience store' called 'In & Out' and is, I discovered later, part of a growing franchise of petrol station grocery shops across India. I stepped inside, and shivered at the strength of the air-conditioning. It was if I had left India, and entered a shrine to the global brand. There were no signs in Hindi; the interior was all steel and plastic. It all looked as if it had just been unpacked. And there on the shelves were a plethora of Western logos:

Hersheys and Heinz, Oreos and Pringles, Red Bull and Huggies, and, bizarrely, a half-shelf of Angostura Bitters. I asked the keen-to-help woman at the counter, in Hindi, whether the Angostura Bitters were selling well. 'Yes. Special promotion. Very popular. Three hundred rupees. Very nice drink,' she replied in perfect, verbless English. The shop, I learned, had been opened just three weeks ago—and, she promised me, with the letter-box smile of a customer-relationship trainee, that it was doing very well. 'Who shops here?' 'Everybody,' she managed to say, without altering the position of her lips. 'Poor people?' 'Everybody.' This conversation was going nowhere. I looked around for something to buy. I spied a box, the size of a pack of cards, on a shelf above her left shoulder, which bore my current favourite word, 'Spiral', and what looked like a picture of the Chrysler building. 'What is that?' She looked behind, and as she passed me the box, her smile crumpled inwards. I turned the box over, and saw that the Chrysler building was actually a picture of a latex prophylactic with a pinched tip, with the words: 'Moods. America's bestseller now in India—spiral condoms'. I was silent, and so was she. And she took the plunge and told me, helpfully, 'For sex'. Or at least I think that's what she said, because her voice had dipped to a mumbling, nervous tremolo—her composure shot, her lips quivering, but still committed to almost total customer satisfaction. Embarrassed by her embarrassment, I left, empty-handed. Outside, a few metres away, I spotted an advertisement for a more dangerous alternative to condoms, on a small placard attached to a streetlight: 'Abortion by Tablets. 100% results. RB Clinic. Tel: 27518472.'

Four hundred metres south of 'In & Out', I reached the first of West Delhi's two overground metro lines, on reinforced grey concrete stilts, high above the city streets. It's still early days for the Metro, and there seems to have been no clear plan of how to use the space at ground level immediately beneath the tracks. In some places, little shrub gardens have been planted, but because they're sheltered from the rain they don't get enough water. This space would be perfect, with a little work, for cycle lanes. And so for now, by default, these narrow, snaking corridors have become rubbish dumps, where clean-up squads of shiny-billed crows loiter and squawk, and a covered walkway, where pedestrians (in West Delhi, that means me, and the very poor) and outdoor sleepers (human and bovine) can get shelter from the sun and rain. I soon turned south-west, away from the serpentine sunshade, past a newly painted multi-coloured mosque and a group of resting female guava-sellers, and entered the Rama Road Industrial Area. This is one of Delhi's many industrial zones, marked, like most of them, by rutted roads, broken pavements, tall chimneys, strange acrid smells and forbidding roll-down aluminium gates: a memorial to old-fashioned manufacturing. These are mainly medium-sized businesses—plastics and printing, lubricants and electroplating—and, by law, have details of stored chemicals inscribed on the exterior of the buildings. A hand-painted notice outside an electroplating workshop warns of the dangers of sodium cyanide. 'Fatal if inhaled or swallowed. Do not breathe dust. Keep away from food. Wash thoroughly after handling.' The watchman tells me that the electroplating is used to make metal jewellery shine. Behind him are rusted metal drums bearing the skull-and-crossbones sign. This does not seem a good place to linger. Further on, the municipal demolition squad had been visiting, bulldozing buildings that had violated planning laws. It could have been a bomb site. Baffled workers were picking through the rubble, stringing up blue plastic sheeting as temporary shelter. A boss screamed insults into his mobile phone. An employee tells me that the authorities had been paid off, and had promised that this factory would be spared.

Like so much of Delhi, Rama Road is in a state of flux. Suddenly, a few hundred metres on, I passed through an invisible curtain that seemed to divide Delhi's grimy industrial past from its scrubbed-clean commercial future. Post-modern metal-and-glass buildings proliferated, with computer-generated toy-town architecture, prefabricated multi-coloured facades, some still under construction. They're for rival delivery firms ('We deliver anytime, anywhere'; 'Our people go to the ends of the earth for you'), car showrooms (Chevrolet

203

and Tata), machine tools and printing equipment. Noritsu—a Japanese 'photofinishing' company—had what looked liked the priapic nosecone of an intercontinental ballistic missile in its forecourt. It turned out to be a reception area. Nearby, a building simply bearing the man-size letters 'VM' appeared to have been made from giant orange, red and white Lego bricks. It was all glossily confident, and determinedly global.

Beyond the Industrial Area, I spied the second of the cross-Delhi metro lines, even higher above the ground, taking commuters to and from Connaught Place. Again I was seduced by the shadow of the Metro, and walked under struts that gently vibrated as the trains passed above. But the shadow was slowly shrinking, because the train track was climbing higher, as if heading for the heavens. I soon found out why. At Rajouri Garden, a gardenless residential suburb, the Metro has to fly over a flyover, an urban transport triple-decker. The two lower layers are sluggish roads of battered trucks and family hatchbacks, and the topmost layer, eighteen metres above me, has sleek blue-and-silver trains speeding past. But the trains are not alone in the newly populated upper atmosphere of West Delhi. For at the same level, is a just completed five-storey shopping mall, part of a huge retail project that has turned much of this area into a building site. I was surprised. I had not realized that West Delhi was rich enough to support this kind of enormous development. West Delhi has the reputation of being a place to avoid, not because it's dangerous or very poor, but because it's an area which people leave as soon as they can afford to.

This is changing. And the metro is part of the reason. Property prices along the metro lines have shot up, and soon so will a series of shopping malls. Rajouri Garden is the vanguard, and a taste of the global future. Inside, air-conditioned, is a huge enclosed courtyard ringed by five layers of shops, linked by escalators, with a low hum of muzak, and the smell of cheap cleaning fluid. I could be almost anywhere. A pigeon is trapped inside. A distressed child watches as it crashes against a glass walkway; she wants her father to do something about it and she says something to him, pointing at the bird. He does not look, but tugs at her hand and pulls her towards the bright lights of McDonalds. A stooped man in khaki uniform is cleaning the marble floor with a motorized circular mop. Unseen by him, two young girls are playing hopscotch with the mop's electric cable. I lift my camera viewfinder to my eye. A security guard gently taps me on the shoulder and tells me I can't take any photographs. He is so mild in his manner that I don't have the heart to protest. I spot a photo booth, which promises, in Italian, for no obvious reason, and with no translation, '*tua caricatura in pochi secondi*'; your caricature in a few seconds. A tight-lipped youth with a proud smile is guarding the booth. He doesn't know why the text is in Italian. I am his first customer of the day. He points keenly to some photos of crumpled, distorted European faces gazing out unappetizingly from the side of the booth. I was about to walk away, when I remembered my encounter with the box-camera man behind the Birla Mandir, two spiral-twists ago, whom I'd allowed to decapitate me for the sake of art and religion. So why not let a more modern machine train its disfiguring lens on me? In return for Rs 150, a decent day-wage for a Delhi labourer, out plopped a version of my face that was distended in every direction and, more alarmingly, was better-looking than the original. I tucked it into my bag, certain that it would amuse my children later in the day.

I took a glass lift to the top floor and found myself in a food court. I felt inexplicably forlorn. I sat down at a formica table close to the walkway, from where I could watch the shopping mall in action. I imagined that each person in my vision had left behind a yellow luminous footprint as they walked, and before long the shopping mall was lit up, in my mind, by strange lozenges of phosphorescence that congregated outside the most popular shops. Dolefully, I began counting the foreign brands and gave up. Almost every shopper was wearing western clothes; the background music was

205

identical (*Bright Eyes*, *Bridge over Troubled Water*) to what I might hear in any British shopping centre. McDonalds had the prime location in the mall, and had taken on a yellow glow all of its own. The pigeon was still flapping around manically. I do not like shopping malls at the best of times, and I was beginning to feel a little like the pigeon. Delhi, this city I had been seduced by, was itself being seduced by the West. Delhi was beginning to be just like anywhere else. Were all big cities destined to resemble each other? With huge air-conditioned shopping malls, with every signboard in English (or Italian), with shops that sell the same brands, with customers who wear the same clothes and eat the same food. This could be Singapore, Dubai, or New York.

Behind me was a series of food counters, with bored young men and women waiting for customers, occasionally stirring pre-cooked food coagulating in silvery Alzheimer troughs. One counter caught my eye. It was called 'Street Foods of India'. I played with these four words on my tongue. Was this a post-modern joke? And would anyone else find it funny? After all, this was just about the one place in India where you wouldn't find street foods. I walked over, and asked a chef with a paper hair-net and a plastic spatula whether customers wouldn't prefer to get street foods on the street. 'No. Not at all. Here the food is clean.' There were a few customers with whom I tried to discuss the subject. They looked at me askance, as if I was the one with the irony by-pass. One samosa-eater told me the food was bland, not as good as on the streets. I felt briefly justified in my distressed amusement. Then, I caught sight of myself, in a mirror at the back of the food court. I was a caricature of myself again, a jabbering, sniggering foreigner, playing pedantic word games. Above my head in the mirror, I saw a white banner, with the words 'THE BEST OF THE WEST' like a caption to the caricature, as if it were a mocking description of me. I felt exposed and chastened; the victim of my own joke. I swivelled round to see the huge banner hanging from the steel and glass ceiling. So, I thought, my heart sinking again, this shopping mall is supposed to be the Best of the West: Nestlé, Reebok, Costa Coffee, and McDonalds. This was my worst of the west—brandname materialism, franchise capitalism. It really was time to leave. I took the escalator down. The pigeon was still there, perched on a handrail, happier now, eating a French fry. I peeped inside McDonalds. It was bursting. The bird-loving girl was blowing bubbles into the residue of her strawberry milkshake. Every table was occupied. This was recognizably McDonalds, with its golden arches[8] and a cut-out of that desperate-to-please clown— but it could also be nowhere else but India. There were no Big Macs here; beef is not on Indian menus. Instead there's Chicken McCurry, Paneer Salsa Wrap and McAloo Tikki[9]. In some unexpected ways, I was beginning to figure out that the West is also having to make compromises as the world shrinks and flattens and homogenizes. And as I left, wondering whether it was possible to be allergic to shopping malls, I suddenly realized that 'The Best Of The West' was probably just referring to West Delhi, and I'd shown a Westerner's arrogance by presuming it to be 'my' West.

[8] India (and Pakistan) appear to disprove Thomas Friedman's Golden Arches Theory of Conflict Prevention which states that 'No two countries that both have McDonald's have fought a war against each other since each got its McDonald's.' McDonalds arrived in India in 1996 and Pakistan in 1998, and they fought an undeclared border war in 1999. Lebanon and Israel are a more recent counter-example to the Golden Arches Theory. Friedman insists his theory was tongue-in-cheek, and in his more recent writings he has espoused the Dell Theory of Conflict Prevention, which argues that two countries which are both part of a major global supply chain will not go to war. Dell, of course, has nothing to do with Delhi—but is an American computer company with a large customer call centre just outside the Indian capital.

[9] Paneer is Indian cottage cheese; aloo tikki is a spicy fried potato patty.

A Ninth Intermission

I HAVE FINALLY come across another Delhi *flaneur*. In 1971, the novelist Ruskin Bond also walked from Connaught Place to Rajouri Garden (he took a more direct route than me) for no better reason than that he enjoyed walking, and that he thought he'd see more of Delhi if he walked. Bond, famous in India for his gently humorous tales of life in the Himalayan foothills, describes in his memoirs how he arrived at the house of his friend, Kamal, in Rajouri Garden. When he explained to Kamal's family that he had walked there from Connaught Place, they 'greeted me with a pained and bewildered silence. Finally my friend's mother, a practical Punjabi lady, asked: "How did you lose your money?"' Bond records that the consensus of opinion in his friend's house was that he was a little mad. They had never heard of anyone in Delhi walking from choice[1].

Except for the occasional stroll in the park, the rich of Delhi almost never walk. They prefer to shop. India's leading news magazines now have free 'lifestyle' supplements, devoted to conspicuous consumption, and packed with ads and plugs for expensive and not-terribly-useful luxury items. The cover story for a recent 'Life & Style' magazine supplement was an interview with a gamine Delhi socialite and businesswoman who had just been appointed Dior's 'brand ambassador' in India. When asked about 'must-haves' for the Indian woman, she replied, 'Every woman should have one nice classic bag, even if it is for 25,000 rupees'. That's more than $500. It would take at least one-and-a-half years for an Indian woman on the minimum wage to earn that kind of money. And it would take her ten years to earn enough money to buy an unprepossessing man's watch advertised elsewhere in the same magazine, and several lifetimes to get her hands on the bottle of 1787 Chateau d'Yquem discussed by one of India's leading sommeliers in a tailpiece article. Being rich, and wanting to be rich, are 'in'; there is a pandemic of affluenza, that phantom disease that creates an insatiable hunger

[1] Ruskin Bond: *The Lamp is Lit* (Penguin India, 1998). Bond was born in India of British parents in 1934, was named after John Ruskin, and has lived most of his life in the Himalayan foothills.

for things one does not need. Delhi is a city on the make. The wealthy fear only the taxman. There is no shame in acquisitiveness; and no vulgarity in broadcasting the costs of acquisition.

Another lifestyle magazine rhapsodizes over a limited-edition Boucheron mobile phone, 'exclusively designed' for the Indian market, which has a diamond-encrusted cobra encircling the key-pad: 'the ultimate in cellular chic'. Each cobra-phone costs almost sixteen million rupees each, or three for a million US dollars. The promotional literature declares, quite accurately and with great pride, that 'they are completely beyond the reach of the man on the street; [but] nevertheless the phones carry huge aspirational value.' As someone who has lost four cell phones in the past two years, the Boucheron mobile would certainly be wasted on me. I'm not sure what 'the man on the street', presumably a walker, would make of it. A friend told me that his cousin, a private banker and profligate gadget-collector, had bought one. Apparently, it helped establish his credentials with his billionaire clients.

But my friend, a veteran observer of Delhi society, also assured me that there were signs of hope. He told me the tale of a Delhi businessman who, over a period of about forty years, had transformed himself from a down-at-heel spiv to a hyper-rich philistine and was now showing an unexpected interest in the environment, intermediate technology and Delhi's heritage. In Europe or Britain, that transformation normally takes many generations.

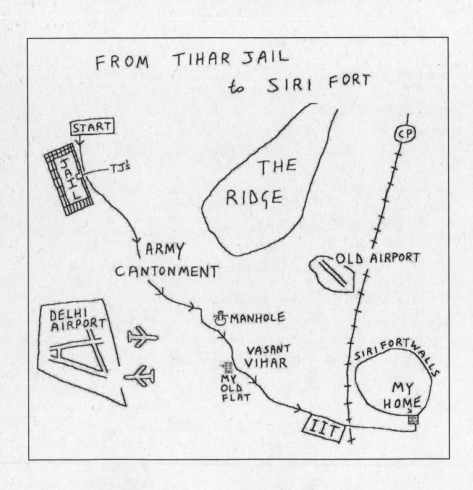

Chapter Ten: In which the Author tries to break into jail, falls into a manhole and encounters several tiny terrorists

OCTOBER 2006: ASIA'S largest prison is searching for a hangman. There have been no executions at Delhi's Tihar Jail since 1989, when two Sikhs who took part in Indira Gandhi's killing were sent to the gallows. But a Delhi court has just set a date for the execution of Mohammed Afzal Guru, a Kashmiri who has been on Tihar's death row for four years. Guru was convicted of organizing the 2001 terrorist attack on the Indian Parliament, in which 14 people were killed. As I resume my walk, this morning's inside-page update is that although the gallows have been recently refurbished, a new rope is needed and Tihar will need to borrow a hangman from another jail, somewhere else in India. Guru is due to hang in just two weeks, there are street protests in Kashmir, and it's possible that he is innocent.

'TJs' is a retail brand. It has a logo of its own, a red bird that appears to be carrying the letters T and J from its beak, like a stork delivering a baby. The main retail outlet for TJs products is a rather unusual gift shop, with the same name. It stands all alone, far from any shopping mall or street market. Its entrance is set into the wall of Delhi's longest urinal. I spotted seven drive-by pissers—two cyclists, one autorickshaw driver, and four car passengers, their vehicles clumsily parked on the kerbside. The stench of urine was overwhelming by the time I reached the iron gates of TJs. The urinal is in fact the eastern wall of Tihar Jail, whose initials give the brand and the shop its name; and the gifts inside are all made by prisoners.

TJs is dank and poorly lit. A bald man was at the till, seated and fast asleep, his body contorted on his chair so that his head could rest neatly on the counter. A lone black ant crawled along the ridge of a skin-crease towards the nape of his neck. Inside the shop, there were neat piles of off-white cotton shirts and woollen shawls, shelves of coloured candles and woven rugs, prisoner-painted greetings cards, five-litre plastic bottles of mustard oil, potato crisps and biscuits, all of it Tihar Jail produce. Each item bore the TJ's logo, and a request for 'help in the rehabilitation of a prisoner'. The bald man woke up with a start, scratching his head where the ant had just crossed and asked me, gruffly, what I was doing. 'Shopping,' I said. He eyed me suspiciously. He had not been on a customer relationship training course. I asked him what was behind the locked door at the back.

'The jail.'

'Can I have a look?' I said, trying to peep through a tiny crack.

'No. What do you want?'

'Just looking . . . Is this all made by the prisoners?'

'Yes'

'Even the mustard oil?'

'Yes. They have fields inside.'

'How many customers have you had today?'

'I'm not sure.'

'Ten, twenty . . .'

'Umm . . . none. Some people came yesterday, but they didn't buy anything.'

'It must be boring.'

'Very boring,' he said with feeling. He was beginning to warm up. 'I'm a prison officer, and it's like a punishment for me, working here. It's much more exciting inside.' He pointed at the padlocked door. I was reminded of the morning's death row headlines.

'Have you met Mohammed Afzal Guru?' I asked.

'Who?'

'The man who's going to be hanged.' I could not remember the Hindi word for 'hanged', and grabbed by own neck, using my hand as a noose.

'The terrorist? No, haven't met him. He's in Jail No. 3.'

'Should he be killed?'

'Yes. All terrorists should be killed.'

'What if he's innocent?'

'He's not. The court says he was guilty.'

'Judges make mistakes.'

He gave me a look of exasperation

'So what. Innocent people die all the time. Why is there all this fuss about a terrorist?' He decided to change the subject. 'Do you want to buy anything?'

212

'What should I buy? Are the coconut biscuits good?

'Very dry.'

'And the candles.'

'They burn OK. But they're cheaper in the market.'

TJs was someone's great idea, a unique venture, but it's also an anomaly in a market-driven world. The shop pays no rent because it's on prison land; it's staffed by prison officers, and its products are the result of the modern-day equivalent of slave labour. It doesn't matter if it has no customers, or no profits. It is not clear, however, that it serves any purpose, apart from keeping the prisoners busy. I left with a tiny striped carpet as a present for my daughter, and a packet of crisps.

Striding on towards the main entrance, past two more unembarrassed urinators, I wondered whether, if I looked confident enough at the gates, I could break into Tihar Jail. There have been plenty of famous break-outs[1], after all. I opened the crisps, which were translucent, coated in grease and unusually chewy. I noticed a crushed ant on the back of the packet. At least it was on the outside. I reached the gates. An autorickshaw had drawn up with two female passengers: a uniformed prison officer and a woman with a large bloody bandage around her head and a big smile on her face. She stuck her tongue out at me, and curled it up to touch her upper lip, in a show of exaggerated lasciviousness. I offered her a crisp. The prison officer, coy and apologetic, stepped between us, explaining in English that she was escorting a prisoner who had been to hospital to have a large cyst removed from the side of her head. I tried to follow them in.

'Where are you going?' a male guard asked me.

'Inside. Just visiting.'

'Who are you visiting?'

'I am visiting Mohammed Afzal Guru.' I said with the assumed confidence of a regular visitor to Tihar.

'He is not a woman.'

---

[1] Most famous were the serial killer Charles Sobhraj, who drugged his guards with some doped birthday cake and strolled out of Tihar in 1986, and Sher Singh Rana, accused of killing the 'Bandit Queen', Phoolan Devi (who was by then an MP). Rana left Tihar in the company of a friend who was impersonating a police officer. Both Sobhraj and Rana were later recaptured.

My confidence was shaken by this unexpected response. There is lot of confusion about Guru's activities before the attack on the Parliament building, but his gender was never, to my knowledge, in doubt. 'Definitely not,' I replied, wondering quite where this conversation might go next.

'This is the entrance to the women's prison.' He pointed to a signboard above my head which I would have seen, had I approached from the main road, rather than having slithered my way past the pissers along the eastern wall of the jail complex. This was in fact the entrance to what has become notorious as the 'mothers-in-law' section of Tihar. Women accused of setting their daughters-in-law on fire are incarcerated behind these gates[2]. I was clearly not going to be allowed in and followed the overhead road signs to Delhi Cantt.

'Cantt' is short for Cantonment, and is home to more than 125,000 people occupying a huge area of south-west Delhi only slightly smaller than Manhattan. Here, and only here, the Indian armed forces are

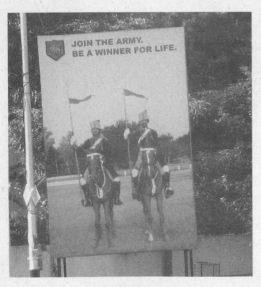

supreme. Unlike most of its neighbouring countries, the Indian military has never been seriously tempted by political power. However, Delhi Cantt is much more than an extended barracks, and has become a city within a city—with its own schools, hospitals and cinemas, a railway station and a golf course. Its sleepy streets are cleaner and emptier than the rest of the city, and are named after British and Indian Generals. There are no high-rises, and the buildings—

[2] Every week the Indian media carry gruesome tales of 'dowry-deaths' and 'bride burning', in which new brides have had kerosene poured on them and then been set on fire by their in-laws, because their families had not provided them with a big enough dowry. The bridegroom can then remarry and receive another dowry. The in-laws usually say it was an accident and that the end of the bride's sari caught fire when she was cooking in the kitchen. These days the police tend to take the side of the dead, and arrest the living. But it has proved hard to convict and many of those in the mothers-in-law jail have been released.

many of them from British days—are set back from the road, surrounded by trees, well protected from prying eyes. Civilians can walk, cycle and drive through some parts of Delhi Cantt, but most of it is off-limits and I was forced to deviate from my preferred route. A military policeman told me to delete all my photos when I took out my camera to take a picture of a recruitment poster showing two overdressed cavalry officers on horseback ('Join the army. Be a winner for life'). It wasn't worth arguing—and I pretended to obey.

I reached the Delhi Cantt market, where three men in khaki were queuing at a cash-point. The gutters were clean, and high-ankled army boots were laid out in neat piles in front of a series of military supplies shops. No one was shouting, and there was a serious shortage of street foods. I went into a small empty vegetarian restaurant to check that I hadn't really deleted any photos, and there I saw, on a mute TV, images of a small, bemused, dark-haired boy. The shot zoomed out, and the boy was holding a woman's hand. They were accompanied by a large crowd, with lots of news cameras, and the boy and his mother were walking through the main gates of Tihar Jail. I had worked out that the boy was Guru's son, Ghalib, whose name I'd remembered from my morning newspaper for its echo of Delhi's best-known poet. They had come from Kashmir to visit Guru, and to meet the President to appeal for clemency. I asked the restaurant manager to turn up the sound. He did, but then drowned out the commentary with a breathless tirade against all terrorists, in which category he included most Kashmiris and all Muslims. He was silenced briefly by a report on an outbreak of dengue fever in Delhi, which had killed more than twenty people. He scratched his arms furiously as if this might ward off the dengue-carrying mosquitoes[3] . He then told me that anyone who opposes the hanging of terrorists should also be hung. Now, I am opposed to capital punishment and so was faced with a mild dilemma. Should I reveal myself, even before I'd ordered lunch, as, in the restaurant manager's words, a terrorist-lover, deserving of the gallows? I decided to limit myself to a cup of tea, and nervously told him that I thought the death

---

[3] Dengue is also known as breakbone fever because of the pain it causes in the bone and joints. In 1999 dengue returned to Texas after a gap of 20 years when a minor epidemic hit the border town of Laredo.

penalty should be abolished. He smiled, and became ingratiatingly pleasant. For a moment I thought he was trying out his customer relationship skills, but actually he was just practising the art of sarcasm. 'Of course nobody should be killed. You are right. Nobody should die. We should abolish death, all death. No more dengue, no more death penalty, no more car crashes, no more cancer.'

He screamed 'Chai lao' (bring tea) at a young boy who had been wiping the tables, very ineffectively. He could not have been much older than Ghalib. I asked the boy why he wasn't at school. He didn't answer. I told the restaurant manager that later this month it would become illegal for him to employ children under fourteen.

'Well, he'll lose his job, then. He's useless anyway.'

'Shouldn't he be at school?'

'That's not my business.'

'Where does he stay?'

He pointed to the bench I was sitting on.

'So where will he go?'

'Bihar, I suppose. That's where he came from.' The manager fell silent, and used his remote to flick through the channels. He stopped when he found another update on the Guru story—street riots in Srinagar, as local politicians warned that Guru would become a martyr. The manager snorted. I paid and left, before he could tell me that they should also all be hanged.

I headed out of Delhi Cantt towards South Delhi, with Guru and the Guru-hangers on my mind. I imagined debating the issue in public with the TJs prison officer and the Delhi Cantt restaurant manager, trying to resurrect the clichés of late-teenage late-night arguments about the death penalty. But Guru's execution had become a question of patriotism and a matter of faith, and neither his possible innocence, nor my moral queasiness about capital punishment, would carry much weight. In my mind's eye I saw the kernel of an argument that might win them over. Why should terrorists be given the satisfaction of an early and violent death, which so many of them clearly crave? Surely they will suffer more by being incarcerated, despised and then forgotten for the rest of their natural lives. It was a powerful, if disingenuous, argument; and in my mind I had won over the Guru-hangers. I savoured my imaginary victory, applauded by my fellow debaters, my head held high. I then fell into a manhole.

I had fallen into one of the few manholes in Delhi that was dry and clean, and broad enough for a large human. It had been built recently as part of a scheme to widen the main road to the airport. I was standing in a circular hole, over a metre in diameter, and the top half of my body, north of the navel, was visible to a tribe of bemused construction workers. The  subterranean lower half of me seemed intact. I could feel a dribble of liquid warmth trickling gently down my bare left shin. My bad knee moved only a little less smoothly than it had earlier. But I was shaken and embarrassed, and a little bloody—and had forgotten all about the Guru-hangers. One of the construction workers helped me clamber out. A comedian among them asked me what I was doing there. The other workers thought his question very funny and applauded. I failed to join in the banter or to ask them why they had left the cover off the manhole. I sat down on a reinforced concrete slab, perforated with steel, and dabbed my injured shin with a paper tissue. And as I watched the blood congeal, and an alpine scab form, wallowing in self-concern, I briefly considered ending the spiral early. But I looked up and around. I realised that beyond the construction site, and some half-built flyovers, and more unwatered manholes, was my former home in Vasant Vihar, an upmarket residential area guarding the western boundary of South Delhi. I was about to reach the start of the Delhi that I know best. But for now, I could now only limp in the direction of an autorickshaw driver, who took me home.

Five days passed. Tihar procured a rope. The deputy superintendent of Tihar travelled more than 700 kilometres to the town of Buxar to collect it personally. The sixteen-foot wax-coated rope was made out of twenty separate yarns spun from Manila hemp[4] by prisoners in Buxar jail. Technical specialists were consulted to assess how long the

[4]Not actually a hemp, but a product of the leaf of the abaca tree, or *Musa textiles*, a relative of the common banana that is native to the Philippines.

gallows 'drop' should be. Too short—and death would be very slow. Too long—and there's a chance of decapitation. Indian news websites gave the English-speaking, computer-using elite a chance to take part in the debate. The hangers outnumbered the non-hangers by roughly ten-to-one. On the website of the acronymically-challenged CNN-IBN, one of India's newest and most professional news channels, there was a section entitled 'How to kill Afzal. Needle or rope?' Among the suggestions sent in by e-mail were that he be buried alive, have all his limbs chopped off and then allowed to bleed to death, or that medical students practise their surgical techniques on him while still alive, and without anaesthetic. 'Anand' asked, rhetorically:

> What the heck does it matter whether killers like Afzal Guru live in this world or not . . . are they going to contribute any good to the country . . . they shud be hanged the day the judgement is given . . . Hang him till his body rots and falls off the noose . . .

'Satya' had a potentially more effective way of ending the debate about clemency:

> Afzal Guru should be hanged in PUBLIC and those who are seeking for clemency for AFZAL GURU should be SHOT DEAD in public as they are even more dangerous than AFZAL himself . . . jai Hind

'Madan Tiwary' was almost alone in challenging the verdict:

> i personally feel that afzal guru didnt get fair chance to defend himself. I am an advocate and i have gone through several cases in which person spending life in jail is fully innocent. I demand retrial of afzal case and use of lie detector and brain mapping test.

There were Google links to the right of the CNN-IBN Internet forum that took you to a huge range of international 'death penalty resources', including directessays.com which can provide you with wide range of high school and college essays on capital punishment for just $19.95; there's a gruesome litany of botched executions, and a long list of exonerated 'criminals' who had spent more than a decade on death row[5] . Back on the CNN-IBN home page, dengue (more than

---

[5] Most bizarre of all, is deadmaneating.com—a website devoted to the last meals of Americans shortly before they are executed. Cheeseburgers are very

thirty-five now dead in Delhi) briefly replaced death-row fever. The cover of the *Outlook* news magazine had a magnified photographed of the zebra-striped, dengue-causing *Aedes aegypti* mosquito, under the headline 'The Tiny Terrorist'. The tiny terrorists will die when the cold weather comes, about the time Guru is due to hang.

With eight days to go before the execution, I returned to the manhole, still coverless, now full of swirling eddies of slate-grey water—and headed, with mixed feelings, towards my old home in Vasant Vihar. In early January 2003, I moved back to Delhi from London, after a ten-year absence and at very short notice. I had been posted, almost literally, to India. My colleagues and friends conspired to find us a flat in Vasant Vihar. It was considered an appropriate place for someone like me: a foreigner with kids who was moving to India for a few months and who worked for an international company. Vasant Vihar (it means 'Abode of Spring') has lots of other foreigners; it's very near the airport, and it has children who go to international schools. It has a grocery store that sells Brussels sprouts, South African grapefruit juice, imported head-lice medicine and other essentials. There's a nearby McDonald's and TGI Fridays. Short leases on flats are possible, if your company is prepared to pay the full rent up-front and at twice the normal rate. By the end of my first fog-laden January week in Delhi, I had taken a violent, visceral dislike to Vasant Vihar. I ranted to anyone polite enough to listen that Vasant Vihar was the worst of South Delhi, an odious, characterless place; an upmarket transit camp for expatriates and Delhi's nouveaux riches. After a few months, I had modified my view, and began to realize that South Delhi and even Vasant Vihar had hidden depths.

I was now skirting through a series of familiar side streets, avoiding Vasant Vihar's main drag, past legions of three-storey whitewashed stand-alone modern houses, a flat to each floor. These are what are known as builder flats. They are usually constructed without much involvement from an architect, to a modular design, with whatever

popular. Mauriceo Brown, executed by lethal injection for murder in Texas in July 2006 ordered 'fifteen enchiladas heavy with cheese and onions, onion rings or fries, eight pieces fried chicken and eight pieces bbq chicken, eight whole peppers, ten hard shell tacos with plenty of meat, cheese, onions and sauce, four double meat-double cheese-double bacon burgers, a boneless T-bone steak with A1 Steak Sauce and a pan of peach cobbler'. It is not clear how much he actually ate.

foreign-looking fittings and embellishments the builders have been able to pick up on the cheap. The streets are wide, and the pavements have become car parks. Most residents seemed to have at least two cars (and two drivers) and never use public transport. And most buildings have a side driveway, ensuring a smooth transition from air-conditioned flat to air-conditioned car without encountering Delhi's climate or its less affluent citizens. A saluting uniformed watchman in a wooden sentry box was receiving a regal wave from a white woman, barely visible through the tinted side windows of her SUV, as her driver sped her away to an air-conditioned office or beauty salon or lunch at a five-star hotel. I then reached a mini-conclave of minor embassies that signalled my proximity to our former home. My over-used *bon mot* of that time, when trying to find something nice to say about Vasant Vihar, was that our flat was handy for the visa sections of the Belarus and Namibian Embassies, where queues never formed.

Our very modern flat had a central corridor long enough to double up as my son's cricket pitch, enough large bedrooms to squeeze in several more families, marble flooring, a broken jacuzzi and, most bizarrely for Delhi, a sauna—perfect for storing suitcases, or as a hiding-place for children. Below us lived an Israeli diplomat whose security team would sometimes turn away our visitors as they attempted to enter the building, and whose modern-for-2003 IT system introduced me to free wireless access to the Internet. There was a nearby gym, where I once was thrown off the treadmill, cart-wheeling cartoon-like to the ground, as the result of a power-surge. The gym was still there, and so was the caretaker of our building who seemed pleased to see me. He told me the Israelis had left, and so had their hyper active security team. More foreign families had come and gone, there had been problems with the lift and the generator, but nothing much had changed.

I was in full nostalgia mode. I stood outside my old flat and spun around, executing some excited mini-spirals, as I remembered how I had begun, on foot, from this spot, to discover another side to the city, to replace my Delhi-detestation with a Delhi-addiction. And I could easily have missed out on my epiphany if I hadn't walked—and we all might have left Delhi when my original six-month posting was over. My unfortunate adventure on the treadmill forced me onto the streets. I became a *flaneur* in Vasant Vihar, chancing upon new routes that took me to unexpected places.

Like many upmarket areas in Delhi, Vasant Vihar and its buildings face inwards, coiled up, as if they don't really want to be part of the rest of the city. The only vehicular exits are usually major arterial routes. And so, unknown to most of its more affluent, non-pedestrian residents (including, for a while, me), Vasant Vihar is ringed by congested villages (aka slums) where sweepers, washerwomen, rubbish collectors, urban cowherds, odd-job men and gardeners reside, set among surviving tracts of rocky wilderness, dotted in turn with dilapidated medieval tombs and mosques. On the northern edge of Vasant Vihar, on one of my earlier walks, I came across the crumbling walls of an ancient fort, with a newly built golden gate, enclosing two well-tended pre-Mughal mosques, which serve as a boarding-school for more than a hundred young Muslim boys. They sat outside, on freshly mown lawns, in perfect symmetrical lines, dressed in white as if on call for the Indian cricket team, chanting in response to their bushy-bearded teacher. I had discovered a hidden footpath to the southern Ridge, where huge black-bristled pigs rolled about in ebony puddles, and young children played out their cricketing dreams, on sloping pitches of dust, with a rock for stumps, and a stick for a bat, all clamouring to play the part of the heterodox hero-batsman Virender Sehwag, born and raised in a Delhi suburb. The footpath no longer leads to wilderness, but to a construction site—for four shopping malls—that has swallowed up a large chunk of the southern Ridge[6].

Back on the spiral, I got briefly lost in the fourteenth-century remains of Delhi's earliest landscaped garden, now a tangle of thorns and a concealer of turds, before discovering a black pond the size of a baseball diamond. Its stagnant surface fizzed with insect life, the perfect breeding ground for tiny terrorists. Dengue fever was still spreading in Delhi, and just a short-haul mosquito flight away are hundreds of anxious Vasant Vihar expats. Their embassies told them to flush their toilets regularly and to dry their shower cubicles in order to stop the mosquito larvae from pupating. Hungry female mosquitoes suck the blood of the wealthy and powerful quite as eagerly as that of their less well-connected victims. The newspapers relate that two

[6]The site will house, boast its proud supporters, the largest shopping complex in Asia, and the fourth largest in the world. Its opponents say it that will cause serious environmental problems, and that its developers have broken India's planning laws.

of the prime minister's grandsons are recovering from a severe attack of dengue fever. But the poor and undernourished are still more likely to die since they are usually less healthy and lack access to good medical care. The big 'terrorist', Guru, was still head-to-head with dengue for the lead story.

His family returned to Kashmir, and the Indian President was considering his family's plea for clemency. A hangman was appointed, but he had never hanged anyone before, a virgin executioner—and a very experienced hangman complained to the press, saying the job should be his.

I fled the malarial, denguiferous borderlands of Vasant Vihar in the direction of my current home, half-a-morning's walk away. My route took me through the sleepy, well-tended campus of the Indian Institute of Technology or IIT, a creation of Nehru's India when tertiary education was seen as the key to development. Its famously impressive ex-students have served the rest of the world, and particularly Silicon Valley, extremely well. IIT Delhi became notorious, not only for exporting geniuses, but also for the bullying of new students—in a way that often involved nudity, penis measurement and public masturbation. I peered into several hostels, half-expecting to see the legendary conga of naked IIT freshers dance past, each (except the one at the head) holding the penis of the man in front of him. A notice-board declared that 'ragging' was forbidden, and, just below, that Ms Puneeta, of the Department of Chemistry, who had been bestowed with the 'Best oral award' for a presentation whose title alone merited some kind of prize: 'NMR studies of styrene/methyl methacrylate copolymers prepared by atom transfer radical polymerization'. It's something to do with plastic.

Panchsheel Park is in the heart of South Delhi, the city of the well-to-do. The super-rich live to the north in their Lutyens-style 'bungalows', or in 'farmhouses' along the city's southern borders. In the 1950s, most of South Delhi was farmland and villages, and as the poorer newcomers built to the west and east, the well-off moved southwards. These were, quite literally, greenfield sites. Today, South

Delhi is the haunt of the junior diplomat and the senior journalist; of expatriate aid workers and retired mandarins. This is Anglophone, blinkered, comfortable Delhi with its large pockets of well-hidden poverty, away from the main roads, away from the unprying eyes of its more affluent residents, who travel to their offices and golf clubs and sports centres in smart new cars (with chauffeur, of course—except on Sundays) and do not venture off-piste into the congested slums where their sweepers and washerwomen reside. Nowadays fewer people want live-in staff, and the minuscule servants' quarters get transformed into mini-gyms, or hobby rooms or dens for drum-playing teenagers. The rich of South Delhi live in flats and they know their square-footage. The shrunken, nuclear household is gradually becoming normal. Servants and grandparents will have to live out.

Panchsheel Park is much less of a transit camp than Vasant Vihar, and has an air of settled bourgeois sensibility. We live at the end of a cul-de-sac, at the top of a house built in the late 1960s, which is overshadowed by the crumbling stone walls of Siri Fort, built two-thirds of a millennium earlier. Unlike our earlier flat, there is no lift, or generator, or marble flooring, or sauna. A previous tenant tried and failed to retrofit the bathtub with a jacuzzi. The toilet seat (on which I experienced my first earthquake) is broken, and nips my left buttock every morning. The water dribbles from the shower, the plug points have been installed sideways on, or upside down, much of the woodwork is rotten, and rainwater leaks through the window frames. But its idiosyncrasies are not life-threatening, and it is deliciously eccentric in a part of the city where modular similitude prevails. This is a home that I love, and from which I have finally made my peace with Delhi. And best of all, only twenty metres away, just inside the walls of Siri, is one of those magical patches of half-tended wilderness, hidden away, unknown to the rest of Delhi. At sunset, I walk and run here, waving at or exchanging local gossip with other regulars, who, like me, want to keep this perfect place a secret.

We have a more comfortable life than in London, despite the inconveniences of power cuts and mosquitoes. We're ripe for teasing by western visitors, who are shocked, and perhaps envious, to see us with a maid, a cook and a driver. In Britain, this would be entirely unthinkable, and even a little tacky. In India, newly arriving expatriates are firmly advised that life is impossible without staff, and that you are helping the local economy by employing as many people as possible. A few puritans and privacy-lovers try to do without. They almost always fail, and their households stealthily grow. They are sucked back into a 'normal' South Delhi existence, in which tradition dictates that one spends a large chunk of one's week discussing 'staff' problems with one's friends. My eavesdropper's tally of three favourite topics for discussion are what to do about servants who have 1) 'absconded', or 2) who have bad body odour or 3) who want a regular day off each week.

The rich of South Delhi, expat and Indian, exist and proliferate in a strangely distorted economy, largely caused by the enormous disparity between the cost of land and labour. Rents are sometimes as high as in European cities, mainly because of scarcity at the top end of the market, but domestic workers' salaries remain, in relative terms, very low. Four thousand rupees, or just under fifty pounds, is seen as a good monthly salary for a cook. Some of the richest people in the world are Indian, including fifty-four who are dollar billionaires[7]. So are a large percentage of the poorest. Domestic servants sit somewhere in between. There are many signs of change. Servants with good English are finding better-paid jobs elsewhere, in shopping malls or call-centres; the arrival of so many more foreigners in Delhi has pushed up salaries, and some of the middle classes[8] will have to manage without, or employ new migrants to the city. Every day the Delhi newspapers have terrible tales of people who have been killed or robbed by their servants; and the Delhi police placed advertisements advising, 'you must verify your servant with police; his antecedents are important to be checked and don't allow visitors to stay with him overnight'. Recently, expatriate Delhi was thrown into a frenzy of fear when a Belgian diplomat living in Vasant Vihar

[7]According to Forbes 2007, at least twelve of India's fifty-four 'dollar billionaires' live in Delhi. There are more than 500 'rupee billionaires' in India.
[8]There is an interesting comparison to be made with the situation in pre-World War One Britain—when more than ten per cent of adult females were in domestic service. My grandfather, brought up in Edwardian England, used to say that you were middle class if you had one servant.

was murdered by her driver. This quickly transmogrified into a frenzy of moral posturing when it was revealed that they were lovers, and that the killing was, so the media informed us, 'a crime of passion'.

The date set for the execution passed. The virgin hangman was still a virgin. Guru was still alive, still on death row, his clemency appeal pending, with no official stay of execution and with no new date. The Guru-hangers were furious. Meanwhile, millions of tiny terrorists were suffocated by Diwali celebrations: mosquitoes murdered by the festive firework-and-cracker-induced air pollution—which just as predictably increases the incidence of bronchitis and emphysema among humans. Less dengue, more lung disease. Cold weather would soon kill the remaining mosquitoes, and, inevitably, a few of Delhi's least affluent residents. Back at Tihar, Guru was joined by a newcomer on death row; a lawyer, this time—convicted of stalking, raping and strangling a fellow law student in her South Delhi flat in January 1996. His father was a high-ranking police officer in Delhi at the time of his first trial—and he was acquitted. A second trial, held largely as the result of some very persistent public and media pressure, led to a death sentence. The Internet forums now demanded public castration. They also demanded the execution of another man, the son of a politician accused of shooting dead a woman who refused him a drink after closing time at a South Delhi nightclub.

As I sat in my study, slowly trawling through Internet newsgroups, forums and blogs, collecting Delhi opinions on the death penalty, and flinching at suggestions for gruesomely slow ways of torturing and executing murderers, two men began screaming at each other outside on the street. They were arguing about money. I went out—where a small crowd had gathered. The younger man had just knocked the older one to the ground, and was kicking him. I told them to stop in my bookish, honed Hindi, using the politest of imperatives. They briefly fell silent, looking at me as if I were a ghost, a white man speaking in tongues. The younger man helped the older man get up, and they staggered towards the main road. Before long they had resumed their drunken curses, threatening to chop each other into little pieces. My neighbour told me they were brothers. I returned to my study, disconsolate, to the verbal violence of the Internet forums, reflecting despondently on the brutality of my adopted city.

A Tenth Intermission

WHEN I FEEL melancholy or need to clear my mind, there is a special Delhi place where I go. I have always had such places. In London, it was the Thames near Albert Bridge, or Brompton Cemetery. When I first lived in Delhi, it was Humayun's Tomb, when it was wildly and romantically overgrown, not the prettily manicured World Heritage Site which it has now become. More recently, I have headed south to Delhi's earliest fortifications, one thousand years old—abandoned, broad, crumbling and deserted. There, walking along the walls of Lalkot, I sing to myself and no one can hear. I love to sing, and to hear myself sing, but over the years have been made to realize that I am tone deaf. I have been banned by my family from ever singing in public, even softly as part of a large group. But on the walls of Lalkot, there is not a soul. And my singing seems to scare away the mosquitoes and attract the local goats—as if I were some kind of Pied Piper. They're particularly keen on Bob Dylan's *Walls of Red Wing*, a near-tribute to my place of wandering[1]. But they all turned tail when I tried *Lonely Goatherd* from *The Sound of Music*, and pranced down a steep path into the forests of the southern Ridge.

When alone on the walls of Lalkot, and not entertaining the goats, I stand and stare and look around in awe: astonished to be so alone in the midst of one of the world's largest cities; astonished that such magnificently monumental ancient ruins are barely visited, astonished at the spectacular views of the surrounding forest, like a thick pile carpet beneath me, and also astonished by the sight in the mid-distance, rearing out of the carpet, of a single extraordinary building, instantly recognizable, towering, beacon-like, priapic, over southern Delhi.

If Humayun's Tomb is the most beautiful of Delhi's great monuments, the Qutb Minar is the most distinctive. It has dominated the landscape of this part of Delhi for the past eight hundred years. Seventy-two metres high and like a huge embossed, tapering chimney,

[1] Lal means red, and kot means fort. But no one refers to Lalkot as the 'Red Fort' to avoid confusion with the other, Mughal 'Red Fort' in Old Delhi.

it was for several centuries the highest tower in the world. It is clearly and impressively visible shortly before landing at Delhi airport, and from close-up the effect is no less dramatic, with the intricate carvings of Koranic verses in the red sandstone barely damaged by centuries of monsoon rains and Delhi grime. And it continues to attract large numbers of tourists, who visit the Qutb (they are no longer allowed  to climb its staircase, for safety reasons) and the adjacent mosque, and who run the gauntlet of snake-charmers and souvenir sellers, and then depart for the other sights of Delhi or the comfort of their hotels. But by doing so, they miss out on an experience that is perhaps just as rewarding: a walk along the walls of Lalkot and a wander around nearby Mehrauli, an extraordinary jumbled-up collection of mosques, wells, tombs and palaces, dating as far back as the eleventh century.

This city is littered with ancient ruins; so many that it is easy to become blasé about them. One modern gazetteer lists more than a thousand. In the park near my home, I have found several more unlisted buildings, almost certainly dating back to the fourteenth century. One of them is a cathedral-like structure three storeys high, peeping over the trees. Anywhere else, I can't help thinking, this beautiful, forgotten building would be a major tourist attraction.

And a new area of wilderness near my home was opened up recently by construction workers laying a water main. And there, on my third or fourth visit, I found a half-ruined stone-built mosque with perfect squinches and beautifully carved rosettes with Arabic calligraphy in the centre, standing deep in the forest, accessible to only the most determined walker. I could find no record of it in all the gazetteers and guidebooks. I fear it may be dismantled for building materials or bulldozed as part of a 'redevelopment'. And I've tried to interest other people in the mosque. I tell people about it at Delhi

227

parties—and they yawn. I telephoned a leading historian of the Sultanate period, who promised he'd get back. A guide-book writer did come to see—and she tells me it will be mentioned in the next edition. But I've failed to get anyone else half as excited as me, and I've found it hard to make the case that this archaeologically super-rich city would be much poorer without this one old half-mosque.

I do, however, find it very beautiful and care very much about its survival. And so I am trying out a new tactic: Geocaching. Near the start of my walk, at Jantar Mantar, I found an American, grubbing in the dust, who introduced me to the wonderful world of the geocache. It's a kind of international treasure hunt. The idea is to hide something—usually valueless objects such as some old buttons or badges—and post details of the 'cache' on the Internet. And so, one summer evening, I filled a plastic jar with coloured paper clips, together with a small log-book, a pen and a lay person's guide to geocaching. Watched by a furious peacock, fanning its magnificent tail at me, I placed the plastic jar in a niche in the mosque, well out of the reach of goats. I posted details of the cache on geocaching.com—and went away to Europe, checking my e-mail regularly to see if a flow of intrepid treasure hunters came to my obscure mosque. Just one wandering geocacher searched for it, and e-mailed me claiming the coordinates were inaccurate, and that he anyway been had chased away by an irate pig.

Postscript: I returned to Delhi after a long summer break, and on my first evening back walked to the broken mosque—to check my coordinates, and make sure the cache was still hidden in the wall-niche. I was astonished to find that the half-mosque had disappeared—indeed there was no sign that it had ever existed. The co-ordinates had been correct but the building had been bulldozed. In its place squash and badminton courts were being constructed for

228

the Commonwealth Games. I felt responsible. I had not tried hard enough to protect a place I had known was threatened. But now there was nothing I could do. The mosque was lost to history.

BEFORE

AFTER

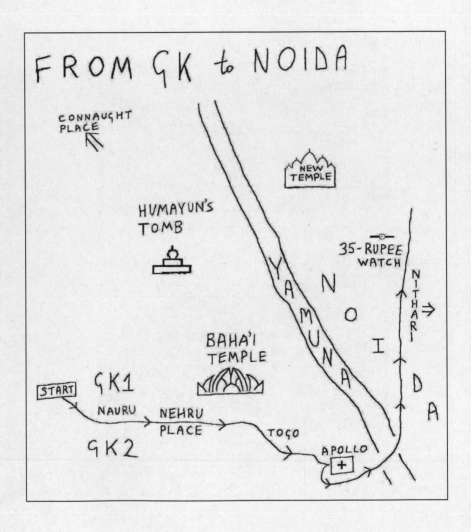

Chapter Eleven: In which the Author is phlebotomized, meets a human yo-yo and avoids the cannibals of Noida

IT IS THE fate of rapidly growing cities to have unimaginative place names. Delhi has four Gandhi Nagars, three Rajiv Colonies, three Indira Vihars and three Nehru Nagars. The city has innumerable sectors, phases, pockets and blocks. They are lettered or numbered, not necessarily in order, or have a broad range of alphanumeric combinations, often containing a backslash or a hyphen. South Delhi has no less than eight contiguous low-density, up-market neighbourhoods each with Kailash as part of its name[1]. Greater Kailash, abbreviated in speech and writing to GK, the name borne by three of these neighbourhoods (GK I, GK II, GK III), has had a life of its own on the Internet and has been the subject of a wiki[2]-war, or minor skirmish in cyberspace. An April 2006 entry in Wikipedia, declared that GK is a 'pretty posh locality and one of the best places to stay in Delhi.' In June, another Wikipedia contributor and GK-hater, changed a few words so that it became: 'It is an unplanned congested locality and one of the worst places to stay in Delhi'. To which the published response was 'Whomsoever wrote this is a jerk and probably [can] not even afford a shanty in GK. Loser.' This slanging match was deleted in its entirety by July from the main entry on Greater Kailash, but is stored on Wikipedia's easily accessible archive. Then in August, the anonymous, canophile admirer of a GK pet shop (its owner, I suspect), with the moniker 'Delhidude', re-

[1] Greater Kailash One, Two and Three; Greater Kailash Enclave One and Two; Kailash Colony, Kailash Hills and East of Kailash. Kailash is a mountain in Tibet, sacred to Hindus as the original home of the god, Shiva. Most of the Kailashes are divided into lettered blocks, but not in alphabetical order.

[2] Wikipedia is an Internet-based encyclopedia, written by members of the public, which dates back to 2001. 'Wiki' has a become a catch-all prefix for almost any kind of publicly created collaborative online content, but wiki comes originally from the Hawaiian word for fast. Wiki has become a backronym for 'what I know is . . .' 'Backronyms are words that have retrospectively turned into acronyms, where the words are chosen to fit the letters. 'Backronym' itself, like 'Wikipedia' and 'cybertrash', is a portmanteau word of recent origin.

edited the GK entry to declare that 'Rio Grande' is the 'best place in Delhi to shop for pet accessories, pet food etc. (so you can get lot of stuff for your adorable dogs).' This too was quickly erased. It broke the cardinal NPOV (neutral point of view) wiki-rule, and now the Wikipedia entry on Greater Kailash has some stability, though a semi-literate mischief-making wag had surreptitiously inserted the most minor of wiki-edits. The text used to say, quite incorrectly, that GK is 'the most affluent area in Delhi'. The first letter of 'affluent' had been changed to an 'e'.

The Greater Kailashes are typical South Delhi residential areas, a little less affluent than Vasant Vihar or Panchsheel Park, with smaller plot sizes. To outsiders, the GKs are barely distinguishable from each other, by name or by look, with untidy ranks of polyzygotic three- and four-storey buildings, a family (plus servants) to each floor. A Punjabi friend described the Kailashes as 'Puppieland'. A 'Puppie' is a late 1980s word for an upwardly mobile Punjabi, a Punjabi yuppie, legendary for their love of gadgets and their lack of taste. But the Puppies were out at work when I passed through, and GK I was full of vegetable sellers and rubbish collectors pushing handcarts through the streets, and women berating tradesmen on their doorsteps. Hans Raj Gupta Marg, until recently a major shopping street, well-known for its jewellers and clothes stores, was quiet and empty. All the shops have been closed down, or, in the Delhi jargon, 'sealed'. The window displays are empty; large hastily written notices provide contact information for customers. At Stanley Boutique, purveyor of sofas and beanbags, there is a sign saying 'Showroom sealed as per Hon Supreme Court Directive'. According to the Supreme Court's interpretation of Delhi's zoning laws, these shops were all illegal, because this land was intended only for residential use. Thousands of other factories, shops, guesthouses, schools and restaurants have been 'sealed' all over the capital. In Seelampur, across the Yamuna, five people were killed after the police open fire during a protest against the sealing of small businesses. But in GK I, there were just a few tears, as shopkeepers wailed for the TV cameras. One retired resident, sitting on an easy chair in his front garden, overseeing his driver wax his SUV ('Don't forget the wheel arches'), told me he was pleased that there was so little traffic, and that it was easy to park, and very quiet. But then, he said, hand to his temple, as if it was the first time that this had occurred to him, 'a lot of shop-workers and watchmen have lost their work, and it has become a bit boring around here. ' And, on reflection, he told me that he'd changed his mind, and now felt some shops should be allowed, especially those that served the local community. 'Now everyone has to go the shopping malls'. And he's right: the big winners in the sealing controversy are the mall-owners whose income from retail space is at record levels.

I wandered on through the uninspiring byways of GK I looking hard for something interesting. I very nearly drew a blank. I was saved by the Consulate General of the Republic of Nauru on an unnamed backstreet. The two-storey house bore a large heraldic shield, with a coat-of-arms incorporating the alchemist's symbol for phosphorus and a cartoon bird on a perch; above, the motto 'God's Will First'. A friendly watchman, in a bright red shirt, told me that no one was at home. And no, he could not tell me where Nauru was,

despite a lot of prompting, or what exactly happened inside the Consulate (he giggled wordlessly), or whether it had opening hours.

'For what?' he asked, incredulously.

'For visas.'

'What visas?'

I knew that Nauru was a Pacific island, I even remembered a description of it as 'a mountain of fossilized birdshit[3],' but wasn't absolutely sure that it was an independent country for which one might need a visa. I dropped the subject and I asked the watchman for

[3] Nauru is a less-than-idyllic South Pacific island about the size of the Kailashes, and with a much smaller population (13,000). The island's sole significant export used to be its huge phosphate deposits—a result of its prehistoric role as a enormous bird toilet. Both the birds and the phosphorus are referenced on its coat-of-arms. By the 1990s when all the phosphates had been mined, Nauru was used as a money-laundering centre, and as an Australian detention camp for asylum-seekers. It is an independent country—and has had periods under both German and Japanese rule, as well as a long period of UN trusteeship administered by Australia, New Zealand and the UK.

directions to Nehru Place. This he knew. He pointed towards the next road junction, and said, in English, 'Nehru Place—there', in that hesitant way that indicated an excited desire to tell me something very funny. He pointed at the building behind him and said 'Nauru Place—here'. I felt a frown and a smile collide on my face, and forced myself to laugh. I enjoy bad puns more than most, but this was quite the worst that I had heard in all my years in Delhi.

According to its hyperbolic street-sellers, Nehru Place is the world's largest computer market, renowned for the cheapness of its pirated software. Just to the north is a crescent of high-rise buildings, with 'visa facilitation' centres, the 'Oh Calcutta!' restaurant, and corporate offices for lots of IT companies, including Microsoft. On the streets below, in the shadow of the high-rises, is a seen-better-days pedestrians-only open-air shopping plaza that feels far from modern ('old and rusty', according to one Wikipedian), but is full of the latest technology. The hardware is just cheap, while the software is, in both senses of the word, a steal. Boys, in their early teens, stand outside hardware shops, with typewritten lists of every imaginable computer programme. I failed to think of anything the boys didn't have—from Microsoft Vista, to high-end photo, video and design programmes, all stored in CD folders that they keep stuffed up their shirts, or in small wooden cardboard boxes. I asked one boy for Quark Express 7, a top-of-the-line publishing software that I knew cost over $1500 in the West.

'Of course. Just Rs 300.'

He took out a single CD, with Quark Express scribbled across it.

'That's very expensive,' I joked. He didn't realize that this was a joke and immediately lowered the price to Rs 100, less than 0.2 per cent of the price of the unpirated original. In these circumstances, it's unsurprising that most Indians would smile at the idea that you might buy unpirated software for private use. My attempt to suggest to the youngsters that they were doing something illegal produced gales of laughter. They became a little more serious when I asked about police raids, but they said the police usually just wanted a cut. Occasionally there was a big raid, and that's why teenage children did the actual selling, since they couldn't be sent to jail. At the end of the last millennium, a Microsoft-commissioned marketing agency brought an elephant to Nehru Place, and in front of invited journalists and photographers, it was made to trample on confiscated pirated software CDs. But nothing has changed. India has one of the lowest usages of legal software in the world. And the youngsters told me, unverifiably, that even Microsoft staff bought software from them.

As I continued eastwards, towards the river again, I momentarily caught sight of Delhi's most stunning and serene piece of twentieth-century architecture, the symmetrical white curves of the shimmering Baha'i Temple. It takes the form of a giant lotus bud, its nine petals just opening, with a huge auditorium inside. It stands alone, raised above the Delhi maelstrom by a landscaped hillock amid a well-tended garden. It is as if the Sydney Opera House were a distant relative, or just an unfinished prototype, or an unsolved three-dimensional puzzle, left strewn on the ground, in bits, by an impatient child; and some enormous genius had patiently slotted the pieces together to create the sublimely sumptuous Baha'i Temple. It is open to the public, of any or no faith, and is a calming, silent place to linger and dream, where I have tarried several times in the past. But today I am in a hurry. I've promised to donate blood at my next destination, the Apollo Hospital, still an hour's walk away. Yesterday, I received a text message from a friend looking for O-negative[4] blood donors. An O-negative friend of hers was being treated for cancer at the Apollo, and would need repeated transfusions.

My impending hospital visit encourages me to develop an enervating kind of hypochondria. I imagine myself to be bearing mysterious diseases that will be revealed when my donated blood is screened. These will reduce my family to tears, and cut short my spiral, or I will have to complete it in a wheelchair. I could feel tears welling in my eyes as I strolled blindly across the outer ring road,

[4] I had recently discovered during a health check-up that I was O-negative, and could give my blood to anyone, but could only receive O-negative.

cars and autorickshaws honking. I suddenly found myself stranded on a narrow spit of land, a 'grade separator', marking the point at which a road divides, with one half descending from a new single-carriageway flyover. I try to cross, and for the third time on my spiral, a moving rickshaw brushes against me, more of a kiss, the yellow canvas hood glancing off my side. It was my fault. Almost every Delhi rickshaw driver has an instinctive feel for the precise dimensions of their vehicle; I don't have the same millimetre-perfect knowledge or control of my own body. A minor prioperceptive failing, a minute wobble, is enough to cause an accident. In my hypochondriac's stupor, I remounted the grade separator, felt my hip and my side, searching for pain or a premature leakage of blood, wondering if I might have to prepone my visit to the Apollo, or even be consigned immediately to a wheelchair. I was entirely unscathed, slightly to my disappointment. I resumed the difficult task of trying to cross the road, and just could not find a gap in the traffic. I realized that the only way I could get across the road was to get a rickshaw to take me there, all of five metres. The driver had a laugh—and didn't want my money. I gave him a ten-rupee note; at two rupees a metre, it was, pro rata, one of the most expensive journeys ever made. Worse still, I had not walked. I had committed sacrilege by breaking the spiral.

I continued towards Apollo Hospital through an industrial estate, full of small hi-tech businesses and car dealerships. I spotted the tristar Mercedes-Benz logo next to a green-and-yellow flag with a five-pointed star.

'It is the flag of Togo,' the security guard told me, 'in Africa.'

'Why is it here?'

'This is the embassy of Togo.'

'In a car showroom?'

'Yes, sir. It is a showroom and an embassy.'

I banged my head with the palm of my hand, out of disbelief and delight at the discovery, in a car showroom, in an industrial estate, of another diplomatic mission almost as obscure as the Nauru Consulate. No-one will believe me. I banged my head again.

'Is everything OK, sir?' asked the guard, with genuine concern in his voice and on his face. It seemed unfair to burden or confuse the guard with my tale of coincidences, of diplomatic ley lines, of embassies without a purpose, secreted away in the strangest of locations. Maybe I could come up with a good pun instead, better than 'Nauru Place'. 'Togo', after all, seemed like a gift to punsters. 'Way to go, Togo!', or 'If you've got to go, you've got to go,' both seemed promising; but the worried look on the face of the guard, along with his basic English, made me lose heart. And with a more modest 'Got to go', I made my way, across the main Delhi-Agra road and railway line, past an odourless 'sewage farm', to the Apollo Hospital, an imposing 1990s' pastel-pink palace. It faces south, so those patients rich enough to have their own balcony don't overlook the hundred-acre sewage farm, but instead have a view over a manicured park and a sports centre. Inside it's like the entrance to a modern European railway station or airport, where the real purpose of the place has been hidden away, and instead it has been created in the image of a shopping mall. I peeked into the empty 'Platinum Lounge', aimed at foreign 'health tourists' who travel from all over the world for a cut-price operation, and slip in a little sightseeing. I pick up a glossy pamphlet that informs me about Apollo's fifty-two 'Super Specialities' (including, I take careful note, knee replacement surgery), and a wide range of operations from liver transplants to liposuction. Unlike the Hindu Rao Hospital in North Delhi, penis amputation is not available, or at least it is unmentioned in Apollo's publicity literature. But all major international credit cards are accepted, and trips to Agra and Jaipur can be arranged.

The blood donation centre has a more economy-class feel to it. But the staff are efficient and busy, and more polite than at a check-in counter. They presume, rightly, that I'm here to give blood for someone specific; they don't get many donors coming in off the street. My finger is pricked to check my haemoglobin levels, and having passed this first test (unlike the anaemic waif in front of me) I'm led along a corridor to a room with six couches. I feel a little like a cow in a milking pen. There are no words of comfort or gratitude; and there is no choice of couch or arm. There's a little fumbling around by the phlebotomist, searching for a decent vein, as I clench and unclench my fist, but there is no eye contact. I have never been able to witness the actual moment when a needle pierces my skin, and I shuddered, blinking my eyes for that shocking split-second of subcutaneous penetration, but then happily watched my near-purple lifeblood being pumped into a see-through plastic sachet.

I looked around, noticing my fellow blood-givers for the first time. The other couches were all occupied, and the room didn't have the funereal atmosphere of a British blood donation centre. Here, it's a social event, a public gift-giving ceremony; and most of the donors (all male) seemed to be having a good time. There were two young men, migrants from Bihar, who were workers at a garment factory owned by a friend of the person to whom I was donating blood. They too are O-negative, and have given blood before. It's a day away from a work, and they're having fun. They deny that they're getting paid, but then laugh so much that I don't quite believe them. There's a man from Jaipur, in a suit and scarlet tie, who is giving blood for his uncle, and is trying to check the label on his plastic sachet, without disturbing the needle. He's worried that his donation will end up in the wrong bloodstream. He says twenty male members of his extended family had come from Jaipur to give blood, but only three of them were the right blood group. And his uncle, he explains, doesn't want blood from women or strangers. He is toe-to-toe with a noisy twenty-something in embroidered black denims, an extravagantly self-confident veteran of the advertising industry. He is talking on his BlackBerry (despite a half-hearted telling-off from a nurse), discussing taglines for a jewellery campaign in a fruity English accent. 'Gold is gorgeous,' he screams into his handset. He behaves as if none of us were there.

'You'll never guess where I am,' he tells his interlocutor.

'Dracula's castle. My body fluids are being sucked out of me. Ha, ha, ha. And there are,' he finally looked around at the rest of us, 'five men staring at me.' He waved at me. 'Hi.' And then he sniggered. 'There's a white man,' he continued into his BlackBerry, 'wearing a green hat and a fifty-rupee watch.' How could I not have taken off my hat? I felt my head with my free hand, and snatched it away. The adman guffawed at my embarrassment, and then screeched across the room at me: 'And why are *you* here? Ha-ha.' But he wasn't interested in the answer, and started screeching about bloodsuckers and leeches into his phone. The only person in the room who had not spoken, a wan, middle-aged man who clearly did not enjoy giving blood, gave me a consoling smile. The nurse returned, extracted the needle, dabbed my arm with a piece of cotton wool and told me to sit in a desolate cubby-hole, furnished with a small table, some chairs and two half-eaten packets of biscuits. I felt too woozy to walk, and took a rickshaw back home, pondering the politics and demographics of blood donation. The room I had just left is possibly the only place in Delhi where such an eclectic group of people might be thrown together, and the occasion had a classless, almost interplanetary feel. It was a reminder of just how segregated Delhi can seem, how its occupants normally occupy parallel universes, and how rarely the rich and the poor have the chance to interact, and never as equals. But the blood of a migrant worker is as revitalizing as the blood of a maharaja or a marketing executive, despite the multiple mythologies that proclaim the opposite. Blood donation suddenly seemed subversive, almost revolutionary. Perhaps the apartheid tyrannies of caste, religion and gender might be overwhelmed by the democratic realities of phlebotomy. But I was fantasizing again. Most people in Delhi do not give blood, and have no intention of doing so unless a friend or relative is ill.

When I resumed my journey three days later, I was, for the first time in Delhi, part of a huge crowd of walkers. There were mainly Bihari migrants, many thousands of them, of all ages, heading towards the Yamuna river, for the religious festival of Chhath. They had reclaimed the roads, bringing all traffic to a halt, swarming around the stationary cars, peering in through the tinted windows at discontented businessmen trying to reach the satellite city of Noida across the river. The walkers veered off down a dust track towards the river bank and I pushed forward, sidestepping the amblers, trying to get to the front. I spotted a gap in the crowd, and moved stealthily into it, imagining myself to be waif-like. But I tripped over a leg, and went sprawling in the dust, next to a near-naked man who was lying on his stomach and seemed even more surprised to see me than I

was to see him. The gap I had spotted was not in fact a gap, but the space the crowd had given to the man I was now lying next to. He jumped to his feet, in one lithe movement, and moved forward two paces. Then, to my further consternation, he threw himself to the ground again, raising a spectacular cloud of dust that briefly concealed him. He was like a human yo-yo, spending alternate periods of five seconds lying on the floor, before leaping to his feet, and then plunging back down to the ground. And each time he lay on his stomach, he would move his arms forwards, and mark the Delhi dust with an outstretched finger, and then, when upright, would move his feet to this mark, before diving, like a footballer trying to win a penalty, to the ground again. He was, unsurprisingly, making slow progress, and was far too busy prostrating himself to talk to me. A fellow pedestrian, carrying a large basket of fruit and vegetables on her head, and trying to stop her children from imitating the human yo-yo, told me that he must have committed a serious sin and had been told by a priest to do penance in this way. We began to talk. She told me she was new to Delhi, though her husband had lived in the city for several years, working on construction sites. She had left her village in Bihar because her husband now earned enough to rent a small room for them and their three children. She told me she wanted to leave the village because the schools were better in Delhi; but she'd had problems getting her children into school. The head-teacher had wanted a bribe. Today was a holiday, but her husband's employer wouldn't give him time off work. Each member of the family had a new set of clothes, and at sunset they would make offerings of fruit and vegetables to the sun-god on the banks of the Yamuna.

I forged ahead and stepping out from behind some trees was startled to see a truly extraordinary scene, as if from a Hollywood version of a Biblical epic. The river banks were invisible; they had disappeared beneath waves of humanity; hordes of people as far as I could see, brightly dressed in crimsons and saffrons and turquoises, and all facing in the same direction. I could not see any land at all, and very little water. Many worshippers were standing up to their chests in the  shallows of the chill autumn river, holding coconuts and garlands of marigolds, and staring at the setting sun. But strangest of all were what appeared to be huge snowdrifts floating on the surface of the river, as if a melting Antarctic ice-shelf had drifted up the Yamuna. It has never snowed in Delhi, and the snowdrifts, I later learned, were a poisonous bubble-bath of blinding-white froth, created by pollutants spilled into the river at a nearby weir. Small rowing boats sliced their way through the froth, delivering worshippers to an invisible island in the middle of the river, entirely hidden from view by the crowds that were standing on dry land and in the water.

Chhath is Delhi's largest outdoor gathering. But because it is a festival celebrated mainly by poor migrant workers, the affluent Anglophones of South Delhi (except those stuck in their cars) are almost entirely unaware of it. Migration is changing this city, though, and Chhath-celebrants are now part of what is probably Delhi's largest community, the people of Bihar and eastern Uttar Pradesh who refer to themselves as Poorvanchalis[5]. Delhi's politicians do know the electoral importance of the Poorvanchalis and will try to visit as many stretches of the river bank as possible, and pay for huge advertising hoardings, featuring their own

[5]When I first lived in Delhi, the city was dominated by Punjabis, many of them migrants from Pakistan at the time of partition. The census figures are not definitive, but it is likely that Poorvanchalis had overtaken the Punjabis as the largest community by the late 1990s.

photograph and obsequious declarations of their deep reverence for the festival of Chhath.

A gerrymandering tongue of India's most populous state, Uttar Pradesh, crosses the river by road bridge, and surreptitiously licks the eastern banks of the Yamuna. By looking over my shoulder, at the battered, faded 'Welcome to Delhi' signs, I know that I have left the capital. The bridge goes to Noida, a new urban centre, officially outside Delhi's city limits, but contiguous with the capital, and part of what's known as the National Capital Region. Noida has a population of more than half a million—and is probably the world's most populous acronym. It was born in 1976 as the New Okhla Industrial Development Authority, a largely greenfield site, parcelled up into 168 sectors, many of which are still being developed. It briefly captured the attention of the international media in 2005, with the proposed construction of the world's tallest building, to a design that bore a striking resemblance to the Disney version of Cinderella's castle. 'Penis envy' was the scathing headline in one of India's best-known blogs. When it was pointed out that the area is earthquake-prone, and that its soil is sandy, the glory-seekers of Noida quietly shelved this attempt to get into the Guinness Book of Records (there is no category for populous acronyms).

In the dying days of 2006, the media returned. They were visiting Noida's 'House of Horrors', not a funfair ride, but a quiet suburban residence, in Sector 31, where the decomposing body parts of more than twenty people, most of them children, had been found. Two men were arrested—the house-owner and his manservant. There was a New Year media frenzy, with tales, some true, some false, of cannibalism, vampirism, organ-selling and necrophilia. The house-owner, it turned out, was well-connected, and educated at elite Indian schools. The TV stations tracked down his former classmates, who scratched their heads to find anything interesting to say about him. His son blamed the servant. The servant's wife blamed her husband's employers. The parents of the dead grieved in front of the TV cameras, and a hypnotized, disbelieving public were interviewed in the streets and the shopping malls by bright-as-a-button reporters. 'How could this happen?' asked the voice of the people. 'Because no one listened to us,' responded the

242

grieving parents. It gradually emerged that the police had ignored the parents, had sent them away when they tried to report their missing children. Most of the parents were low-caste and poor, and seemed unsurprised, though very angry, at the way the police had treated them.

I hurriedly skirted Noida. It had become, temporarily, a synonym for serial killing. And Delhi's politicians seemed delighted that the killings had happened on someone else's turf. Noida is neither Delhi, nor not-Delhi. It is a protrusion into Delhi's natural space, a kink in the city limits. It certainly feels like the rest of the capital. But because Delhi has no jurisdiction here, it is a place with even weaker planning laws, where many of those escaping from the sealing laws have relocated. Factories cravenly pump bilious smoke into the atmosphere, and there is a very significant (for a walker) lack of pavements. One main road did have a pavement—and a man who appeared to be guarding a yellow bucket. I peered inside. The bucket was full of water, submerged in which was a large and varied collection of wristwatches. I asked the bucket's guardian why the watches were underwater. He looked at me as if I was very stupid, and said with a look of disdain, 'because they're waterproof'. As a regular purchaser of cheap and unreliable waterproof watches, I had never been shown such evidence of their effectiveness, and asked the price. *Paintis*—Rs 35. I couldn't believe the price: it was as if I'd been offered a Salvador Dali for twenty dollars. I was too stunned to bargain and handed over the money, less than the cost of two cigarettes in London. The watch had a smart utilitarian black plastic finish, and told the time. Ever since I've taken pleasure in asking my more plutocratic, materialistic friends to guess how much my watch cost compared to theirs.

As I examined my new purchase, using my fingernails to detach a sliver of loose plastic, a convoy of television outside broadcast vans drove past, heading for the House of Horrors. Relatives of the dead children were holding a public protest against the police. But Sector 31 was not on my route, and I was secretly relieved: the house and the drains outside had become a macabre tourist destination for the people of Delhi. And the 'tourists' were shown glum-faced on TV, helping to look for bone fragments in the open drains, as if panning for gold. 'Sicko', as my children might say; though still not one-hundredth as sicko as the original crime. In all my time in Delhi, nothing has shocked its inhabitants so much as the Noida killings. But no one quite dares mentions the worst of it: these children, all children of the poor, were tortured in terrible ways before they died; dismembered, according to one account, while they were still alive. Panning for bones might be one way of dealing with the trauma.

As the weeks passed, the coverage of the Noida killings disappeared into the inside pages, and spawned a series of sidebar stories. Noida's reputation, as a middle-class sanctuary for those who can't afford South Delhi prices, has been badly damaged. House prices dipped dramatically, and some local residents have called, successfully, it seems, for the media to refer to the 'Nithari' killings after the Noida slum where most of the victims lived. Then there is the great drain debate—in which it was pointed out that if the drains had been covered, as many local residents had been demanding, the body parts might never have been found. Others point out that if the drains has been cleared more regularly then the body-count would never have reached double digits. And the great death penalty debate has returned, with Afzal Guru still hanging out on death row. The Internet news forum sadists are back on form, demanding that the 'killers' should be executed without trial. One of them says, 'give them wounds that could not be healed, let them rot by the roadside to be eaten by stray dogs'; another demands that they be treated like the children they killed, and be cut into small pieces by the relatives of the victims—though *lex talionis* doesn't appear to extend as far as cannibalism. Most bizarre of all was the way the alleged killers themselves became victims, when making a regulation courtroom appearance. A group of lawyers dealing with other cases heard that the Noida killers were in the building and rampaged through the corridors searching for them, in full view of the TV cameras. The manservant was wearing a balaclava and managed to avoid being identified by the lawyers. The house owner was less fortunate. The lawyers pulled at his arms, as if they wished to dismember him; they grabbed his hair and his beard. He collapsed on the ground, unconscious, and shielded from the lawyers, but not from the TV cameras, by some terrified policemen, who stretchered him off to hospital.

An Eleventh Intermission

THE YEAR 1999 was one of the worst in Delhi's history. Air pollution reached record levels, there were daily power cuts and water shortages, rioters took to the streets, a tornado struck the south of the city, there were huge fires in the largest industrial area; a plague of locusts descended on Delhi's suburbs, space junk landed in the city centre and the Yamuna turned into a raging whirlpool. The population halved in the course of the year, with people fleeing to the neighbouring countryside, and the city went bankrupt. Delhi's long-standing mayor, Shyam Mitra, leaned back, stared at his computer screen, and felt he had no option but to resign. Or he could go back to his previous saved version of SimCity, when Delhi was still a flourishing metropolis.

Until my son introduced me to SimCity, I thought all computer games were about killing or winning, or both. In SimCity you can't win, and no one ever dies (even during an earthquake). Instead, you build your own 'simulated' city, call it what you want, become its mayor—and see how successful you are at running it. As the clock of history ticks by, at your chosen speed, on the toolbar at the bottom of the screen, your city grows and shrinks. People ('Sims') migrate to your city when it's an attractive place to live and work in. And they leave if they don't like it, perhaps because you haven't built enough schools or there are too many power cuts, or because it's too boring. I became a secret addict. It's unexpectedly realistic, and because there is a serious side to it—like a beginners' course in urban planning—I felt able to pretend that I was hard at work.

SimCity has a number of pre-installed cities—real and invented—including London, Los Angeles and an all too plausible Dullsville. But there's not a single city from the developing world. So, no Delhi. I felt it was time for me to have a shot at running this city that had become my home. First, I had to recreate the terrain of Delhi on an empty greenfield site, carefully sculpting, with mouse-and-toolbar, the contours of my virtual city. Delhi would not be Delhi without the Ridge and the Yamuna, and I was able, god-like, to raise and sink the land to create the ancient topography of Delhi on my computer screen. I then had to skip the next few millions of years of

Delhi history, since the game automatically gave me a formal start-date of 1 January 1900.

I hurriedly created Old Delhi first, with a central street, just like Chandni Chowk, as its main east-west axis. I carefully placed homes, factories and shops around Old Delhi in a way that mimicked the real city at the start of the twentieth century. I could lay out the streets as I wished, and had a choice between residential, commercial and industrial buildings of low, medium or high density. The population began to grow. I laid railway lines, created landfill sites, built hospitals and schools. The architecture of the building was very Western, so compromises were necessary. For the Red Fort I had to make do with a Disney-style Cinderella's castle; a lighthouse became the Qutb Minar, surrounded (this was the early 1900s) by a small village. The only nod to India in the entire pre-packaged SimCity game is the Taj Mahal—which, quite appropriately, I was able to place on the site of its precursor and inspiration, Humayun's Tomb.

In 1920, I began building British New Delhi. The avenues of India's new capital were laid out according to the plans of Lutyens and Baker, with the Arc de Triomphe and the White House proving suitable substitutes for India Gate and the Viceregal (now Presidential) Palace. I moved on quickly to the concentric circles of Connaught Place. The city's population continued to grow slowly. The new parts of the city were too low-density, I was told by Constance Lee, one of a series of virtual advisers.

I soon came upon the 'disaster' menu, a drop-down list which allowed me to summon up a wide range of catastrophes. And so, at the click of a mouse, I was able to replicate the great North Delhi tornado of 1978. Similarly, the partition riots of 1947, the anti-Sikh riots of 1984, the anti-Muslim riots of 1992 all took place (this time without serious casualties) on the streets of SimDelhi.

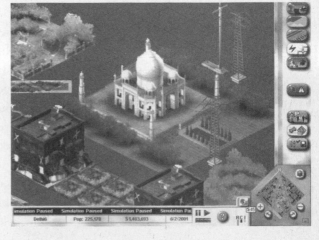

However, the SimCity computer model was not working like the real Delhi in a number of telling ways. Sims are a lot more fussy, or spoilt, than the people of Delhi. By the late 1990s my city only had a population of just over half a million—a twentieth of the size of the real Delhi. If the roads aren't kept in perfect conditions, or there are a few power-cuts, Sims leave the city in droves. They began demanding a Metro as early as the 1920s, and would not put up with what were, by Delhi standards, rather low levels of pollution. Sims won't move into homes without an underground 24-hour water supply.

As mayor of Delhi, I became more and more frustrated, and began to run out of money. Most of the city's income came from taxes, and its residents kept moving out if I raised tax rates. In early 1999, an old electricity generating station became overloaded, and blew up. I didn't have enough money to buy a new one, and all the other electricity plans tripped. Suddenly Delhi had no power, not even enough to work the water pumping stations—and my lovingly created city had no water either. In the real Delhi, poor people would have used handpumps and wells, the rich would have used water tankers and generators. But Delhi just collapsed. A self-destructive anger, born of impotence, overtook me. I pressed every disaster button, and went to get a beer from the fridge. My city was black with the carcasses of deserted buildings by the time I returned a few minutes later. In two SimCity years, the population had dropped to almost nothing. I realized that I hadn't destroyed the city quite as quickly as the British had following the 1857 Uprising, or as Mohammad Tughlaq had in 1327; but I had come pretty close. Delhi was dead.

I searched out my son, and told him my tale of woe. And he told me a secret. He taught me about cheat codes. Most computer games have them, he told me with a slightly patronizing air, as if I were the child. 'With SimCity, you just need to type in the special code, and everything is free.' He reverted to my older stored version of SimDelhi from 1993, held down four keys at once (Ctrl-Alt-Shift-C) and up jumped a little dialogue box. He typed 'I am weak' and suddenly I had unlimited credit. Everything was free. Another cheat code 'nerdz rool' converted all my old industrial buildings into hi-tech ICT businesses. I began to create the perfect Delhi, my version of Amir Khusro's heaven on earth.

Like the Delhi's city planners of the 1960s and 1970s, I was able to ignore reality. They just pretended it was a middle-sized city without major infrastructure problems. I could just print money, and buy any solution I wanted. I did still try to keep the city authentic. So the Metro appeared in 2002, and an earthquake shook the city in 2005. Lots of sporting facilities sprang up across the city in time for the Commonwealth Games of 2010, by which time the Metro had spread across all of Delhi; there were still more sports stadia for the 2020 Olympics, and I was delighted when my city became an international hub for space travel in the 2045.

As the population continued to grow, I felt pleased with myself, despite the double artificiality of a city which exists only on a computer hard drive and in which construction costs are zero. But it did raise the same issues which remain at the heart of Delhi's modern dilemma. I had chosen population growth as my indicator of success; recognizing that improved services mean more migrants, which puts greater pressure on services. If these services can be improved, the city's population would—well—spiral.

SimCity has a limited number of pixels, or land squares, on which I can 'grow' my city. And in the end I ran out of space, with a population of just over two million. There are no geographical limits—no mountains and no coastline—to the expansion of the real Delhi; it could, for better or worse, continue to grow in every direction, and it may once again become the most populous city in the world.

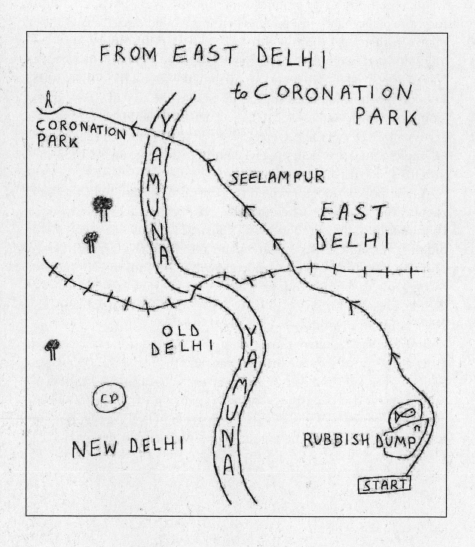

Chapter Twelve: In which the Author climbs a malodorous mountain, reflects on poverty and hope and falls at the feet of King George V

I CROSSED THE state border into East Delhi, and a series of monuments to excretion and garbage. Delhi's Far East is a forgotten world of detritus and poverty. I was greeted first by one of the world's most unpleasant bus stops. In large white letters on the side of the concrete passenger shelter were the words 'Dallu Pura Sewage Pump', and behind was a noxious, sludge-filled wasteland, twinkling in the sunlight, as if tinsel had been stirred into the slurry. There were no passengers to be seen. They had walked to the odour-neutral bus stop round the corner. The view from here was also a slight improvement. Delineating the horizon was a towering table-topped mountain of rubbish. An open sewer, blue-black, and spluttering methane bubbles into the atmosphere, snaked its way towards the mountain. Children in rags were racing along its banks. One small boy, in shorts and a green woollen hat, stood in the shallows of the sewer, using a stick to retrieve a tennis ball from its thalweg. I asked him why he wasn't at school. He looked at me suspiciously and said nothing.

I trod slowly along the sewer-bank towards the distant mountain of rubbish, which was steaming in the winter sun; the warm, rich smells of putrefaction drifting on the morning breeze. As I got closer, I realized that this was no mere garbage dump. This was Ghazipur, Delhi's largest landfill site. It's a complex piece of engineering, carefully constructed in layers, like a step pyramid. It

was also buzzing with life. There were municipal dump-trucks spiralling their way up towards the summit, where crows and pariah kites circled in small clouds, waiting for their next meal to be delivered to the mountain top. Feral dogs gambolled and snarled their way around the base of the mountain, foraging in the foothills. I felt fortunate to be protected from them by the sewer. I spotted, on the furthest slopes of the mountain, small shadowy figures stooping over the rubbish. Too small for humans, I thought; too solitary for simians. I screwed up my eyes, and tried to focus. And then I realized. They were small children at work, rag-pickers, each carrying a bag. One of the children spotted me, and called out, waving. He wanted to show me a trick, and sat down theatrically on a piece of plastic and elegantly slid down the side of the mountain to the next level, as if he were an Olympic snowboarder. He tried to scramble back up, but it was too steep—and he resumed his work, as if he were taking part in a treasure hunt, searching for anything that could be resold.

To get closer to the mountain I had to take a long detour. First, I had to cross the sewer by a perilously unfinished bridge. This involved walking along a narrow downward-sloping beam of uneven concrete. A man ahead of me nonchalantly carried his bicycle on his shoulder as he strolled along the beam, and then turned back, solicitously, to watch me cross. I nervously sat down on the beam and bum-shuffled my way across, tearing my trousers on a protruding shard of steel. The bicycle man seemed to be trying to hold back a laugh. I sat down on a low wall, embarrassed, head down, cocooning myself from the outside world, and inspected my trousers, which had a neat two-inch rip down the inside left leg, and beneath, my pale thigh, which bore, a little disappointingly, the most minor of weals.

Then I stood up, ready to walk on towards the rubbish mountain. I looked around, and blinked, and blinked again. I was greeted by a tableau of extraordinary complexity, even by Delhi's impressive standards. There were a hundred minor dramas being played out, in a spectacle of quite exhausting hyperactivity. It deserved the title, '*Where's Wally in Purgatory?*' (with me as Wally[1]). And for the

---

[1] The '*Where's Wally?*' cartoons, are complex themed drawings by the British cartoonist, Martin Handford, each involving many hundreds of figures, amongst which the reader has to find Wally and his friends. Wally became Waldo for the American market, Ubaldo in Italian and Effy in Hebrew.

unlucky few who haven't been engrossed by Martin Handford's seminal late-twentieth-century '*Where's Wally?*' cartoons, it was a scene straight out of Breughel or Dickens, with a cast of characters to match.

To my right: an old man in a woollen hat stood in the rutted road, pulling chickens out of a cage, half-cutting their throats with a knife, and throwing them, one-by-one, wings still flapping, into a huge blue plastic barrel. An albino dog, with half a tail, and a pus-filled hole where his right eye should have been, was standing on his hind legs, and trying to leap up and catch the dying chickens as they went on their final brief journey through the foetid air of Ghazipur. Behind the old man, another butcher sat on a stool plucking and disembowelling the recently slaughtered chickens. He leaned against a low brick wall that marked the edge of a stagnant tributary of the sewer I had followed all the way here, and beyond the wall was a huge signboard that proudly announced the entrance to Delhi's main wholesale poultry market. In the foreground, to the left of the butchers, was a small boy trying to kill a black scorpion with a stout stick. The boy's aim was spectacularly bad, and within seconds his angry mother had dragged him away, pulling at his arm as if were a leash, and kicking at the scorpion with her open sandals.

Straight ahead, was a different kind of market, whose smells overpowered even the stagnant sewer and the mountain of rubbish. This was Delhi's main wholesale fish market. A fish porter drove past on a cycle cart, narrowly missing the scorpion. On the back of his cart was a pyramid of ten huge fish, each as fat as a sumo wrestler's thigh, and with great lolling fish-tongues like frankfurters, which wobbled around as the cart struggled over the uneven surface of the road. In the mid-distance, a group of five men swaggered towards

me, each of them wearing a black leather helmet, perfectly flat on top; they waved at me and veered off to a small covered building full of plastic crates of seafood. They helped each other stack the crates three and four metres high onto their helmets, and then staggered back towards the main market—water dripping from their headgear, and fish tails and crab claws sticking out of the sides of the plastic crates. The albino dog followed them briefly, trying to drink the dripping water until it spotted the scorpion. The dog wagged its tail out of excitement, and splayed it forelegs to the ground as if it wanted to play. Its nose was less than three inches from the scorpion which raised its tail as if it was about to sting. The dog lost its nerve and headed dolefully towards the mountain of rubbish.

I followed the dog, and finally reached the foot of the mountain, a melange of taupes and bistres, the deep browns of composted vegetation. There was a light dusting of glittery colour, courtesy of some wind-blown crisp packets, and scraps of food packaging. Underfoot, the mountain felt like an old mattress, softened and mildewed by years of bedwetting, with a smell to match. I counted

at least thirty rag-pickers on the lower slopes, and many more in the distance. There was one group of men, women and small children in outsized clothing, trussing up separate piles of rags and plastic; but most of them were solitary, pulling scraps from the rubbish, or sorting out their pickings. I asked a child to tell me her name; she turned away from me. A man shook his head, as if to warn me off. I walked towards a huge haystack of rags, to which someone had laid a makeshift path with bits of wood and stone. On closer inspection I saw it was more of a tent than a haystack. And then I realized that I was standing outside someone's home. Inside were some more rags, and a tin cooking pot. And I looked about, and saw that there were several shacks just like this one, constructed out of rubbish. This was not just a place of work. People live here, hundreds of them; in the heart of this mephitic rubbish dump.

I have seen some insalubrious homes on my travels, but this seemed like the worst. I began to rant rhetorically to myself. How could people live like this? How can they raise their children here? And what must they think of people who don't live on rubbish dumps? And how have these people benefited from India's famous economic boom? Whatever happened to the legendary trickle-down effects of economic growth, I wondered? The growth rate is about nine per cent. The rich will often talk about the poor as if they were a different species. My children's Indian school-friends boast of private family jets, of plasma-screen TVs, of safari holidays in Africa. Is trickle-down just a big lie, designed to keep the poor in their place? There didn't seem to be much hope here.

I trudged up the slope a little, two paces behind the albino dog, a small cloud of flies circling near its suppurating eye, along a worn path of compressed rubbish. Then I saw coming towards me a waif of a girl, barefoot and wearing what was probably once a party frock. She was carrying over her shoulder a huge sack that bent her almost double. She had a limp, her left leg shorter and thinner than her right. She did not look up, and I could not see her face beneath a jungle of matted hair. Alone amid the debris of civilization, I was reminded of a film depicting the aftermath of a nuclear bomb. She looked as if she might be the last person left on earth.

Then a few of my preconceptions began to crumble. The dog bounded up to her. She dropped her bundle and took the dog in her arms. It licked her face, and she nuzzled her cheek against its pink nose. She looked up, with a huge smile on her happy face. She saw me, and gave me a cheeky grin, before coyly turning away. I asked her why she wasn't at school. 'Today is a holiday.' I felt a bit stupid. I had just supposed she didn't go to school. She told me she was in the fourth standard, could read and write, and was helping out her

255

parents on the rubbish dump. And they didn't usually stay overnight on the rubbish dump, but in a room about twenty minutes' walk away. She picked up her sack, and with an albino dog and a large white man following close behind, headed back down the mountain. Near the bottom, she pointed out a man sitting on a wooden box sorting rags outside one of the shacks, 'Ask him all your questions,' she told me and then said 'goodbye' in two carefully and proudly enunciated English syllables.

Pal Singh, sitting on his box, was not happy. The quality of rubbish arriving at the Ghazipur dump was very poor. There were too many middle men, and the best stuff had all gone. He asked me if I had any servants. I nodded, slightly apologetically.

'Well, they take the best rubbish; then they give what's left to the local rubbish collector with his hand-cart, and he'll take the next best; and take that to the depot where it all gets put in trucks, and the people at the depot take anything else that they might be able to sell. And we get all the rubbish.'

'Or the rubbish rubbish,' I replied sympathetically, trying to make a joke that didn't really translate into Hindi. He made Rs 100 on a good day, selling bundles of rags, or wood, or old bicycle tyres, plastic bags. His parents had been properly educated, he told me, but he had fallen on hard times, and had now been working on rubbish dumps for twenty years. He didn't stay on the dumps at night any more, though they still used the shack as a daytime shelter in the hot season. Others still stayed there, but he and his wife and three children had a small room beyond the fish market. Schools and doctors were nearby; and they had enough food to eat, though not much to spare. He told me he had got used to the smell, though you had to be careful not to cut yourself on discarded razors or syringes. He told me his children weren't working on the dump so much these days, and one of his sons was doing computer studies at college, and spoke good English. 'He wants a job with an international company. Maybe then I'll stop working here. They say they're going to close this dump; that it's too full, and then, I don't know . . .'

An hour later, I left the rubbish dump, unsure what to make of my brief insight into the life of the rag-pickers. They worked in appalling health-endangering, life-shortening conditions, but there didn't seem to be a hint of self-pity. Some were simply uninterested in talking to me, but others spoke passionately of their hopes for their children. There was a sense of the possibility of social mobility, that being at the bottom of the heap was not hereditary. Their lives had little security, they had no savings, almost no possessions and survived each day on what they had earned in the previous twenty-four hours. The trickle-down, if there is one, is not yet economic— instead it is a trickle of hope and optimism, a belief that their children could have better lives than theirs. The work they do is extremely low-status, and my Delhi acquaintances are apologetic that rag-pickers should exist. Their presence is seen as pre-modern and a blemish on booming India. But it's possible to argue that the role rag-pickers play also has a post-modern avatar, a Western rebirth as separators of garbage, as recyclers of waste, and, I began to fantasize here, perhaps we might one day see rag-picking as a trendy, alternative career option.

Back in the real world, large tracts of East Delhi are being reborn. The Metro has impregnated this area, spawning small patches of the kind of identikit urban renewal seen throughout booming West Delhi. This is virgin territory for the middle classes, who are grabbing land for a small fraction of the prices in other parts of Delhi; and the retail developers are following them. But away from main roads, often alongside open sewers and garbage dumps, are the vast resettlement colonies, built to house people evicted from the slums of Old Delhi in the 1960s and 1970s. They usually began as long narrow streets laid out in parallel, with small lanes connecting them: a geometric layout compromised by later rebuilding. The plot sizes are tiny, and the homes, either low-level tenements or individual one-roomed houses, were constructed out of the cheapest building materials, by builders who often used too little lime or cement in the mortar. The exterior masonry has been patched and re-patched, to form a mosaic of greys and browns. The monsoon rains still ooze through the mortar and down the interior walls. Residents have often added extra floors, and overhanging balconies that keep the alleyways dark and cool and a little scary. The connecting lanes have become garbage dumps and piggeries.

Two of the resettlement colonies, Trilokpuri and Seelampur, have been immortalized as places of sectarian murder, where the blood of members of India's minority communities has congealed on the streets of these modern slums. In 1984, in Trilokpuri (which falls under the olfactory footprint of the Ghazipur garbage mountain), more than one hundred and fifty Sikhs were killed as part of the Delhi-wide pogrom that followed the assassination of Indira Gandhi. One street in Trilokpuri was so full of human limbs and burnt corpses that journalists had to walk on tiptoes to pass through. The same journalists spotted a truck laden with four burnt bodies near a police station. They found that one of the 'bodies' was still alive, and able to talk. He'd come to Trilokpuri from Punjab to visit relatives, when he was attacked by an anti-Sikh mob, who poured kerosene over him, and set him on fire. His host had been hacked to pieces by men wielding machetes. Inside the police station, the journalists were told that nothing could be done about the dying man until their boss arrived. The man died shortly afterwards[2].

The next major communal riots in Delhi took place eight years later. By the time I arrived in East Delhi to cover the Seelampur riots of 1992, the streets had been cleared of the dead. I had by then lived and worked as a journalist in Delhi for two years, and had never crossed the Yamuna, except en route to a Himalayan holiday. Seelampur was just one of many places in India with mixed Hindu-Muslim populations where riots had broken out following the destruction of a mosque by Hindu militants in the town of Ayodhya[3]. By the time I got there, the killings were over, more than twenty Muslims were dead and Seelampur had become a ghost town. Apart from some broken windows, smouldering tyres and a single burnt-out car, there was little sign of the violence that had erupted. The police, who refused to tell us anything about what had happened, had cordoned off the area, but let us enter at our own risk. A local journalist pointed out some dried blood on what passed for a pavement. I picked up a small rock to protect myself from the dogs who patrolled the street, and whose desolate barks punctuated the Seelampur silence. I wandered off alone. There were no proper maps of Delhi then, and it was hard to orient oneself in the narrow alleys.

[2] For journalist Rahul Bedi's account see carnage84.com
[3] The sixteenth-century mosque was built on what some Hindus believe were the ruins of an ancient temple marking the birthplace of the god Ram.

There was no one to ask for help. All the doors were locked, the windows shuttered. A young boy, eight or nine years old, high up on a parapet, threw a stone at me, and missed, only just. I looked up, dropping my own rock and holding out my palms to signal my neutrality and lack of weaponry. I saw, to my amazement, that the uneven rooftops of Seelampur had become an elevated walkway, busy with silent, shuffling pedestrians. The streets may have been empty, but dozens of people were moving around, carrying provisions and keeping watch on what was happening down below. They were making preparations for the possible return of the killers by fortifying their rooftops[4].

On my return fifteen years later, all the activity in Seelampur had reverted to the streets, though the back alleys continued to function as dumps and latrines. A few months earlier, there had been yet another riot in Seelampur. 'Only' four people died, in the series of Delhi-wide protests against the sealing of unauthorized commercial premises. The people I asked seemed unconcerned about the latest riots and the latest deaths, as if this were quite normal here. Seelampur is full of small buzzing hubs of activity: training centres, schools, workshops, and market-places. It is clearly part of both the global economy and the village economy, a jaw-dropping melange of the old and the new. A young vegetable seller, seated cross-legged on the roadside next to two huge white radishes and a pile of mustard leaves, talks broken English into his mobile phone. A gaggle of giggling, niqab-wearing young women emerge from the computer training centre at the Babool-Ulm Madrasa. Their shoulders are shaking with laughter, their faces invisible, but their eyes dance flirtatiously through the slits in the cloth that covers their heads. Teenage boys recycle computer waste. They burn and strip electric cables in order to resell the copper wire; they dip circuit boards into baths of nitric acid to recover traces of lead and gold . The fumes are toxic. The workers know this, and complain of coughs and lung infections, but this is quick money. The failure of the world to implement a realistic

---

[4] Only later did a slightly clearer picture emerge of what happened in Seelampur. Many of the dead had been set on fire and burnt to death by a triumphant mob of Hindus, celebrating the destruction of the mosque in Ayodhya. According to local Muslim residents the police stood watching during the attacks, and at one point opened fire on Muslims.

electronic waste management system is slowly killing the e-waste workers of Seelampur, and poisoning the air of the city in which I live. The thought of this, the ultimate depressing irony of globalization in the computer age, prompts a staccato coughing fit. And I head, hurriedly, towards the placid and pestilential waters of the Yamuna, which I would soon be crossing for the final time on my journey.

A little before Delhi's northernmost bridge over the Yamuna is a small square park, set amid fields of vegetables planted on the floodplain, and severed from Seelampur by huge overhead water pipes, each large enough to enclose a rowing boat. The pipes come from the nearby Sonia Vihar water treatment plant, the largest in India, which opened in 2006 to a tsunami of unjustified optimism about Delhi's water problems[5]. The park was waterless, with gentle gusts of wind whipping up whorls of dust. Some withered stalks were all that remained of a flowerbed surrounding a memorial column at the centre of the park. This was meant to be a place of remembrance for dead children, the casualties of a road accident involving a school I had already visited. I stepped up to the memorial, and read the words 'Ludlow Castle. List of Students who left us for their Heavenly Abode on 18-11-97'. Twenty-eight names, all children who drowned in the river, when their bus skidded off the bridge; I noticed that the youngest, Ruchika—a six-year old in 1997—had the same birthday as my daughter, and as I walked across the bridge I sank into a mournful melancholy, imagining Ruchika's last dark moments in the ebony Yamuna.

North Delhi is the city's most underdeveloped quadrant, as if someone had started building here and had run out of money. It

---

[5] Some parts of Delhi did get greatly improved water supplies, but there is still a significant shortfall, which is expected to grow exponentially. The plant has diverted huge quantities of water from previously water-rich agricultural areas far away from Delhi.

feels deserted. Its roads are bordered by scrub and marsh, sewers and sewage plants, scattered residential townships and shrinking strips of farmland. It might easily have been so different; this area could have become the centre of modern Delhi. At the heart of this North Delhi wasteland is a clue to what might have been, yet another forgotten memorial, a stone obelisk in a deserted park. The obelisk marks the site of the most momentous announcement in Delhi's history, the first step in Delhi's transformation to a megacity. For this park was the location of the Durbar of 1911, where King George V, the only reigning British monarch to visit the subcontinent, stunned his audience of princes, officials and soldiers by declaring that Delhi would replace Calcutta as the capital of India.

After the final collapse of the Mughal Empire in 1857, Delhi had been despoiled by the British and allowed to turn into a shrunken, provincial backwater. Now, it would be transformed into a majestic imperial capital, and the original intention was to build the new city, New Delhi, at the site of the durbar. But after two years of arguing, New Delhi's planners chose a site twelve kilometres to the south, at Raisina Hill, from where India is still ruled. The British had decided that North Delhi was too marshy and too flat; it was too far from the ruins of ancient empires; and the architects wanted to build an enormous Viceregal palace on a hill-top, so it would command an impressive vista, and, most important of all, create a sense of awe among Britain's Indian subjects. The Durbar site became an overgrown reliquary known as Coronation Park, with busts and statues of long-dead British rulers, noses held high in the air, peeping through the foliage. Today the park has a large population of squirrels and pigeons, who have made their home amid the debris of empire. Several of the busts have disappeared from their plinths, presumably taken as souvenirs. The plinths themselves serve as vertical race-tracks for the squirrels, and the statues have become perches and latrines for the pigeons. King George still reigns supreme in Coronation

Park. A fifteen-metre full-body statue in white marble towers above his viceroys and governors. I was walking round the statue, staring up at the imperious monarch, thinking how his facial hair immediately identifies him to any former philatelist, when I tripped over a sleeping watchman. I stumble and the watchman leaps to his feet, helping me back up on the way. He tells me that almost no one ever comes here. 'It's too far away from the rest of Delhi. Some old white people come sometimes. One of them tried to take one of the statues. He said it was his grandfather. But it was too heavy.'

For more than eight centuries, Delhi's centre of gravity had crept slowly northwards—as if it were on tiny castors. From its oldest standing ruins in the far south of Delhi to Siri, and later Ferozebad, Shahjahanabad and Civil Lines. But, in the aftermath of King George's seismic announcement at what is now Coronation Park, the direction was reversed. Delhi's centre of gravity began to creep southwards. After half a millennium with farm animals for company, the ruins of older empires, of previous versions of Delhi, were being swallowed back into the growing city—and the creep became a crawl. Today, Delhi is galloping southwards, beyond where it began, beyond its own borders. Like Delhi itself, I was changing direction at Coronation Park, the most northerly point on my spiral, and was now trotting towards the city's Deep South, Delhi's most modern avatar, on the final arc of my journey.

A Twelfth Intermission

THERE ARE NO tickets on the Delhi Metro. Passengers buy a small circular plastic token, like an overgrown tiddlywink, which is scanned at the entry gates, and swallowed up at the exit gates. There are lots of rules to be followed: don't eat or drink; don't carry more than 15 kg of baggage; don't ride on the roof of the train; don't use the lift, which is only for the physically challenged. Loitering on the Metro is definitely not allowed, and anyone who does not complete their journey within two hours is fined Rs 10 per additional hour or part thereof.

As a child in London in the 1970s, I would loiter happily on the Tube. After school, a friend and I would regularly ask train drivers to let us ride in the cab for a few stops. And most of them would, letting us work the brakes, showing us the emergency communication equipment, and pointing out long-deserted 'ghost' stations. We also collected tickets, stealing used ones from unattended booths at station exits. We were trying to get a ticket from each of the 250-plus stations. One time, we tried to break the record for visiting all the stations on the Tube in the shortest possible time, which then stood at fifteen hours. We gave up after forty-five hungry, exasperating minutes, when we realized that we had not planned our journey in advance, and were not carrying any food. By the 1980s, Tube geeks were using computer programmes to work out the quickest way of travelling to every station— and the 'Tube Challenge' is today overseen by the *Guinness Book of World Records,* and has its own website and its own complex set of rules[1]. By 2007, the Delhi Metro had passed the fifty-station mark, and I decided I would try to redeem my London failure with a Delhi triumph.

And so, one summer's day, I set off on my own invented Metro challenge. I didn't need a computer programme to plan my journey. With just three metro lines, networked in the shape of a double dagger,[‡] there wasn't a great choice of routes, and only two intersections. My speed would depend on how quickly I could change at the intersections,

---

[1] Tubechallenge.com . The current record is higher than in my childhood, because there are more stations and stricter rules.

[‡] The double dagger is usually used to denote the third footnote on a page, after an asterisk *, and a single dagger † or obelisk.

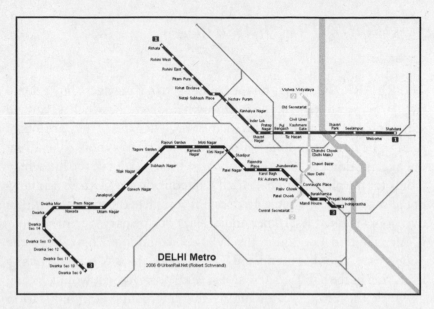

Connaught Place (aka Rajiv Chowk) and Kashmiri Gate, and on the famed reliability of the Delhi Metro. I bought the highest value token (Rs 22) and set off from distant Dwarka Sector 9, the station furthest from central Delhi, surrounded by farmland and building sites. The broad train, with a continuous open carriage from front to back, filled up quickly with commuters heading into the city. My neighbours on both sides were Indian women wearing western clothes, jeans and a T-shirt; the one on my right was listening to Coldplay on her MP3-compatible mobile phone and moving her lips, singing along silently. On my left was a woman entranced by Enid Blyton's *The Famous Five Versus the Black Mask* in French. Unlike most Indian trains, there was very little chatter between passengers, just a low-level Coldplay hum, interrupted by brief business-like mobile phone conversations. I interrupted the Famous Five fan, and asked her why she was reading Enid Blyton[2] in French. 'I'm training to be a primary school teacher, and for these international schools you need to be able to teach a little French, and I thought this book would be easy. I borrowed it from the

[2] I later discovered that Enid Blyton, the creator of Noddy and Big Ears, as well as the Famous Five and the Secret Seven, did not write this book that bore her name, and that my fellow traveller was reading the book in its original language. The author was Claude Voilier who wrote twenty-four Famous Five books, all published after the death of Blyton, eighteen of which have since been translated into English.

Alliance Francaise.' She told me that it used to take her 90 uncomfortable minutes by bus from her home in Dwarka to Connaught Place. 'Now it takes less than half that. And it's clean; it's reliable, and,' she added, looking me up and down, 'men behave properly on the Metro.'

Most of the Delhi Metro is elevated so high above the ground that I had an almost aerial perspective of many of the

places I had walked through. I watched Delhi fly by, past the Metro's highest point at Rajouri Garden, and then down underground and up again near the Pragati Maidan Exhibition Centre. Particularly striking was the pestiferous sewer that backed onto the regional headquarters of the World Health Organization, as well as the West Delhi apartment built so close to the Metro that I could read the time on a wall-clock in someone's bedroom. At Connaught Place, I strode across the station concourse from whose roof-cum-park I had started walking many months earlier, and descended into its depths to catch my connection. It was the only time I had to hurry, throwing myself through the closing doors of a departing train, and landing in a heap on the spotless floor of the carriage. I brushed aside offers of help, leaping to my feet, and smashing my head against a hand-strap for standing passengers, designed for people a good six inches shorter than me.

My desperate dive at Connaught Place saved me a few minutes, and I was elated when I reached the fifty-fourth and last station in less than two and half hours: 2 hours 28 minutes 9 seconds, according to my stopwatch. The journey had been without a hitch. The Metro had lived up to the hype, and I was enormously impressed. I walked down towards the exit, putting my token into the slot. But the electronic gates would not open. So, I thought to myself, the Metro isn't quite perfect. I went to the customer information kiosk, and asked to be let out of the station. I was told, in a firm but polite manner, that since I had spent more than two hours on the metro, I had 'incurred' a fine of Rs 10. I paid up, apologized, and left.

265

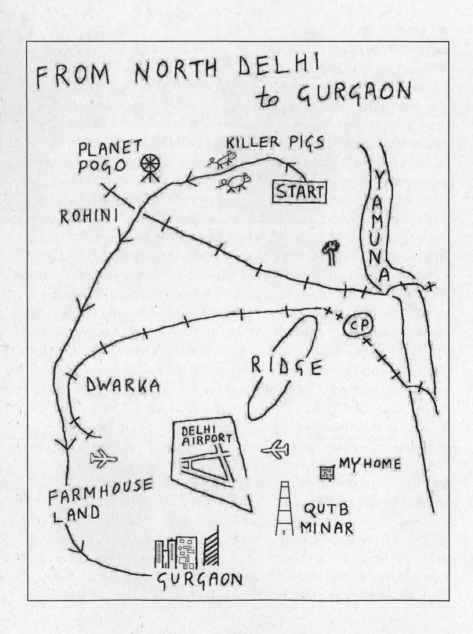

Chapter Thirteen: In which the Author is chased by killer pigs, meets the 'Magnet Man' of West Delhi and has a doleful wander through the Millennium City

I NOW HAD about forty kilometres to go—little more than two hours for a top marathon runner, but a full day for a man with a creaky knee. I put on my trainers in the foolhardy belief that, with a little light jogging, I might be able to buy some early time with a rapid escape from North Delhi. I had plotted my route in advance, with the help of Google Earth, for I was now spilling over the edges of my well-worn city map. I would take an arc that would brush past the most westerly stations of the Metro, like a spider linking up the spokes of its web, before dropping down into Delhi's Deep South. My final destination, or so I hoped, was the schizoid, bulimic satellite city of Gurgaon—a city which isn't a city, which is both Delhi and not-Delhi, and which is so engorged by the fruits of modernity that it needs a regular anti-emetic.

The broken pavements of the outer ring road were slowing my early progress. A bridge I had planned to cross, turned out to be a railway line, with no railing or pathway. Two men *were* crossing, strolling between the rails. The arrival of a train would have crushed them or forced them into the sewer below; I watched them, heart in mouth, as they walked to safety. With a spring still in my step, I took a less dangerous but more circuitous route over a foot-bridge and trotted along a small road beside the sewer. I was distracted by a fine view of a smart new jail on the other bank, and stepped into a

muddy puddle that was deeper than I thought. A malodorous semi-liquid black sludge went over the top of my left trainer. I sat down on a low wall, not far from a group of snuffling black pigs, and began cleaning myself off with some large leaves. The two largest pigs, both sows, didn't seem pleased to see me, and began making a guttural noise that was more roar than oink. I got up, and began to walk away. They followed me, at my pace. I stopped, and look back at them with the firm stare of authority. This made no difference; the two pigs kept coming towards me. I picked up a stone, and threw it a little short of them. They didn't flinch. I began to feel a little uneasy. I picked up my speed. And so did they. I had never realized that pigs could run so fast. My trot had turned into a sprint. They were gaining on me, and I was scared. I felt I was running for my life. I clambered up and over a small brick wall, thanking God that not only were pigs wingless, but they weren't very good at climbing. They circled on the other side, sniffing each other—and their fun over, they ambled back to their families. I had pulled a calf muscle, and was limping. There was no way I was going to get to Gurgaon that day. I stopped to rest at a tea-stall. I told an old woman about the pigs. She said I was lucky that they hadn't eaten me. I laughed. She glared back at me, and told me how a herd of pigs in this colony, Badli Samaipur, had recently eaten a child. I didn't believe her, but it later turned out she was telling the truth[1].

I struggled out of sewerland. A dull fibular ache was slowing me down, and I gave three undernourished piglets a wide berth. I entered a more affluent area, the borders of Rohini, one of three 'subcities' created by the Delhi government, with smart new tenement blocks, marked 'MIG housing', for 'middle income group' residents, not fighter pilots. Amid an enormous construction site was a newly laid-out park, almost empty and large enough for a golf course, with

[1] In November 2006, a three-year-old boy, Ajay Yadav, was eaten alive by a herd of pigs. According to the *India Abroad News Service*, 'Manish Agarwal, Deputy Commissioner of Police said a case has been registered against Jachche, the owner of the pigs, who is absconding. Police said the civic authorities immediately took the pig to an animal hospital'. Attacks by pigs on humans are rare, but have a long history. In Chaucer's *Knight's Tale*, the shrine to Mars carries an image in which 'The sowe freten the child right in the cradel'. 'Freten' is Middle English for 'devour'.

separate formal, scented and informal gardens, a vandalized animal-free mini-zoo, a boat-less boating lake and a 'refreshment area'. There weren't the usual courting couples. The park had been designed without hiding-places. The trees were all high-branched, providing shade but no privacy. A loud green notice screamed 'Maintain Proper Decorum. This Is A Family Park.' I sat down underneath the sign, and, lifted my left trouser leg and begun massaging

my aching calf, trying to jab my thumb deep into my soleus muscles to reach the source of my pain—still wandering what had made the pigs so aggressive. I peered up, and in the distance spotted a strange tangle of pastel-coloured towers and battlements, and spidery blue structures, decorated with stars and spirals, as if I'd stumbled on Disneyland in outer Delhi. A fluorescent green disc suddenly swung into view, high on the horizon, and disappeared just as quickly. Five seconds later it reappeared again, briefly. Hypnotized, my calf forgotten, I followed the flying green disc into the distance.

And it *was* a kind of Disneyland. Under construction, in Delhi's equivalent of the boondocks, is a shrine to Planet Pogo—the Disney Channel's chief competitor in India. Pogo is a huge brand here. It encourages Indian parents to give their children an American childhood. There's a shopping plaza that you have to pass through before you get to the amusement park. McDonalds, Pizza Hut and Levi's have pride of place here, alongside a 'US dollar store', where everything—from Cornflakes to Heinz Baked Beans—costs Rs 99, or roughly two dollars. There's nothing that would be out-of-place in an American store;

269

none of the signage or products labels are in Hindi, there is nothing to indicate that this is India—except the customers, who are all Indian, and the staff, most of whom cannot speak more than a few words of English. Many of the fairground rides (Cyclone, Side Winder, Derby Devil, Air Pogo) are still under construction, but I was able to see the flying green disc from close-up. Twelve brave-hearted youngsters and I were strapped into our seats, harnessed at our shoulders, turned upside down, and sent spinning through the air at great speed. It was even worse than being chased by killer pigs.

Planet Pogo is strategically placed a short walk from the last station on Delhi's oldest Metro line (DoB: 24 December 2002). The elevated railway tracks extend a few hundred metres beyond the station, before ending dramatically, like an unfinished flyover. It's as if the Metro builders had, mid-sleeper, simply run out of money. In fact, it's incomplete because the new 'subcity' that this Metro line will eventually serve is largely unbuilt. Most of Rohini does not yet exist, though the land has been sliced up into alphanumeric plots, and the auctions have begun. Rohini is due to house more than a million people by the end of the second decade of the third millennium, but it's only one small part of Delhi's land-guzzling gigapolitan future.

In 2007, the government published, with great fanfare, its 'Master Plan Delhi 2021', in which it finally seems to accept that it is unable to limit the growth of this city's population. Instead, it declares its intention to make Delhi 'a global metropolis and a world-class city',

and it expects the city's population to grow by almost half-a-million souls each year. For the wider 'National Capital Region', the Master Plan predicts a population in 2021 of an astonishing sixty-four million people (more than the population of the UK). About twenty-three million people—and that's already looking like an under-estimate—are expected to live within Delhi's formal city limits.

Delhi, which had one-sixth of the population of London, in 1950, will have almost three times London's population by 2021[2].

Rohini, and two other six-lettered 'subcities', Dwarka and Narela, are central to Delhi's plans for growth and are part of a construction project which is far, far larger than the Metro. They are each, individually, larger in scale even than those previous planned cities, British New Delhi and Mughal Old Delhi. The western arc of Outer Delhi is quite simply one of the world's largest construction sites—in what may become the world's largest urban conurbation. And these burgeoning subcities, built around older suburban and village settlements, are getting a brand new infrastructure—underground sewers, electricity substations, giant water pipes, arterial highways connecting them to inner Delhi, a grid-like interior road network, and, of course, the Metro—as well as the Planet Pogo Amusement Park, which, because Rohini is only partially built, is not very busy.

The subcities have been speared onto the end of long spokes that radiate from the older British and Mughal Delhis—and are well out-of-sight for the average Delhi-ite or visitor. Almost thirty kilometres from Connaught Place at the furthest, they are still within those official, 'pre-independence' city limits. The subcities were a belated response to Delhi's failure to deal realistically with its own growth. It's a failure that has had dramatic consequences for Delhi. It led to the growth of Noida and Gurgaon, huge satellite cities that mushroomed on the other side of Delhi's borders with neighbouring states. And it led to the emergence of hundreds of unauthorized colonies, for the poor and the rich, that sprang up in almost every part of the city.

---

[2] According to a November 2007 study by the independent Washington-based Population Reference Bureau (PRB), Delhi already has a population of more than twenty million. It argues the criteria used previously for defining Delhi's urban limits are too restrictive, and different from those used to define other Indian urban areas. Under the PRB's new criteria, Delhi overtook Mumbai as India's largest city in 2002—and this would put it in second place globally, behind Tokyo. It is then easy, though possibly disingenous, to argue that the definition of Tokyo's urban limits—which spreads into three neighbouring prefectures—is too broad, and that, therefore, Delhi in 2008 is already the world's most populous city.

For too many years, Delhi's administrators ran a city which existed only in their imagination. It was a fantasy city, born of the same loins as the real Delhi, but it was small and neat, and everyone obeyed the law and respected the planning process. The unauthorized colonies were the most obvious by-product of this utopianism. Officially they did not belong in this city, but they grew to overwhelm the fantasy Delhi. A senior city administrator once admitted to me that the majority of Delhi's population lived in homes to which they or their landlords had no legal title. It's easy to draw a further conclusion: that the growing divergence between these parallel cities, the fantasy Delhi and the real Delhi, bred a contempt for the laws and for the processes that seek to guide this city's development. It helped inculcate a culture of corruption involving the police and civic authorities, a more overt disregard for civic values than in any other large Indian city, and a widespread disloyalty towards the city on the part of many of its residents. This is changing, but slowly.

Today, it is accepted that Delhi is, for better or worse, a megacity—and it needs an infrastructure and a civic culture to match. It is also recognized that an improvement in the quality of life for new migrants to this city will spawn a further cycle of migration. For this reason, the current guesses about Delhi's population are almost certainly underestimates. And the only real way of keeping people out of Delhi, is to make life in the villages and towns of India a lot more attractive. It is pretty well impossible to find a disincentive to migration, so long as new migrants would rather live on the banks of an open sewer in a big booming city than return to the poverty of their more picturesque homes elsewhere in India.

There is still plenty of land into which Delhi can expand. As I hobbled southwards from Rohini subcity towards Dwarka subcity, I was struck by the low density of the housing, often single-storey. The air is fresher. There are small copses and little chunks of vestigial agricultural land. There's hardly a soul to be seen. And the roads are almost empty. Despite my limp, I overtake an eccentric cyclist, who appears to be trying to break the world record for slow-pedalling. Hanging from his kerbside handlebar by a piece of wire are the innards of a car speaker, just skimming over the surface of the road. I ask him what he's doing. It turns out he's got one of the world's more unusual occupations, a cycling recycler, collecting roadside metallic emissions from vehicles. Bir Singh uses a speaker magnet to attract iron traces[3] from the kerb, and gets Rs 15 a kilo. He picks up the speaker, and shows me the magnet, covered with a carpet of iron filings, all standing erect, which he then brushes with an ice-lolly stick into a bag hanging from his other handlebar. This road, he

tells me, is not very good, because there is little traffic, so he only comes here once a year. The biggest roads and the highways are too busy and dangerous, and the iron traces disappear down the roadside drains whenever it rains. The police stop him sometimes, because they say he's too much of distraction to drivers, and might cause an accident. But bullock carts and bicycles are the main form of transport on this road, on Delhi's rural fringe. There is now more farmland than buildings, and the small settlements are recognizably villages. Women toil bent-backed in the fields. Men sit cross-legged discussing the problems of the world over tea and *bidis*. Small children gambol near the village well, throwing water at each other. Buffalos wander aimlessly along dusty country lanes—and yet this is all still Delhi. According to the Master Plan, seven per cent of Delhi will remain agricultural, but it's hard to imagine, whatever the planners say, that all of this won't be urbanized within a decade.

Gradually, the city re-emerges from the countryside. The fields slowly shrink from football-pitch size to tennis-court and smaller. There are many more houses, the traffic increases, men work on lathes and die-stamp machines or beat metal in small, cluttered workshops. My eventual arrival in Dwarka is signalled by the sighting

---

[3] Sadly, the cycling recycler is unable to remove lead, the most toxic of vehicular metal pollutants, because it is not magnetic.

of one of this enormous subcity's eight Metro stations, its unmistakable green-blue curved roof thrusting itself above the semi-urban skyline. Dwarka, like Rohini, is half-built. I follow the Metro line as it curls like a shepherd's crook around this land of pile-drivers and scaffolding. But unlike Rohini, the Metro in Dwarka already reaches the voids planned for future development. The magisterial Metro station for Dwarka's Sector 14, raised high above the ground, presides over a wasteland. There's hardly a soul who lives or works close enough to use it. My aching calf tells me to end my marathon early, and I propel myself towards this deserted monument to the future. I stagger, exhausted, up the station steps. The platforms are pristine and empty. There's a faint rattle from the rail, a train bound for Connaught Places slides almost noiselessly into the station, and, with a gentle electronic sucking noise, the doors open. There's no one in the carriage—except for me. There are moments when the Delhi Metro seems just a little ahead of its time. And I left thinking that they really should have built a bit more of Dwarka first.

By the time I returned to Dwarka, a full month later, quite a bit more *had* been built. My swine-induced injury had delayed the final stage of my journey, despite the attentions of a smiling, playful physiotherapist who squeezed jelly on my calf twice a week, and then smeared it around very slowly with an ultrasound stick. As she fondled my calf, she advised me to rest. 'Why do you need to do all this walking?' she asked, implying that only the poor or insane would wander Delhi on their own two feet. (I hadn't even mentioned the killer pigs.) This question brought forth a tidal wave of emotion— as I poured out my heart, incompetently explaining the importance of walking in cities, and the pleasure and insights that it gave me. I told her, sotto voce, that I had walked in a spiral around Delhi, and needed to finish my journey. From the look on her face, I thought she might refer me upstairs to the psychotherapy department, where an over-zealous receptionist had sent me on my first visit. 'Do you want to come with me to Gurgaon?' I teased, 'I might need a physiotherapist. Only another ten miles to go.' She laughed in my face. I think she would have rather drunk from the Yamuna.

This time, Dwarka Sector 14 station was a little busier. A 'camp' for building workers, with bright blue tents made out of plastic sheeting, had been set up nearby. They were newcomers from Bihar, all of them planning to stay on in Delhi. They are an important part of the city's growth cycle, a spiral of another kind: migrants who came to this city to build homes for future migrants, though these unskilled workers are not going to be able to afford the kind of homes they are building. Instead, they become urban nomads, moving between building sites, and setting up their temporary homes nearby. Over the last month, the construction workers of Dwarka had been very active. The intestines of the western half of this subcity had emerged from the wasteland. Chimney-like protuberances from the earth announced the completion of deep sewer lines. There are huge trucks delivering concrete to be poured into skeletal steel structures, the foundations for residential skyscrapers and shopping malls. Further to the south, like a mirage in the desert, I came upon a completed housing development, stranded on its own—again built too early for the rest of Dwarka. A developer had jumped the gun—and gone ahead without proper planning permission. One mournfully resident told me that it had been declared an unauthorized colony[4]—and that there were plans to have it demolished.

Dwarka is being built on fields of mustard. And beyond today's construction sites, I could see acres and acres of spindly mustard plants, taller than a grown man; a gorgeous yellow carpet of flowers, swaying

---

[4] The colony is tagged on Google Earth, with this intemperate, but not entirely unfair diatribe against the Delhi authorities, from a correspondent who calls himself Morphonx: '[This is a] low income residential area. NOT A SLUM. People BUILT the roads here, laid the sewer lines, even though they paid taxes. What do they get in spite of paying taxes? Regular power outages, a dirt track for a road, not even sewer lines! And what does the government call it? An "unauthorized colony", right in the heart of India's capital. When the people went to their leaders to get it authorized, the leaders asked for bribes. And now

in the spring breeze, perfect for a Bollywood song-and-dance routine, or a secret assignation. In the West, mustard has become little more than a tangy hot-dog accompaniment, but in north India, mustard is a major crop, and full of symbolic resonances[5]. But this is the last mustard crop these lands will ever see. They're the site for a convention centre (seating 12,000 people), hotel (with 800 rooms), and Dwarka's first golf course. Santosh Kumar has farmed these lands all his life, but is reconciled to the change. He is almost tearful when he talks about the past, but he got a decent price for his land, and his children don't want to work in the fields. They look down on agricultural work, they think it's 'dirty' and want 'clean' city jobs working in an office. His second son, he tells me proudly, speaks good English, and is already working in a call-centre in Gurgaon— he says, pointing to the south, and to the serrated skyline of the place that proclaims itself 'the Millennium City'.

The only farmhouses that will remain in this area don't deserve the name. A 'farmhouse', in the modern Delhi vernacular, is a rich person's house in a large walled compound on the outskirts of the city, built on what was once agricultural land. Some of these farmhouses are quite spectacular—little palaces with massive grounds, swimming-pools and tennis courts. They have a slightly exaggerated reputation for debauchery and shameless luxury. And they're perfect for that legendary oxymoron, the privacy-seeking celebrity, and for Delhi-hating foreigners, or anyone really—so long as they've got lots of money and want to pretend they're not in

---

they call this model of people empowerment "UNAUTHORIZED". Shame on you corrupt babus! Google Earth is telling the truth to the PLANET! The people built all these areas themselves, and you shitholes wish to take credit for the entire "New Delhi" The only areas you shitholes "preserve" is the British legacy in colonial Delhi, of all those stupid roundabouts. The real "New Delhi" is the 90 % of Delhi made by the REAL people of Delhi who have built it with their sweat and toil. Now all the sick babus on this planet better ask themselves who has to give AUTHORIZATION to a man to build his own home in his own country?' A 'babu' is a bureaucrat.

[5] Its yellow flowers are known as *basanti*, the word for spring; and the flowering of the mustard plant marks the end of the cold season. The leaves are the key ingredient of Punjab's best known dish, *sarson ka saag*. The seeds are used as a spice, and among poorer families, is the main source of oil for cooking. Mustard oil is also used as a mosquito repellent, as a remedy for constipation, and to massage babies.

Delhi. Originally, many of the farmhouses were second homes, built on the southern fringes of Delhi as weekend escapes. But as the city itself swept southwards, and as Gurgaon burgeoned and grew next to the Delhi border, the farmhouses lost their agricultural hinterland, and became an integral, if rather untypical, part of city life. Patches of communal grazing land sometimes survive nearby— but the fields have gone. The farmhouse walls are high enough to keep out prying eyes, and dogs and security guards stand watch at the gates—though Google Earth reveals the swimming-pools in all their turquoise splendour. Officially the actual farmhouses can't take up more than ten per cent of the area of the compound, and they're supposed to be single-storey, but these rules are widely disregarded and some of these farmhouses are enormous and very grand. There's not a farmer to be seen, but according to an Internet guide for foreigners planning to rent farmhouses, it is essential to have a minimum of three gardeners, as well as at least two cars. Most of the farmhouses have their own sources of water (a tube-well) and electricity (a generator), and are widely decried as environmentally unfriendly and elitist. But with their pristine lawns and privacy-protecting trees, they do create a green belt; and, together with the airport, establish a narrow buffer zone between Delhi and Gurgaon, as this whole engorged region is transformed into one of the world's largest urban agglomerations.

Gurgaon has been trying hard to build a reputation as India's most modern city[6], and it now has the skyline and the shopping malls to match that ambition. In the early 1970s it was a dusty, undistinguished town on the road between Delhi and Jaipur, with fewer than sixty thousand inhabitants. Its own Master Plan now predicts a population of almost four million by 2021. The biggest reasons for Gurgaon's dramatic early growth were the setting up of the massive Maruti car factory, manufacturing India's equivalent of the Model-T, and the unwillingness of Delhi's rulers to allow private developers to build modern townships and new industrial zones within the city limits. At the time, the Delhi authorities, misled by

[6] Bangalore was the undisputed hi-tech city for much of the late 1990s, although it was challenged at the start of the new millennium by Hyderabad—nicknamed Cyberabad. Bangalore's fall from grace came as its infrastructure crumbled because of the speed of unplanned growth in the city.

the contemporary dogma of urban planning, wanted to create 'counter-magnet cities', much further from Delhi, as a way of limiting the growth of the capital. But migrants and businesses weren't attracted by the 'counter-magnets' and big Delhi developers bought up agricultural land just across the border in the state of Haryana, and began building big new residential colonies, with houses and flats at much cheaper prices than Delhi. A huge residential area of northern Gurgaon is now simply known as DLF[7], after the largest of these developers.

The Maruti factory, now producing more than 350,000 cars a year, began as a government-sponsored project; one of the many controversial pet schemes of Sanjay Gandhi, the imperious prime ministerial son, who wanted to manufacture a car which would be affordable to the new middle classes of urban India. But the factory did not produce a single vehicle until he was dead, and the Japanese Suzuki company had taken a major role in the project. The early Marutis were like a tin can on wheels, crumpling up like a concertina at the most minor of accidents, and their twisted, rusting remains still decorate the kerbsides of many Indian highways. But the Maruti also played an important role in a social revolution. The middle classes could now afford cars, and therefore live further away from their offices, often in purpose-built apartments that were springing up in places like DLF in Gurgaon. The small car revolution in turn encouraged Delhi to grow spatially, increased overall traffic congestion, and eventually spawned the huge road widening and flyover building programmes that are transforming Delhi and its satellites into an American-style city of highways.

It's appropriate that Gurgaon should have first gained national fame as a car city, the Detroit or Dagenham of India, for it remains very much a car-drivers' city, appalling for public transport and even worse for pedestrians. Unlike the real Delhi there's almost no street life, and walking through Gurgaon was a soulless, dispiriting, lonely experience. The main places of social interaction are not the streets

[7] DLF (an acronym for Delhi Land and Finance) is a family-owned company which developed large areas of south Delhi before turning its attention to Gurgaon in the late 1970s. 'DLF City' now has five 'phases' in Gurgaon.

but the shopping malls (always pronounced to rhyme with ball, not shall) with their air-conditioned food courts, boutiques, and multi-screen cinemas. One shopaholic, pizza-guzzling, mall-lover told me, with glee and provocation in her voice, that there were sixty malls either under construction or already completed in Gurgaon. Despite the speed at which it has grown, Gurgaon is very spread-out—more than thirty-three kilometres from north to south (and half as wide) now that the further-from-Delhi, less-developed Manesar area has been brought under its thrall. It has huge undeveloped voids, mainly future construction sites. There are few pavements, an antiquated bus system, and no railway network, though Gurgaon will soon be connected with the Delhi Metro.

Gurgaon has become a place of middle-class aspiration, a westernised urban utopia where owning one's own palatial flat is not a pipedream. The Delhi newspapers carry full-page advertisements for new residential developments in Gurgaon, mainly condominiums in pastel-shaded tower blocks, surrounded by neatly manicured lawns. 'Dream' is the key motif of the marketing message: *Dream Homes—Dream Lifestyle'*, *'A paradise in the making'*, *'Homes to recreate the essence of royalty'*, *'Make your dream come true'*, *'At last the enriched lifestyle you've aspired for becomes unbelievably affordable'*.

The names resonate with suburban America—Rosewood City, Malibu Towne, Belvedere Park, Carlton Estate, Scottish Castle, Maple Heights, Greenwood Plaza, Hamilton Court. The advertisements promise luxurious living: floors made of 'Italiano marble', a 'jacuzzi in master toilet', 'wooden cupboards and fancy lights', 'European-type modular kitchen with breakfast table of granite' and, more mysteriously, 'POP Cornish'—which I later learned referred to plaster-of-Paris cornices. And many Gurgaon residents are gloriously content with their gleaming new homes, which have provided them with exotic comforts and a sound investment. They will tell you proudly that they never need to come in to Delhi any more, or that they feel they are living in the West or Dubai. They used to get snobbish sneers and sarcasm from the smart-set of South Delhi. But as more multinationals moved to Gurgaon and the value of residential property doubled and redoubled, the sneers began to droop a little.

The American-style condo is not the only contribution Gurgaon has made to modernity. It has become a major international business centre, and a rack of intimidating glass-and-steel office buildings loom and cavort for several kilometres along the eastern kerb of the Jaipur highway. There's one that looks like a transparent ark with a few real animals grazing and snuffling on the wasteland nearby (including an unusually sedate herd of pigs), another with an off-centre finger-like pinnacle pointing meaningfully at the sky. They seem curiously out of place here, as if they've strayed into the Indian countryside from Manhattan or Shanghai, where no one would give these baby skyscrapers a second look. But here they're imposing, forbidding even. Not places to visit without an appointment. Inside there's nothing to indicate that you might be in India; most of the tenants are modern multinationals of the kind you'd find in any world city (Nokia, Alcatel, Canon, Convergys, Sapient); the language of conversations in the lift is English, and pizza is the omnipresent canteen food.

Gurgaon today is more cosmopolitan and less conservative than Delhi. It's become a place of liberation for some youngsters and newly weds, who can afford to escape the constraints of a joint family. If you speak good English, there are plenty of jobs. Call-centre salaries are rising, and suddenly twenty-somethings can have a place (and car) of their own. Offices are open-plan, centrally air-conditioned and, I'm assured, the best place in the country to conduct serial, and occasionally overlapping, relationships with members of the opposite (or same) sex; a whirligig of trysts and romantic longing which have spawned two recent call-centre novels. Gurgaon now has lots of young foreigners for whom a spell working in India is no longer a hardship posting, but a relatively normal part of a career in telecoms, or outsourcing. This is a place where everyone knows what BPO stands for (though one Gurgaon blogger proposes 'Brain Paralysing Outfits'), and that outsourcing has led to prosperity for Gurgaon, and untold wealth for a small number of Indians, the super-rich entrepreneurs of the global economy, who are the most envied role-models of modern India.

But not all is well in the Millennium City, this city of dreams. Call-centre workers complain of burn-out, of permanent night-shifts, or that foreign workers in India are being paid indecently high salaries. Gurgaon was wracked by riots in 2005, as a demonstration by striking workers from the Honda motorcycle factory was broken up by the police in a shockingly violent manner that was televised around the world. And many of the blogs from high-connectivity Gurgaon (the housing ads promise wireless broadband—one developer even threw in a free PC) don't paint quite such a happy picture of those dream homes. There is not always enough water for the jacuzzis, or electricity for the fancy lights. Like most people in and around Delhi the dream-home residents have to endure power cuts and water shortages. The grander condos have private generators, and their own water supply, for which they pay extra, and live apart from the rest of Gurgaon. But even then they complain that they can't get servants who are willing to travel so far for work, or stay so far away; or that the roads are not repaired, and that they're fed up with living in the middle of a building site. And for others, there's a kind of anomie that overwhelms them, a sense of purposelessness now that they achieved a major aim of their lives—a smart new flat in Gurgaon.

For me, a refugee from post-modern monotony, Gurgaon was worse than going back home—even if it's easy to see how for many it has become a dreamtown. I, however, had come all this way to escape places where the streets are lifeless; places where people are too world-weary or too preoccupied to smile and to talk. Were India's cities becoming like anywhere else? Were all cities destined ultimately to resemble each other? Nothing, nothing at all, happened to me as I wandered through Gurgaon. I wasn't chased by killer pigs; I didn't step into a sewer; no one harassed me; I wasn't hit by an autorickshaw; I wasn't threatened by butchers; no one asked me to sing; I didn't have shit squirted onto my shoe. I suppose I ought to have been happy, but I wasn't. I missed the bustle, the noise, the colours, and the smells.

For better and worse, Gurgaon is probably the future, and Delhi, and other Indian cities, will become more and more like Gurgaon.

I had now finished my spiral. But I kept walking round in small circles, pirouetting and gyrating through Gurgaon, awaiting a revelation, hoping that something would happen to me before I began slouching back towards Delhi. The blackening skies suddenly opened and let loose a tirade of hail-stones, some as big as marbles. Stung to the quick, I sought shelter in a security guard's hut, and in the invigorating company of a garrulous Japanese businessman, a flirtatious teenage Gurgaon college student, and our smilingly attentive host, we watched the storm pass by.

Acknowledgements

I have a large number of people to thank for the help they gave me in writing this book. Too many of them are dead. Kate Jones, my agent, died suddenly in 2008—and she, who had never been to Delhi, got the point from the first. My wife's stepfather, Tony Mango, who migrated to India a good sixty-five years before I did, was a source of inspiration and humour from the moment I set foot on Indian soil. He shared my study in Panchsheel Park on many long afternoons, and contributed to this book in more ways than he would ever know. He died, aged 92, in May 2008. On one of my first trips to Delhi, I was welcomed with great warmth by my future wife's uncle, Kersi Satarawala. His wisdom and sense of history would shape my views of a country that I grew to love. He passed away in 2001. My Panchsheel Park landlady, Rajmohini Vikram Singh, whom I knew as Kaki Bua, told me many fine Delhi tales. Sadly, she died in 2007.

There were several people who read early versions of this book. They include my friend and fellow primagravida Mohammad Hanif, who was pregnant with his remarkable novel about the strange death of General Zia at the same time as this book took embryonic shape. I have benefited enormously from his detailed comments over the last few years, and omitted a few absurd metaphors at his behest. Rafil Kroll Zaidi, Sue Preston and Lucy Peck also read the entire manuscript and gave me lots of useful suggestions. Andrew Whitehead, my friend and BBC colleague, was unstintingly helpful and had lots of good advice. Thanks also to Mala Singh, Alexandra Pringle, David Godwin, Jane Lawson and Sachin Mulji who all gave me feedback on parts of the book. Sachin also makes a poorly-disguised appearance in the sixth intermission as a devotee of Hank Williams.

In Delhi, there are many people who helped me in a great variety of ways. These include: Deepika and Gautam Mehra, Ferida and Noni Chopra, Tejbir Singh, Sushil Kanti, Priya Paul, Anjali and William Bissell, Sagarika Ghose and Rajdeep Sardesai, Syed and Sameera Zaidi, Olivia and William Dalrymple, Vineeta Dwivedi, Seema Chishti, Shernaz Italia, Harish Saluja, Valeria Corvo, Gaia Giammusso, Pan Singh Bisht, Raj Kumar Sharma, Clementina Lakra, Raju Kumar, Anushree Ramchandani, the late General Adi Sethna,

Mark Tully and Gillian Wright, the Sarai reader list and its contributors, Phil Goodwin, Abhishek Madhukar, Renuka Chatterjee, Satish Jacob, Sunil Arora, Manvendra Singh, Ashok Nehru and Ravi Agarwal. Around the world: Georgia Miller, Ardashir Vakil, Daniel Miller, Yvonne Andrews, Catherine Goodman, Iris DeMent, Deepak Mehta, Anuradha Awasthi, Barry Langridge, Abbas Nasir, Chloe Paidoussis, Ella Saltmarshe, Jeroo Mango, Freny Satarawala, Jonathan and Rachel Miller, Capt JM Nath, Jack Bauer, Jack Turner, Christina Noble, Robert Schwandl, Pascale Harter, Claire Doole, Jerome Senanayake, Rajiv Saurastri, the late Richard Wollheim, Chris Cramer, Hugh Barnes, Andrew O'Hagan, Kathryn Williams, Jo Johnson, Anjan Dutta, Julian Rothenstein and Hiang Kee, Ed Luce, Andrew Robinson and Jennifer Terran.

Ranjana Sengupta was an inspiration long before I met her, as a careful reading of the text will make clear, and I was particularly delighted when she became my editor at Penguin India. Thanks also to her colleagues Bena Sareen, Hemali Sodhi, Bhavi Mehta, Ravi Singh, Mike Bryan, Dipali Singh, Manju Khanna and Manmohan, the long-distance compositor. Karolina Sutton, Laura Sampson, Octavia Wiseman, Margaret Halton at ICM, which mysteriously transmogrified into Curtis Brown, were all of great help, particularly after the death of Kate Jones. Thanks also to Dan Franklin at Random House in London, who is publishing the UK edition of the book.

I'm grateful to Merchant-Ivory Productions for permission to use stills and quote passages from *The Householder*, to Moulinsart for permission to reproduce a cartoon from *Tintin in Tibet*, and to Raghu Rai for permission to reproduce his superb photograph of Agarsen's Baoli.

My parents, Jane and Karl Miller, have read every word I've ever had published, usually more than once. *Delhi: Adventures in a Megacity* is dedicated to them with great love and thanks, and a vague memory that I once swore to them that they would never catch me writing a book. And undying love to my indomitable wife, Shireen, who brought me to her country all those years ago, and commented wisely and forcefully on almost every page of this book. Finally, a special 'Yo' to my beloved, easily-embarrassed, computer-hijacking children, Zubin and Roxy. They are almost certainly responsible for any errors that have crept into this book.

Index

101 Dalmatians, 23
1787 Chateau Yquem, 208
1857 Uprising, 9, 60n^{14}, 98n^{17}, 113, 186n^{10}, 189, 196, 248
Aarhus, 208
Agarsen's Baoli, 47, 49, 77
Agra, 41, 113, 237
Akshardham Temple, 160, 168–72
Albania, 1
Alexander the Great, 101n^{19}, 138n^9
All-India Sports Council of the Deaf, 66
American Embassy School, 138, 147–48
American Women's Association, 139, 147
Amritsar, 85n
Antriksh Bhavan, 30–32
Ants, 99–100, 131, 211–13
Apollo Hospital, 235–37
Aravalli Hills, 66
Asclepius, 34n^{17}
Ashoka Pillars, 100, 197, 199
Asian Games, 45, 155
Athens, 1, 4
Aurangzeb, 4n^3, 108n^2
Ayodhya, 258–59

Badli Samaipur, 268
Baha'i Temple, 235
Bahadur Shah Zafar, 97
Baker, Herbert, 18n^4, 72, 247
Bakri Eid, 175–76
Bal Bhawan, 52–53
Bangalore (see Bengalaru)
Bangladesh, 157–58, 182
Barakhamba Road, 33, 37, 47
Barreto, Dr, 101
Baudelaire, 6

Beatles, the, 103
Bedi, Rahul, 258n^2
Bengalaru, 41, 277n^6
Bengali, 33n^{15}, 157–58, 171
Bernoulli, Jacob, 10–13, 35
Bihar, Biharis, 157, 216, 238–41, 275
Birla House, 83–87, 93, 101
Birla Mandir, 68–70
BlackBerry, 238
Blood: author's, 217, 235–6; human, 53, 101, 257–58; animal, 120–23; donation, 198, 235–39
Blyton, Enid, 264
Bogota, 76
Bolivar, Simon, 137–38
Bombay *see* Mumbai
Bond, Ruskin, 208
Bosch, Hieronymous, 130
Bourgeois, Louise, 12
Brahma Kumaris, 131–32, 135
Breasts, 26–27, 50, 64, 165
Breughel, 253
Britain, 33n^{15}, 191, 209, 224, 261
Brown, Mauriceo, 218n^5
Buddha, 43
Buffy the Vampire Slayer, 30
Bungalows, 33, 73–75, 88, 93, 154, 191, 196, 222
Buxar, 217

Cairo, 4, 160
Calcutta *see* Kolkata
Campa Cola, 37–39, 53
Carrots, 64–65, 129*ff*, 159
Cemeteries, 65, 88–89, 226
Chanakya, 138n^9
Chanakyapuri, 138, 149

Chandler, Tertius, 4n^3
Chandni Chowk, 113, 115–16, 247
Chaucer, 268n^1
Chekhov, Anton, 170
Chennai, 32
Chhath, 239, 241–42
Christo, 118
Civil Lines, 191, 194, 196, 199, 262
Clemenceau, Georges, 72–73
Clitoris, Green Plastic, 165
CNN-IBN, 217–18
Coca Cola, 38, 86n^7
Cochin, 90
Cockroaches, 46, 198
Coldplay, 264
Colosseum, 18, 45
Commonwealth Games, 171, 229, 249
Communist Party of India (Marxist), 66
Connaught Place, 15–27, 31, 33, 37, 39, 41, 42, 50, 66, 129, 160, 208, 247, 265
Connaught, Duke of, 17n^3
Cornflakes, 63, 269
Coronation Park, 261–62
Correa, Charles, 28n^{10}
Coryate, Thomas, 101n^{19}
Cricket, 7, 18, 42, 84, 100, 155, 194, 199, 220–21
Crisps, crisp packets, 51, 56, 91, 117, 213, 221, 254
Curzon, Lord, 30
Cyrus, Prince, 143–45

Dali, Salvador, 243
Damodaran, Ramu, 143n^{13}
Daniell, Thomas and William, 44, 46–47
Daulatabad, 9n^5
Delhi, Louisiana, 4n^3
Delhi Cantonment, 186, 188, 199, 214
Delhi Development Authority, 179

Delhi Flying Club, 150–51
Delhi Master Plan, 270, 273, 277
Delhi State Industrial Development Corporation (DSIDC), 19
Delhi University, 186–87, 199, 201
Dengue Fever, 56, 215–16, 218–19, 221–22, 225
Dettol, 37
Dhanu, 78n^{12}
Diamonds, 9, 115n^7, 143, 209
Diarrhoea, 2, 63
Dickens, Charles, 85n^5, 253
Dikshit, Sheila, 163
Disney, Disneyland, 59, 167, 242, 247, 269
Diwali, 67, 152, 225
DLF, 278
Dogs (and puppies), 16, 20–21, 87–88, 137, 144–45, 149, 172, 183–85, 232, 244, 252–56, 258, 277
Durga, 69
Dwarka, 264–65, 271–76
Dylan, Bob, 226

Ears: cattle ears, 119;
ear cleaners, 22, 101
Eicher, 7, 112, 172, 188, 199
Eiffel Tower, 58, 84
Eisenhower, Dwight, 74n^{10}
Eliot, TS, 6n^4
Eno, Brian, 2

Faecal matter, 28, 40, 87, 156, 161, 281
Faridabad, 4n^3
Feroze Shah Kotla, 60n^{13}
Fiddler on the Roof, 65n^3
Finland, Finnish, 22, 89n^{11}
Flaneurs, 6–8, 17, 208, 220
Friedman, Thomas, 207n^8

Gandhi Peace Foundation, 51
Gandhi, Feroze, 76–77

Gandhi, Indira, 2, $17n^3$, 75–78, 83, 85, 93, 99, $107n^1$, 150, 163, 180, 196, 211, 258

Gandhi, Kasturba, 30

Gandhi, Mohandas, $33n^{15}$, $65n^3$, $69n^8$, 72, 76, 83–8, 92–5, 101, $107n^1$

Gandhi, Rajiv, $17n^3$, $20n^6$, 77, $78n^{12}$, 85, 151, 153

Gandhi, Sanjay, 150–1, 153

Gandhi, Sonia, 163

Gandinnovations, 94–95

Ganesh Nagar, 172

Gates, Bill, 52

Geneva, 52, 59

Geocaching, 37ff, 228

George V, King, 10, 251ff

Ghalib, 9, 215–16

Ghaziabad, $4n^3$

Ghazipur, 251, 253, 256, 258

Goats, 46, 60, 135–6, 175–76, 226, 228

Godse, Nathuram, 84

Gole Market, 66

Gondwana, $67n^6$

Google, $4n^3$, $39n^2$, $112n^4$

Google Earth, 139, 172, 178, 267, 275–77

Gopal Das Bhavan, 24, 68

Goyal, Pradeep, 24

Greater Kailash, 231–32

Griggs, Dawn, 133–34

Guinness Book of World Records, 242, 263

Gujarat, 168, $193n^1$

Gunn, Thom, $35n^{18}$

Gupta, Hans Raj, $33n^{15}$, 232

Gurgaon, $4n^3$, 16, 32, 267–68, 271, 274, 276–82

Guru, Mohammed Afzal, 211–13, 218, 244

Haddock, Captain, 149–50

Hailey Road, 49

Handford, Martin, 252–53

Harcourt Butler School, 67

Haryana, 278

Heinz, 202, 269

Hendrix, Jimi, 168–70

Hergé, $149n^4$

Hindi, $3n^2$, 7, 11, $31n^{14}$, $33n^{15}$, 39, 41, $44n^4$, 55–56, 63, 66, 79–81, 97, 100, 103, 121, 126, 130, 173, 178–79, 185, 191, 201–02, 212, 225, 256, 270

Hindu Rao hospital, 196–99, 237

Hindus, 21, 26, $33n^{16}$, 47, 69, 85, 87, 89, 92–4, 103, 119, 130–31, 135, 153, 161–62, 167–69, 175, 180, 183, 189, $231n^1$, 258–59

Ho Chi Minh, 76, $87n^8$

Householder, The, 2–3, 44, 103, 105, 108, 111–12

Humayun, 92

Humayun's Tomb, 7, 158–9, 226, 247

Hyderabad, $131n^3$, 196, $277n^6$

Ibn Battuta, $9n^5$

IMAX, 170

Imperial Hotel, 46–47, 114

Index, 285

Indian Institute of Technology (IIT), 222

Indian Life Insurance building, 27–29

Indira Gandhi Indoor Sports Stadium, 99

Indraprastha, 92

Israel, 90, $175n^5$, $207n^8$

Israeli salad, 64

ITO, 98

Jacobs, Irwin, 96

Jains, 43–44, 131

Jaipur, 44–45, 237–38, 277, 280

Jama Masjid, 31, 113

Jamaica, 76

Jangpura, 156–57
Jantar Mantar, 3, 44–47, 104, 108, 228
Japan, Japanese, 44, 200, 204, 233n^3, 278, 282;
Jawaharlal Nehru Stadium, 102, 155
Jesus, 49, 84, 142n^{11}, 175n^5
Jews, 88–91

Kabari Bazaar, 53–54
Kalam, APJ Abdul, 168n^1
Kapoor, Shashi, 3
Karbala, 153–54
Karol Bagh, 135
Karzai, Hamid, 148
Kashmere Gate, 8
Kashmir, 9n^5, 58n^{11}, 193, 211, 215, 222
Khair, Tabish, 17
Khan Market, 87–88
Khomeini, Ayatollah, 52
Khushak Drain, 156
Khusro, Amir, 8–9, 249
Knees, 35, 43, 45, 49, 51, 54, 100, 111, 116, 156, 165, 170, 217, 237, 267
Kohinoor diamond, 9, 115n^7
Kolkata, 3, 9, 10, 32, 67n^7, 234, 261
Kook-a-doodle-do, 46
Krishna, Lord, 47
Kumble, Anil, 100n^{18}

Lahore, 69
Lajpat Nagar, 152n^8
Lalkot, 60n^{13}, 90n^{13}, 113n^5, 226–27
Laredo, 215n^3
Lesbianism, 26
Liechtenstein, 1
Lodi Colony, 154
Lodi Gardens (Willingdon Gardens), 87
London, 1, 4, 8, 10, 23, 49–50, 58, 60, 76–77, 79–80, 84, 88, 103, 125, 127, 160, 200, 219, 223, 226, 243, 246, 263, 271
Lord of the Rings, 90
Lovely, Arvinder Singh, 175n^4
Ludlow Castle, 191ff, 260
Lutyens Bungalow Zone (LBZ), 73–74
Lutyens, Edwin, 18n^4, 72, 247
Lutyens' Delhi, 29n^{13}, 88, 113n^6

Madras. see Chennai
Mahabharata, 89n^{11}, 92
Mahatma Gandhi Marg, 87, 99, 102
Mahavir, 43–44
Malcha Mahal, 137–38, 142–45, 150
Malta, 47n^7
Mandir Marg, 66–67, 70, 136
Manesar, 279
Manhattan, 214, 280
Maruti, 24, 277–78
Matisse, 147
McDonalds, 86n^7, 136, 204, 206–07, 219, 269
Mehrauli, 227
Mehta, Harshad, 44
Merchant-Ivory Films, 2, 105
Metro, the Delhi, 15ff, 66, 97, 103, 136, 160, 179, 185, 191, 199, 202, 204, 248–49, 257, 263–65, 267, 270–71, 274, 279
Microsoft, 20, 95, 195, 234–35
Millerites, 51n^8
Minnie Mouse, 23
Mitra, Shyam, 246
Monkeys, 71, 87, 131
Moses, 56, 142
Moses, Edwin, 142
Moses, Grandma, 142
Moses, Menacheim Daniel, 89
Mother Dairy, 172–74
Mozart, 167ff
Mumbai, 3, 9, 10, 32, 79, 84, 90, 184, 196

Municipal Corporation of Delhi (MCD), 29, 180
Muslims, 21, 25–26, 54, 69, 85, 91–93, 119, 156–58, 175, 187, 189, 215, 221, 247, 258–59
Mustard, 211–12, 259, 275–76
Mutiny Memorial, the, 197, 199

Nadir Shah, 9, 115
Naidu, Leela, 111–12
Naipaul, VS, 79
Napoleon III, 5
Naraina, 102–03
Narasimha Rao, PV, 143n^{13}
Narela, 271
National Bonsai Park, 87
National Capital Region, 29n^{13}, 242, 270
National Capital Territory, 29n^{13}
National Defence College, 83
National League of Pen-Friends, 66
National Project for the Eradication of Rinderpest, 155
Nauru, 233–34, 236–37
Nehru Park, 149
Nehru Place, 234
Nehru, BK, 151n^6
Nehru, Jawaharlal, 52, 74–75, 85, 107n^1, 138n^9, 180, 222
Nehru, Kamala, 75
Nerval, Gérard de, 6
New Delhi, 2, 10, 18, 20, 29, 30, 4', 46, 53, 55, 56, 68, 71, 72, 113, 138, 186, 191, 196, 261, 271
New Delhi Municipal Council (NDMC), 29
New Delhi Railway Station, 41, 53, 55, 56, 137
Newgrange, 52
Nigambodh Ghat, 181
Nizamuddin, 157–59
Noguchi, Isamu, 44
Noida, 4n^3, 231ff, 271

Nuremberg, 73

Octopus, 58
Om, 11, 63
Oudh, 137, 142–44
Outlook magazine, 219

Paharganj, 63, 65, 66
Pakistan, 21, 69, 71, 84, 85, 92, 93, 124, 135, 153, 189
Palika Bazaar, 23
Panchsheel Park, 222, 223, 232
Paris, 1, 5–7, 84, 118, 160
Parsees, 20–21, 76, 90n^{12}, 184
Partition, 21, 84, 92, 93, 102, 124, 131n^3, 153, 158n^{12}, 189, 241n^5, 247
Peacock Throne, 9, 115n^7
Penises: 50, 71, 222, 242
    amputated, 198, 237;
    false, 165;
    shriveled, 43
    unseen , 20
Pepsi, 37–38, 91
Perfect numbers, 10, 11
Perlus, Barry, 45
Phoolan Devi, 213n^1
Pigeons, 16, 55, 113, 142, 204, 206, 261
Pigs, 68, 221, 267ff
Pitampura, 86n^7, 102–03, 199
Pizza, 18, 180, 269, 279, 280
Pogo, 269–71
Police, the (Delhi), 16, 21, 24, 53, 56, 70, 73, 116–18, 126, 134, 151, 157, 177–78, 192, 215, 224–25, 232, 234, 243–45, 258–59, 268n^1, 272–73, 281
Police, the (rock group), 178
Poorvanchalis, 241
Population, 1, 4, 7, 8, 90n^{13}, 116, 149, 177, 199, 233n^3, 242, 246–49, 270–72, 277
Pornography, 19, 23

Pragati Maidan, 93–94, 97, 265
Prem Chand, 137n^7
Psychogeography, 8, 129
Punj Peeran, 156–58
Purana Qila, 90–94
Purgatory, 1, 4, 63

Qutb Minar, 149, 226–27, 247

Raelians, 91n^{14}
Rai, Raghu, 47, 77
Raisina Hill, 71–72, 113n^6, 261
Rajagopalachari, C, 73n^9
Rajasthan, 49, 67n^6, 131, 177
Rajendra Place, 136
Rajouri Garden, 204, 208, 265
Rama Road, 203
Ramayana, 89n^{11}
Rana, Sher Singh, 213n^1
Rashtriya Swayamsevak Sangh (RSS),
     33n^{15}, 69
Red Fort, the, 31, 90n^{13}, 92, 113,
     149n^4, 159, 181n^8, 186n^{10},
     191–92, 226n^9, 247
Regal cinema, the, 26
Ridge, the, 31, 66–68, 70, 93, 136–
     38, 143, 149, 159, 186, 191,
     194, 197–99, 221, 226, 246
Rinder, Lawrence, 12n^8
Rome, 1, 4, 156
Rowling, JK , 40
Rushdie, Salman, 37
Russel, Robert Tor, 18n^4

Sadar Bazar, 118
Safdarjung Airport (Willingdon
     Airport), 149–51
Sakina, Princess, 143–45
Salimgarh, 90n^{13}, 181n^8
San Diego Prostate Cancer Support
     Group, 64n^2
Sanskrit, 6n^4, 44n^4, 87, 89n^{11}
Sarai, 194, 196
Sarojini Nagar, 152–3

School of Planning and Architecture,
     98
Scooby-Doo, 103
Scrabble, 75
Seelampur, 232, 257–60
Sena Bhavan, 73
Sengupta, Ranjana, 154
Seventh-Day Adventists, 47n^7, 49
Shaggy, 103
Shah Jahan, 113, 118
Shahjahanabad, 11, 60n^{13}, 112–13,
     116, 176, 262
Shankar, Ravi, 103
Sheba, Queen of, 6
Shit see faecal matter
Sikhs, 2, 69, 75–76
SimCity, 246–49
Sinclair, Iain, 8, 11
Singh, Beant, 75
Singh, Jagjit, 24
Singh, Khushwant, 50
Singh, Manmohan, 168n^1
Singh, Milkha, 156
Singh, Satwant, 75
Siri Fort, 60–61, 90n^{13}, 223, 262
Sobhraj, Charles, 213n^1
Sonia Vihar, 260
Sound of Music, the, 177
Spirals, 10–13, 16–17, 19–20, 23, 26,
     34–35, 42, 46, 51–52, 59, 66,
     68, 71, 92–93, 98–99, 124,
     158, 175, 179, 202, 205, 217,
     220–21, 235–36, 249, 262,
     269, 274–75, 282
Stella of Mudge, 83ff
Sting, 102–03, 199
Sufis, 1, 25, 158
Sunehri Masjid (Golden Mosque),
     115
Supreme Court, 168n^1, 232
Suzuki, 278
Swaminarayan, 169–70
Swastikas, 89, 91–92, 119
Switzerland, 14, 26, 59n^{12}

290

Taj Mahal, 113, 158, 247
TGI Fridays, 18
Thatcher, Margaret, 76
Thums Up, 37
Tibet, 2, 231n^1
Tihar Jail, 75n^{11}, 211–15
Times of India, 61, 192
Tintin, 2, 130, 147ff
TJs, 211, 213, 216
Toast, 80–81
Togo, 236–7
Tolstoy Marg, 47
Torr, Diane, 164–5
Trans-Yamuna, 159–60, 172, 174–5
Trilokpuri, 257–58
Trinidad, 79
Trisoft, 19–20
Tughlaq, Ghiyasuddin, 149n^4
Tughlaq, Muhammad, 8, 9n^5
Tughlaqabad, 60n^{13}

Urdu, 66, 119
Urinals, 20, 24, 211
Usha, PT, 156n^{10}
Uttar Pradesh, 241–2

Vasant Vihar, 217, 219–24, 232
Verhilion, Claude, 91n^{14}
Victoria, Queen, 17n^3

Vidal, Gore, 43n^3
Vivekananda Camp, 147–48

Wally, 252–53
Warner, Mark, 148n^2
Wikipedia, 231–32, 234
Williams, Hank, 143
Willingdon Airport *see* Safdarjang
    Airport
Willingdon Crescent *see* Mother
    Teresa Crescent
Wolfowitz, Paul, 148n^2
World Trade Centre, 37
World War Two, 21, 83, 224n^8
Wushu Association of India, 155

Yams, 165
Yamuna Pushta, 177–79
Yamuna, river, 13, 31, 60n^{13}, 99–
    100, 107n^1, 158–61, 168,
    171–72, 174–77, 183, 191,
    196, 232, 239–42, 246, 258,
    260, 274
Yaseen, Mohammed, 24

Zeenat mosque, 108
Zeus, 34n^{17}
Zita, Empress, 144
Zoroastrianism, 20n^6, 90n^{12}, 184n^9

Copyright Acknowledgements